JUSTIN TRUDEAU

JUSTIN TRUDEAU

THE NATURAL HEIR

HUGUETTE YOUNG

TRANSLATED BY GEORGE TOMBS

DUNDURN
A J. PATRICK BOYER BOOK

Translator: George Tombs
Copy editor: Cy Strom
Design: Courtney Horner
Cover design: Courtney Horner
Cover image: Robson Fletcher/Metro/Torstar Syndicate
Printer: Friesens

Library and Archives Canada Cataloguing in Publication

Young, Huguette, 1955-
[Justin Trudeau, l'héritier. English]
     Justin Trudeau : the natural heir / Huguette Young
; George Tombs, translator.

Translation of: Justin Trudeau, l'héritier.
Includes bibliographical references and index.
Issued in print and electronic formats.
ISBN 978-1-4597-3572-9 (paperback).--ISBN 978-1-4597-3573-6
(pdf).--ISBN 978-1-4597-3574-3 (epub)

     1. Trudeau, Justin, 1971-. 2. Canada--Politics and government--
2015-. 3. Canada--Politics and government--2006-2015. 4. Liberal
Party of Canada--History--21st century. 5. Political leadership--
Canada. 6. Politicians--Canada--Biography. 7. Prime ministers--
Canada--Biography. I. Tombs, George, translator II. Title.
Titre: Justin Trudeau, l'héritier. English

FC656.T78Y6813 2016   971.07'4092   C2016-902249-8
                                                  C2016-902250-1

1   2   3   4   5   20   19   18   17   16

We acknowledge the support of the **Canada Council for the Arts** and the **Ontario Arts Council** for our publishing program. We also acknowledge the financial support of the **Government of Canada** through the **Canada Book Fund** and **Livres Canada Books**, and the **Government of Ontario** through the **Ontario Book Publishing Tax Credit** and the **Ontario Media Development Corporation**.

In addition, we acknowledge the financial support of the Government of Canada through the **National Translation Program for Book Publishing**, an initiative of the **Roadmap for Canada's Official Languages 2013–2018: Education, Immigration, Communities**, for our translation activities.

Care has been taken to trace the ownership of copyright material used in this book. The author and the publisher welcome any information enabling them to rectify any references or credits in subsequent editions.

— *J. Kirk Howard, President*

The publisher is not responsible for websites or their content unless they are owned by the publisher.

Printed and bound in Canada.

VISIT US AT
Dundurn.com | @dundurnpress | Facebook.com/dundurnpress | Pinterest.com/dundurnpress

Dundurn
3 Church Street, Suite 500
Toronto, Ontario, Canada
M5E 1M2

CONTENTS

To my father, Aurèle, who taught me discipline

To my mother, Rita, who encouraged me to see this project through, *"C'est valable, continue,"* she told me a week before her death

To my husband, Edison, who encouraged me to persevere

To my son, Justin, and daughter, Anika, who continue to enrich my life

To the Library of Parliament and its staff whose help made this book possible

Huguette Young
May 2016

INTRODUCTION

On October 3, 2000, close to 3,000 people poured into Notre-Dame Basilica in Montreal to pay their last respects to Pierre Elliott Trudeau, an extraordinary Quebecker who had dominated the Canadian political scene for more than fifteen years. The former Canadian prime minister had died of prostate cancer five days earlier at the age of eighty.

Many dignitaries took their places in the majestic church: Canadian Prime Minister Jean Chrétien was there, as well as his predecessors Brian Mulroney, John Turner, Joe Clark, and Kim Campbell; former American president Jimmy Carter; Prince Andrew; former French prime minister Raymond Barre; Quebec Premier Lucien Bouchard; the leader of the Quebec Liberal Party Jean Charest; and many others. Actress Margot Kidder, who had often been seen at Prime Minister Trudeau's side, attended the funeral bearing a bouquet of white roses. Sarah, the daughter Trudeau had had nine years before with his lover Deborah Coyne, sat in the same pew as the prime minister's former wife Margaret Trudeau and their son Alexandre. Cuban President Fidel Castro, a friend of the family, seemed conspicuously out of place.

Beneath the blue vault of the church, everyone listened with bated breath to the eulogy delivered by Pierre Elliott Trudeau's son Justin, who had dropped out of sight several years before after moving to Vancouver.

Tall, with wavy, short black hair and wearing a blue-grey suit, Justin wore a red rose on his lapel, just the way his father had often done. He seemed younger than his twenty-eight years.

"Friends, Romans, countrymen," Justin began, with the hint of a smile on his lips. By quoting Mark Antony's funeral oration from Shakespeare's *Julius Caesar*, he captivated his audience. All eyes were riveted on him.

With a theatrical air, Justin began the eulogy by recalling how he had met Santa Claus at the age of six during an expedition to the North Pole with his father and grandfather, James Sinclair. The little boy did not understand the goal of this "top-secret mission" to the ends of the Earth. A Jeep dropped them at Alert, a scientific and military outpost in the Canadian High Arctic. He could make out someone working away inside a red building. He started crunching across the snow and headed for the front door. But his father pointed him to the window.

"So I clambered over the snowbank, boosted up to the window, rubbed my sleeve across the frosty glass to see inside," the young Trudeau continued. "As my eyes adjusted to the gloom, I saw a figure, hunched over one of many worktables that seemed very cluttered. He was wearing a red suit with a furry white trim. And that's when I understood," Justin added, his eyes brimming with tears, "just how powerful and wonderful my father was."

A ripple of shy laughter washed across the crowd, then a wave of emotion and a burst of applause. Justin continued his story with that eloquence for which he is now widely known. He described how Pierre Elliott Trudeau had pushed his sons to test their limits, to challenge anything and anyone standing in their path. He spoke of his father's unflinching principles and of his "genuine and deep respect for each and every human being, notwithstanding their thoughts, their values, their beliefs, their origins."

By way of illustration, Justin told of a misadventure in the parliamentary restaurant in Ottawa when he was eight years old. His father reproached him for making a joke about Joe Clark, the Conservative leader he had succeeded in 1980, after a short and turbulent reign lasting nine months. "Justin, we never attack the individual," his father said, bringing him over to meet Joe Clark and his daughter, Catherine Clark. "We can be in total disagreement with someone, without denigrating them."

The grieving son added that his father's "fundamental belief in the sanctity of the individual" was not taken out of some textbook. It stemmed from "his deep love for and faith in all Canadians."

In his closing words, Justin's voice stirred with emotion. "He left politics in 1984, but he came back for Meech, he came back for Charlottetown, he came back to remind us of who we are and what we're all capable of. But he won't be coming back any more," Justin said, stifling a sob. "It's all up to us — all of us — now. The woods are lovely, dark and deep. He has kept his promises and earned his sleep."

"*Je t'aime, Papa,*" Justin said in his last tearful goodbye. The church filled with applause. The son stepped up to his father's coffin and bowed before it.

This eulogy touched the heart of millions of Canadians and will long be remembered.

Political observers consider this moment to have been Justin Trudeau's political baptism of fire. He had just been propelled — despite himself — onto the national political scene.

English-Canadian journalists fell under his charm. According to the *Globe and Mail*, "as a young man buried his dad, a star was born." The *National Post* went even further: "Then Justin spoke, and the country fell at his feet."

He was praised for his presence, refinement, self-confidence, intellectual independence, and also for his dramatic impact. Some commentators tried decoding his words, in search of a sign the young boy people remembered from Prime Minister Pierre Elliott Trudeau's Christmas cards was now destined to follow his late father into politics. People around Justin denied this was the case: the eulogy was only a sincere tribute paid by a grieving son to his father.

In Quebec, where the father had been more respected than admired, especially by the end of his career, newspapers described the emotion-filled day of the funeral. "But What a Dad!" ran the headline in *La Presse*, echoing Justin's words. *Le Devoir,* meanwhile, described the unleashing of a wave of sympathy for the late head of government and Justin's express desire "to take up his father's political struggle."

"Except that once the grieving is done, political reality is bound to set in," wrote columnist Michel Venne. "Trudeau didn't just have friends across Canada." Venne described the feeling of alienation in western

Canada, where Trudeau's National Energy Program had left deep scars. Nor did Trudeau's vision of federalism have broad appeal in Quebec, as the results of the 1995 referendum demonstrated, when half of Quebeckers voted for separation from Pierre Elliott Trudeau's Canada.

Despite everything, there was a lingering impression that "we have not heard the last from the Trudeau family," as the former Quebec Liberal leader Claude Ryan put it. "We may even be witnessing the emergence of a new dynasty."

CHAPTER 1

24 SUSSEX DRIVE

Justin Trudeau was born a celebrity. He was making the news even before his birth on Christmas Day, 1971. Trudeaumania, a wave of mass infatuation, had swept his father to the leadership of the Liberal Party of Canada in 1968. This phenomenal surge of popularity had since waned, but the charismatic and "sexy"[1] prime minister still had many surprises in store for Canadians.

In fact, nine months earlier, the fifty-one-year-old Pierre Elliott Trudeau had stunned the country by secretly marrying Margaret Sinclair, a beautiful twenty-two-year-old from Vancouver, in a Catholic ceremony. They had met on the beaches of Tahiti in 1967. And now the picture-perfect couple were about to have a baby, which hadn't happened to a ruling prime minister for 102 years.

It was a happy event, and Canadians were overjoyed. Mother and infant (weighing in at six pounds, nine ounces) were doing well at the Ottawa Civic Hospital. The infant's proud parents decided to baptize him Justin Pierre James, the last name in honour of Margaret's father, James Sinclair, who had been an influential fisheries minister in the Liberal government of Louis St. Laurent.

"I had some ideas about my son's name," the prime minister said as he handed out cigars to the journalists and press photographers gathered at the hospital. "But my wife did as well. So he is going to be called Justin Pierre." Then the new father stopped a beat: "I fear he may resemble me."

The arrival of the Trudeaus' first-born late on Christmas Day was announced on television: telegrams and congratulations flooded the little family. Margaret was soon receiving hundreds of hand-knit sweaters, bonnets, bibs, and bootees, as well as thousands of greeting cards. And when news spread that she was breast-feeding, a new avalanche of letters arrived, commending her decision, as she recounts in her book *Beyond Reason*.[2]

It was the beginning of a frenetic lifestyle for the family. By the time Justin was one and a half, he already had his own suitcase. He appeared in public beside his beaming father at the Commonwealth Heads of Government Meeting, where he met Queen Elizabeth for the first time.

Two years after Justin's birth, day for day, came the birth of his brother Alexandre, also known as Sacha. Margaret was ecstatic. She simply couldn't believe her two babies were born on Christmas Day. Justin wasn't shy about speaking in public. When accompanying his father to the hospital just before his mother gave birth, the little two-year-old made his first statement to the journalists gathered for the occasion. What did he want for Christmas? *"Motorcycle!"* came the answer.

Then, just as Justin was on the point of leaving with his father, the toddler turned to face the journalists, saying, "Happy birthday … and Merry Christmas!"[3]

Margaret gave birth to a third son, Michel, on October 2, 1975. Justin's second brother was affectionately nicknamed Micha or Miche. At twenty-eight years old, the ravishing Margaret had three children.

Justin Trudeau's years growing up at 24 Sussex Drive, the prime minister's official residence in Ottawa's embassy district, were recorded by press photographers. He was photographed arriving at Rideau Hall, the governor general's residence, carried like a package under his radiant father's arm, and again in the prime minister's office beside his parents. As a little boy, he often travelled overseas with his father. He was photographed at the Brandenburg Gate in Berlin, at the Acropolis in Athens with his brothers, in the Vatican during a private audience granted to his father by the Pope.

The Canadian photographer Peter Bregg accompanied Prime Minister Trudeau around the world and recalls that the Trudeaus did their best to shield their children from the media. Hired at nineteen by the Canadian Press in Ottawa, Bregg estimates he must have taken tens of thousands of photos of the prime minister, but very few of his children. He says the press kept a respectful distance from the Trudeau children. But exceptions were made when it came to the prime minister's Christmas cards (the first of which showed Justin as an infant), special events, Canada Day, commemorative ceremonies, and official occasions of all sorts.

Not everyone gets to grow up at 24 Sussex Drive. Public life certainly has its ups and downs, and Justin recognizes he had a privileged childhood, although not a normal one. Few children are taken out of class to go meet the Queen of England.... The Conservative leader Joe Clark has said that his daughter Catherine and the Trudeau boys were practically brought up together and were subject to intense media attention. This led to an artificial environment "where the father's perpetual vigilance could have been hard for a child to endure."

Justin Trudeau seems to have adjusted well to the situation. His mother dreaded the overbearing presence of RCMP officers, but he didn't mind the fact they were keeping tabs on the official residence twenty-four hours a day. As he confided in a 2009 interview to his former playmate Catherine Clark, host of the CPAC television show *Beyond Politics*: "We were raised with them always around. They were babysitters, uncles, aunts, drivers, friends; they used to play Frisbee with us; they were part of the environment in which we were raised. And I realize now, looking back, that they were also role-models for me."

The first years at Sussex Drive were wonderful. Jack Deschambault served as chauffeur and drove the family everywhere. Sometimes Trudeau himself loaded the three boys into his Mercedes convertible and drove them to the prime minister's retreat at Harrington Lake. Weekends in the country home were particularly enjoyable. "We were alone there, we went walking in the forest, it was a private place."

Pierre Elliott Trudeau was not only adept at doing pirouettes: he was also a keen athlete. He initiated his children in karate and judo, and took them on canoe trips, ski excursions, and swimming. In the woods, he would imitate a mythical monster, the sasquatch, stomping playfully after the boys to frighten them.

Deep down, Trudeau was an adventurer who in his younger years had gone right around the world, getting himself into trouble and even being jailed for vagrancy. He taught his sons to take risks. One fine morning at Harrington Lake, the prime minister discovered Miche fooling around at the edge of his bedroom window on the second floor. "Please drop now, Miche. I'll catch you."[4] His youngest son obliged, under the anxious gaze of the house guests.

At 24 Sussex Drive, life followed a regular routine. The prime minister would get home from the office at exactly 6:45 p.m. Once he had done his forty-four lengths (never more, never less, Margaret later wrote), his children were expected to be all set to join him in the pool or on the trampoline.

Contrary to popular conception, Trudeau kept office work and home life with his sons completely separate. According to his chauffeur Jack Deschambault, "he would get his foot in the door, set down his briefcase and the boys would jump in his arms. And off they went! Jumping into the pool or onto the trampoline!"

Margaret was getting restless, however. Much to her dismay, Pierre would plunge back into his papers once the boys had been tucked into bed. The young wife would later describe herself in *Beyond Reason* as being a "hippie without a cause." She felt very much alone. She had developed a reputation at British Columbia's Simon Fraser University as a left-leaning activist. Without any meaningful employment of her own, she struggled to find her own space in a public life that bored her and that she eventually would come to dread. In a newspaper interview in 1976, she clearly declared her independence and perhaps her dissatisfaction as well, when she said she wanted "to be more than a rose in my husband's lapel."[5]

Margaret was a passionate flower child from Vancouver who hated society life and official protocol. She found the cocktail circuit suffocating, and would have preferred smoking a bit of grass and making her own clothes.[6] She also made a few faux pas, for example, at an evening at the White House where she made a stunning appearance in a white dress that went down to her mid-calf, whereas protocol required her to wear a long dress. And on a state visit to Latin America, she didn't understand why she was ridiculed for singing a song of her own invention in honour of Blanquita Pérez, wife of the Venezuelan president.

Margaret often felt isolated in her husband's world, given his extremely demanding schedule and the way he could seem cold and distant. She found it infuriating that practically every evening he would go through "those damn brown boxes" of documents from the office until midnight.

As a young woman, Margaret valued her freedom, so when security measures were drastically tightened after the October Crisis broke out in 1970, she took it hard. She was with Pierre on Thanksgiving weekend when the phone rang in the middle of the night, plunging the country into a political crisis. Over the course of the phone call her husband learned that the Quebec provincial minister Pierre Laporte, who had been kidnapped by members of the Front de libération du Québec, was now dead. Pierre Elliott Trudeau had vowed never to negotiate with terrorists, but he had known Pierre Laporte personally and Margaret saw how devastated he was. She heard him sobbing.[7]

From that evening onward, she couldn't ride a bicycle along the Ottawa River without being accompanied by two RCMP officers. For the beautiful rebel, the bodyguards provided by the RCMP were no better than "prison guards." Margaret soon managed to shake them off once and for all, but her children would remain under police protection.

Once the 1974 election campaign got underway, Pierre was persuaded to have Margaret at his side. She enjoyed crossing the country from coast to coast, often bringing little Sacha along, and becoming a celebrity in her own right. The public found this twenty-five-year-old woman delightful, and warmed to the anecdotes she shared about her family and young children and her life as a mother. She managed to humanize Pierre Elliott Trudeau, who was increasingly considered cold and arrogant. She definitely contributed to his election victory, but once the campaign was over she returned sadly to oblivion. She waited for a phone call, a word of thanks or congratulations, but in vain. It was at this point that she began to feel exploited, broken. Official protocol and never-ending ceremonies were now a nightmare for Margaret, and she fled them whenever she could. Her marriage suffered as a result.

One day, in a fit of anger, she tore down a piece of a Canadian quilt work hanging in the stairwell of the prime minister's residence because it bore an embroidering of Pierre Trudeau's personal motto, "Reason before passion." She ripped the letters off the quilt one by one and threw them at the bottom of the stairs. Margaret would later write that her husband found this behaviour "inexcusable."

The children sometimes witnessed their parents quarrelling, for example, when Pierre would criticize Margaret for what he considered her extravagant spending on clothes. There was no reconciliation in sight. In spring 1977, six-year-old Justin lived through the bewildering drama of his parents' separation. Sacha was four and Michel just two. Pierre and Margaret decided to keep their children in the dark about what was really happening. "We told them I was going to look for work and I would come home as often as I could," Margaret wrote in her second book, *Consequences*.[8]

On March 4, the lovely Margaret left her "prison" on Sussex Drive — it was actually her sixth wedding anniversary — and joined the Rolling Stones for a weekend in Toronto. She had an affair with Ronnie Wood.[9] Then it was off to New York, where rumours of her nighttime encounters with the Stones snowballed. Nobody realized she had left the prime minister. World media seized on the story, describing with lurid headlines and sensational but misleading details how the prime minister's wife had taken part in an "orgy" in a hotel room. In an attempt to calm things down, the Prime Minister's Office issued a laconic press release:

> Pierre and Margaret Trudeau announce that because of Margaret's wishes they shall begin living separate and apart. Margaret relinquishes all privileges as the wife of the prime minister and wishes to leave the marriage and pursue an independent career. Pierre will have custody of their three sons, giving Margaret generous access to them.[10]

In theory, this would be a temporary separation lasting ninety days. The prime minister would not pay alimony to Margaret, who would see her children five days every other week.

Margaret shocked people during her first year of separation, sometimes without realizing it. "I filled the time with aimless comings and goings, breakdowns, and getting into publicity scrapes that affected not just my standing in Canada but also Pierre's whole political future," she later wrote.[11]

Her escapades met with public disapproval, but they also fed the media's appetite for sensation. She made "many trips, not all of them respectable," got into mischief at Studio 54, her favourite nightclub in New York, and experimented with cocaine. It later came out that she had affairs with Senator Ted Kennedy and the actors Ryan O'Neal and Jack Nicholson.

And while public opinion grew frankly hostile to her, she noticed people feeling sorry for the prime minister. Actually, the popularity of the world's most famous single father was now soaring.

In 1979 came the definitive breakup between Margaret and Pierre. At first she stayed in the prime minister's official residence in order to be close to the children. "When I was home, I had simply changed one bedroom for another," she later wrote.[12] Finally, she moved to a new home close to the official residence.

There were certainly tough times after the breakup, but the children learned to navigate the rough waters of their parents' troubled lives. Surrounded by maids and bodyguards, the children received a lot of attention at home, as well as many gifts from dignitaries and even from total strangers. Pierre and Margaret maintained their presence. They organized family activities. They did their best to soften the impact of the breakup and "to preserve the image of a united family," Margaret later wrote.

Sacha had an anxious nature: of the three boys, he was the one most disturbed by his mother's absences. His father explained to him that his mother needed to pursue her career. In fact, Margaret took on many new challenges. She did some photography and acted in two films, L'ange gardien (1978) and Kings and Desperate Men (1980).

The Trudeau government went down to defeat in the 1979 election. Conservative leader Joe Clark moved into the prime minister's residence at 24 Sussex Drive, leaving the Trudeau family to move into Stornoway, the official residence of the leader of the Opposition. The move didn't make much difference to the Trudeau boys because they had never been particularly fond of Sussex Drive. At least that's what Justin Trudeau told Catherine Clark during the interview on Beyond Politics.

But the Conservatives only hung on to power for a short time. Trudeau led the Liberals to victory in a sudden election, and the family returned to the greystone mansion Margaret had always found gloomy. During the few months they lived there, Joe Clark and his wife Maureen McTeer had managed to make a few changes to the decoration of the house. Moving back in was straightforward for Justin, since his father had always told the boys that 24 Sussex Drive "was not their house" but belonged to the people of Canada. The maids, the bodyguards, and "the Queen coming for lunch" were not meant to last.

Pierre and Margaret's relationship was not meant to last either. The joys of their honeymoon were a thing of the past. They divorced in 1984, the same year Pierre Trudeau retired from politics after nearly sixteen years in power. He told journalists he had taken the decision to retire during a long walk in the snow in February, after a judo session. He packed his bags and moved to Montreal with his sons. Margaret stayed in Ottawa and often saw their children.

Shortly after the divorce, Margaret married the real estate promoter Fried Kemper. They had two children together: Kyle in 1984 and Alicia four years later.

The Trudeau boys found it hard adjusting to their parents' divorce. But overall, they kept "positive memories" of their lives at 24 Sussex Drive: the pool, the circle of relations, weekends in the country. "It was like a dream," historian John English, the author of an excellent biography of Pierre Elliott Trudeau, recalls in an interview. "The parents were very loving to the children, and the children didn't get caught in the middle as they often do in a divorce or separation. So the parents insulated the children from the animosity they felt towards each other."

Monique Nemni, co-author of a monumental intellectual biography of Trudeau, agrees that the prime minister did everything he could to minimize the impact of the breakup on his children. He was heartbroken by the split with Margaret, but he never spoke publicly about affairs of the heart. "He never criticized the mother [of his children] whether in front of other people or in front of his children. Never.... God knows she said a lot of things about him, but he never reciprocated."

Many years later, Margaret's public image greatly improved after she revealed that she was suffering from bipolar disorder.[13]

CHAPTER 2

THE FORMATIVE YEARS

Despite their many differences, Pierre and Margaret agreed on one thing — their children would have a bilingual education — so they settled on the prestigious Collège Jean-de-Brébeuf, on Côte Sainte-Catherine Road in Montreal, where Pierre had been an outstanding student.

Justin Trudeau would spend seven years at Brébeuf: his high-school years, plus two more years at the Brébeuf CÉGEP (the equivalent of junior college). Scarcely any written trace remains of his years there. He did little worthy of mention at Brébeuf, obtained no academic distinctions, left no memorable writings behind. He opted for the demanding International Baccalaureate Diploma Programme, and distinguished himself in a debating tournament.

More likeable and outgoing than his father, Justin Trudeau was interested in everything and he spoke easily in public. His high-school teachers saw him as a born communicator and a student who made a good impression. He was not at all arrogant, nor did he have an inflated opinion of himself. He loved sharing ideas but, according to one of his teachers, he never "argued merely to prove he was right."

Justin Trudeau's school career would prove very different from his father's. Pierre Elliott Trudeau had been an exceptional intellectual and scholar, already publishing several noteworthy articles while following the classical course of study at Brébeuf. At the age of nineteen he had come first in his class, and had won all the Latin prizes (in versification, translation, and prose composition) as well as prizes for literature, history, English, and physics.[1]

But that was then, and this was now. Justin was less interested in writing than his father had been. If anything, he was more of a social creature, like his mother Margaret: he loved to party and he enjoyed meeting people.

Brébeuf was a whole new world for Justin Trudeau, but he managed to adapt quickly. He had gone to a French-immersion elementary school in Ottawa, where, as he mentioned wistfully during an event highlighting the Semaine de la francophonie in 2007, he had often spoken English in the hallway and the schoolyard. The nannies at 24 Sussex Drive had been mostly English-speaking. Once Pierre settled with his sons in Montreal, however, he insisted on their speaking French at home.

At Brébeuf Justin made lasting friendships with a group of bilingual boys — Marc Miller, Allen Steverman, Mathieu Walker, as well as David Legendre and Gregory O'Hayon — friendships that are still going strong.

Justin Trudeau was tall, slim, attractive, and lively. "He spoke with a loud voice," says Michel "Jim" Lefebvre, for thirty-five years a kind of institution at Brébeuf where he was in charge of Student Affairs. Justin had "communications skills" that drew other people to him. "He would be speaking to two or three people, and three minutes later a group of ten or twelve would have gathered around him. That gives you an idea of his character. He must have been quite persuasive."

Justin had travelled far and wide from a young age, and he was used to crowds. He was comfortable in all social situations, whether with friends or teachers or even total strangers. By the age of thirteen, when he moved with his father and brothers to Montreal, his father's hometown, he had already visited fifty countries.[2] He has been to forty more since then.

Justin's social graces set him apart from his classmates, but also from his more reserved and cerebral middle brother Alexandre and his youngest brother Michel, the most rebellious of the three boys.

It came as no surprise when Justin was elected to the students' council during his last high-school year at Brébeuf.

His father made sure that Justin took his coursework seriously. Pierre had custody of the three boys and was severe with them to the point of intransigence. He had been first in his class, and was therefore very demanding with them. According to Denis Jean, former assistant principal at Brébeuf and Justin's catechism teacher in Grade 10, the father "insisted that the boys pay close attention in class and listen attentively."

The former prime minister came to pick up his sons' report cards in person, and made a point of attending parent-teacher meetings. He stood in line in the hallway like other parents, waiting his turn to meet the boys' teachers. Several other parents found him a charming conversationalist.

"While waiting in line, he would chat with one person, then with another," says Denis Jean, who remembers that period with a wry smile. "We were always impressed by the way he took such a keen fatherly interest in his children. Parent-teacher meetings in those years were well attended — actually, those were *record years* for attendance!"

The teachers were simply astonished to see how attentive Trudeau was with his sons.

The former prime minister was a fervent Catholic and a champion of individual rights, although that hadn't prevented him from suspending those rights during the October Crisis in 1970. He was fascinated by the relationship between human rights and the Bible. When meeting the catechism teacher, he would ask a lot of questions. "He would spend an hour and a half in my office," remembers Denis Jean, "just like that!"

Pierre Trudeau made sure his sons put in their best effort, and insisted on their taking Latin. Justin studied Latin for four years, analyzing long Classical texts and rendering them diligently into French. Denis Jean believes this technique must have served Justin well when the time came to draft his father's eulogy, "which impressed everyone with its structure and soundness." It turns out Justin's friend Gerald Butts had a hand in drafting the eulogy, according to journalist Althia Raj. But Justin's friend Mathieu Walker insists that "Justin wrote most of it."[3]

Like his classmates, Justin Trudeau also studied math, French, and social science. He took courses in drama, a subject much to his liking. He had above all a passionate interest in history. André Champagne, his history and geography teacher and a close friend of the Trudeau family, had a profound influence on him. Champagne told the press that Justin "was incredibly talented and could pull off an 80% average practically without trying."[4] But he wasn't willing to say more, and he was not the first person refusing to talk about Justin Trudeau.

Justin developed a reputation at Brébeuf for being able to discuss a wide range of subjects and always emerge unscathed from the discussion. "He was a likeable and lively student who was open about his convictions," adds Jim Lefebvre, "although he never got the Governor General's Academic Medal."

In short, Justin managed well. Some say he was "above average," while others remember him as a "brilliant student." He got good grades, according to his former physics teacher, Gilles Levert, and without being "top notch" he definitely stood out. "We had some truly exceptional students. I can't say he was extraordinarily gifted. But he was a normal person, with what I would call medium-high intelligence. He was not a genius."

Justin played all the team sports at Brébeuf, from lacrosse to hockey and football to soccer. He was playful and loved to laugh. He sang Harry Belafonte's song "Day-O" in a humorous sketch. "Our favourite Jamaican," reads Justin's entry in the high-school yearbook of 1988–1989, "you sing well for a white man." Even then, people talked about his appearance. Mathieu Walker recalls that his eyelashes were so long, classmates nicknamed him "Tammy Faye" after the American singer and television evangelist.

———

Justin was a smooth talker who didn't always think about the consequences of his actions. He sometimes coaxed his buddies into taking part in his risky escapades. One time in high school, he convinced them to explore an old abandoned manor across the street from Brébeuf. The building was actually a crumbling heap about to collapse, but that didn't faze the young man. By prying a board loose, they could get inside. His friend Mathieu Walker still remembers this unfortunate incident.

"In retrospect, the place was probably filled with asbestos and I remember the floors were rotting, and we were going up these rotting stairs that could have collapsed. It was a dangerous site, the place was off limits but it was an adventure and it was fun … until we got caught."

Once witnesses out in the street had spotted teenagers inside the barricaded building, the police quickly arrived on the scene. Justin inadvertently attracted their attention.

"Had we stayed quiet, probably they wouldn't have come in and they would have left, but when they called out, Justin's reflex was to stick his head out the window," recalls Walker.

The band of teenagers had the biggest scare of their lives, although they got off without being put in handcuffs. They were punished the old-fashioned way by the principal of Brébeuf, who was not the least amused by their escapade. They had to write a hundred times on the blackboard, "Never again will we enter boarded-up houses."

Pierre Trudeau was a sportsman who enjoyed taking risks and skiing down the slopes at breakneck speed. He taught Justin and his two brothers to be afraid of nothing. When he was about fifteen, Justin got into another scrape when he took some of his buddies underground.

While visiting his mother in Ottawa, he convinced four or five classmates from Brébeuf to follow him down into the city's water diversion tunnels at one o'clock in the morning. Clutching little flashlights, the teenagers tried to find their way in the darkness. Justin thrust a dentist's mirror up through manholes to find his way. They wandered in the dark tunnels for an hour and a half, never knowing where they were. They had the impression of walking "for miles and miles." Mathieu Walker, now a heart specialist at St. Mary's Hospital in Montreal, was downright afraid. But, at the time, the whole quest made Justin laugh.

They continued walking, sticking close to walls covered in cobwebs, until they reached a dead end. That's when the group noticed a manhole.

Mathieu Walker still shivers when he thinks what could have happened: "It was in the middle of the night when there were not many cars around, but, as it happened, one car passed as we were about to pop up ..."

Justin's little dentist's mirror shattered into a thousand fragments. This was a narrow escape for the teenagers.

"In the end, we were in the middle of the street. It could have ended there, it could have been dangerous — let's put it that way — but in the end it was fine." Walker still wonders how he got coaxed into joining an escapade the teenage delinquents still haven't told their parents about to this day.

———

Justin also had a knack for creating little diplomatic incidents. The high-school classes continued until June in a stuffy old building without air conditioning. In Grade 10, seeing how hot the summer was turning out to be, young Trudeau and the other boys were jealous of the way girls could wear skirts as long as they respected the dress code; boys had to wear long trousers despite the stifling heat.

Justin and a few other students went to the principal's office to denounce what they saw as an injustice, but they were turned down flat. The physics teacher, Gilles Levert, remembers Justin as a "good negotiator," but the principal stuck to his decision.

"And then, out of the blue, Justin turned up at school on a particularly hot day … wearing a kilt. Which meant he had his skirt!" This stunt led to a hue and cry among the teaching staff. They held long and acrimonious meetings. "The principal was caught in a bind," adds Levert with a chuckle, "he really had no choice. Justin had nailed down the winning argument, and news of his stunt ran through the school like wildfire. Boys started borrowing skirts from their sisters at the convent next door."

Collège Brébeuf finally gave in, changing the dress code so boys could wear Bermuda shorts.

This incident reveals a fundamental trait in Justin's character. Once he sets his sights on a goal, he pursues it with great determination. He strikes when people least expect it. In the political arena, because he is often underestimated, this gives him a strategic advantage. In the boxing ring, Conservative Senator Patrick Brazeau would learn this the hard way.

Justin and his brothers also disliked being dropped off and picked up by limousine at Brébeuf, morning and evening. They were practically the only ones to be chauffeur-driven. They felt the limo cast them as different from other students, and they protested.

Gilles Levert noticed Justin was uncomfortable and raised the question with him one day in the computer lab. "Well, it's unusual, that's for sure," Justin said, before venting his frustrations about the strict attitude his father took toward many aspects of the boys' home life.

"The Trudeau household was run like a tight ship," Levert recalls. "Mr. Trudeau strictly controlled the number of hours they could watch television. Everything was mapped out, right down to what they could watch; there was constant surveillance and control. They couldn't do whatever they pleased at home."

Naturally, the Trudeau boys lacked for nothing, and they often invited their friends over. In the lovely Art Deco house Ernest Cormier had built on Pine Avenue, the floor where the boys had their bedrooms was covered with exercise mats. This was their private realm. They could play-fight or work out without hurting themselves. Justin used to practise boxing there. He learned boxing from his father, just as Pierre had learned the sport from his own father before him.

But unlike many young people from well-to-do families, the Trudeau boys weren't spoiled. Well-heeled students would often turn up at Brébeuf in brand-new cars. Many of them flaunted the latest electronic gadgets, like Walkmans. But the Trudeau boys didn't have them all; their father didn't believe in spoiling them.

The former prime minister had grown up in the lap of luxury but was always tight with money. He had let himself be charmed by a Harley-Davidson motorcycle and of course the stunning silver Mercedes he proudly drove through the streets of Ottawa. But he once told the authors Max and Monique Nemni that he didn't want to be a "slave to material possessions," and he wanted to transmit that value to his sons. He wanted them to be "quite detached from all that."[5]

———

The teachers at Brébeuf had seen their share of children crushed by their parents' divorce. That does not seem to have been the case with Justin, although the separation had more of an impact on his two younger brothers, Alexandre and Michel.[6] There's no doubt that Justin was affected: he just didn't let it show. At least that's the impression several of his teachers had. Justin's friends saw something different.

How could a young person remain unaffected by the separation of his parents when the whole drama was being played out in public? Newspapers and magazines devoted a lot of space to the breakup. Margaret herself let everything hang out, when she wrote juicy details about her troubled relationship with the prime minister, her life as a hippie, evenings with the Rolling Stones, amorous adventures, and her love of marijuana. Justin later joked that his mother was "a bit too much of a hippie."

In Montreal, he shared his grief over the separation with his close friends. According to his Brébeuf classmate Marc Miller, his friends became "his extended family." Justin found solace in the happier atmosphere of his friends' home life.

Justin is discreet about his childhood, but he nonetheless confided in the 2009 interview with Catherine Clark that he realized his parents weren't meant for each other: "They loved each other incredibly, passionately, completely, but there was thirty years between them. And my mom was never an equal partner in what encompassed my father's life, his duty, his country. She was a partner in the child-bearing stuff and the family stuff, but not in his full life."

———

Brébeuf had instilled in Pierre Trudeau "the demon of knowledge." Justin was full of intellectual curiosity, but he wasn't the kind of person to write long diatribes for the pleasure of proving he was right. Justin didn't leave behind a trail of writings as a youth. Naturally, he read a lot and was interested in everything. In this respect he followed his father's lead, as he once explained to Jim Lefebvre: "Oh! My father has always been telling us how important reading is. I got that from him. I try as much as possible to delve into many different subjects."

Collège Brébeuf gave him opportunities to broaden his horizons. Reading was encouraged and there was no lack of subjects. Current affairs were discussed in class. Discussion was encouraged without teachers imposing any single point of view on the students. During his first year of CÉGEP, Justin took part in a debating tournament organized March 2, 1990, by the Bar of Montreal, drawing students from French- and English-speaking CÉGEPs throughout Montreal. The subject was captivating: "Should the 'polluter pays principle' be applied in the interest both of economic development and environmental protection?" Trudeau came second.

Justin's success in the debating tournament might make one think he was already following in his father's footsteps. But at the time, politics wasn't on his mind.

The teachers at Brébeuf were careful not to take a stand on the bitter debate about Quebec's political future. The subject came up from time to time in the schoolyard, although it never dominated exchanges between students. Anglophone students and more nationalist francophone students sometimes clashed over the protection of the French language and Bill 101. According to Mathieu Walker, some francophones were simply "obnoxious" with anglophone students, even to the point of chanting "101, 101" whenever they encountered them. Walker got fed up with the atmosphere at Brébeuf, and left right after high school, opting to do his CÉGEP years elsewhere. Bill 101 came up all the time, he says. "There was a lot of graffiti in the bathrooms and on the walls. Some people would write '101' on their notebooks."

In general, however, students stayed away from hot political issues and didn't dwell on their parents' professional careers. Justin was no exception: he admired his father but he never put on airs.

———

If truth be told, Justin wasn't that interested in politics. Pierre had written several articles for the student newspaper *Le Brébeuf*, but Justin wasn't one for initiating debates. Sometimes, though, news events got in the way.

In June 1990, the Meech Lake Accord, which had sought to bring Quebec into the 1982 Constitution "with honour and enthusiasm," was defeated. The provincial government set up the Commission on the Political and Constitutional Future of Quebec, also known as the Bélanger-Campeau Commission, to study political options for the province. By November that year, a mini-referendum campaign was underway in thirty-one Quebec CÉGEPs, with almost 74,000 students taking part. They were going to answer the following question: "Do you want Quebec to become a sovereign state?"

Brébeuf was no exception. The college would host a vigorous debate on Quebec's political future, reflecting the obvious tensions between federalists and sovereignists across the province, in the aftermath of Meech.

On the day of the debate, Justin Trudeau took up the torch for the federalist side. With his high cheekbones, nasal inflections, and blue eyes, he bore some comparison to his father. The cameras were rolling.

"The Meech Lake Accord was defeated because it was a bad accord," he said with an air of determination. "Quebeckers should not feel they are hated by other Canadians as a result," stammered the former prime minister's son, "because that's just not true."

Buoyed by the applause they were getting, the young sovereignty supporters retorted that Quebeckers should stop letting themselves be dominated by Canada. But Trudeau stuck to his guns.

"Quebeckers are perfectly capable of succeeding in the world as a sovereign state. But I believe they would be even more capable of succeeding in the world with Canada backing them up."

Justin explained to the journalists hounding him that he was taking his own stand, not following the position of his father. Pierre had been a ferocious opponent of the Meech Lake Accord and of any special status for Quebec, coming out of retirement from active political life to make his point.

"I don't take anything for granted," eighteen-year-old Justin said. "I listen. I listen to my friends who believe Quebec should separate, just as I listen to my father who believes in the federal state. I have my own ideas."

In the debate at Brébeuf, federalists were in the minority and were heckled. "Everyone faces pressure at our age," Justin declared to the cameras, shrugging his shoulders. Then he added, with a sly grin, that he had never been affected by such pressures.

Across the CÉGEP network, the "Yes" side won with 82 percent of the votes. At Brébeuf, the sovereignists won 63 percent of the votes, compared to 34 percent for the federalists. This mini-campaign took place five years before the 1995 referendum on Quebec independence, when the "Yes" side would come within a hair of winning.

———

Like his father Pierre before him, Justin was among the francophone elite at Brébeuf. Celebrated graduates included Quebec premiers Robert Bourassa and Pierre-Marc Johnson, the founder of Quebec's modern education system Paul Gérin-Lajoie, the astrophysicist Hubert Reeves, the journalist André Laurendeau, and many others. Many of these graduates were initiated into politics at Brébeuf: Robert Bourassa had even gone around the school saying, "One day, I will be premier of Quebec."

Jim Lefebvre, long in charge of Student Affairs at Brébeuf, says, "That particular story has often been repeated. But nothing like that happened with Justin Trudeau. He rarely talked about his future." The direction he was going to take "was not altogether clear" when he graduated.

His teachers thought he was likely to make his mark in one of three areas: history, his passion; law, which his father had studied; or political science. But Justin Trudeau writes in *Common Ground* that he "fairly deliberately flunked" experimental psychology, which he found boring, "effectively killing any hope I had of going to McGill Law.... I had sabotaged that path, perhaps as a way of forcing myself, and my father, to come to grips with the fact that I would never be the academic high achiever he was." Politics didn't interest him at the time. His real "passion" was English literature. [7]

His friend Mathieu Walker believes that even if the two didn't discuss politics at the time, Justin Trudeau would inevitably go into politics one day.

"That was his destiny," Walker says without hesitation. "I had a gut feeling that's where he would end up. Obviously, there was a clear association with his father, but there was more going on than that, because I wouldn't have said the same about his brothers."

Whatever destiny might have held in store for him, young Trudeau was unaware of it at the time. In fact, he spent years searching for himself. In 1994, he graduated with a bachelor's degree from McGill University in English literature. Then he took time out from his studies, travelling around the world for six months with friends like Mathieu Walker, Allen Steverman, and Marc Miller. He got away from it all, he was an ordinary person, he let himself go … and he enjoyed the experience. "It was good for him to just get away for awhile and to be a regular kind of guy," says Walker, adding nobody knew the Trudeau name in Ouagadougou.

The young Quebeckers visited seventeen or eighteen countries in Asia and Africa, crossed the Sahara by truck with some Europeans and Australians, and went camping. "Sometimes we didn't wash for many days in a row; this was a really primitive way to travel, but it was fantastic," recalls Walker.

In Africa, Trudeau decided on the spur of the moment to cut his hair short, but he soon regretted it. A few days later, he fell on his glasses and had to repair them with adhesive tape. At border crossings, customs agents sometimes demanded bribes. At one point, the young friends worried their passports were about to be seized. According to Walker, this was a character-building experience for Justin.[8]

Once he got home after this long trip abroad, it was time for Pierre Elliott Trudeau's eldest son to work out his priorities. Justin loved the world of teaching, which he saw as a form of public service and a chance to get away from the family mould and his own past.[9] When he announced his decision to his mother, she was overjoyed: "It's a family tradition!"[10]

Justin started teacher training at McGill, but he felt uncomfortable in Montreal where he was often recognized on the street, so he headed for Vancouver. His brother Michel, an avid skier and outdoorsman, was on the West Coast already. His mother Margaret had four sisters there. On weekdays he took a bachelor's in education at the University of British Columbia, and on weekends he was a snowboard instructor at Whistler-Blackcomb.

Some of his friends wondered about his decision to go into teaching. Years later, Justin Trudeau would explain that he had always been aware of living a privileged life, and he wanted to transmit what he had learned to a new generation. He also wanted to avoid doing what he was expected to do — that is, take over the family business: politics.[11]

Vancouver and Whistler suited him just fine. He started as a substitute teacher, taught at Sir Winston Churchill High School, and then got a job at the prestigious West Point Grey Academy, a private school in Vancouver.

For five years, Justin Trudeau lived the life of a bachelor. Girls found his charm hard to resist, but according to Thomas Panos, a friend who had come back to Vancouver to run a travel agency, Justin didn't have any serious relationships.

Going out with Justin was never dull. In the street, people often recognized him and came up to say hello. Justin took it in stride. He was used to it. One day Panos accompanied Trudeau to a bookstore. A lady came up to Justin, saying how much she respected his father: she hoped Justin would also do something important in politics one day. "She gave him a hug and a kiss," Panos recalls. "I saw this quite a few times." Justin seemed to enjoy this kind of gesture, although he never spoke about his family.

But on the slopes of Whistler, the young man blended into the background. The daredevil from Montreal was great on a snowboard and he was great with kids. Sean Smillie hired him to work at his snowboard school. He was impressed by this young instructor with the chaotic but controlled style, who wove his way through the glades at breakneck speed. "Justin always got the wild and crazy kids who ran all over the mountain." Nobody figured this long-haired snowboarder in his mid-twenties was actually from one of Canada's leading families. "I had no idea who he was, for months and months," says Sean Smillie.[12]

When Smillie finally asked his employee whether he was actually the son of Pierre Trudeau, Justin answered with a modest yes. And life went on as before. The two young men became friends, took their meals together, watched movies, and hauled their snowboards in Justin's beat-up old car. Justin often hung out on the sofa, while Sean described video game scenarios he was working out in his mind. He eventually became one of the creators of the very popular "extreme snowboarding" game SSX3, for the video game company Electronic Arts.

Life was good in Whistler-Blackcomb. The young men loved the magnificent trails and they loved snowboarding — "the ride," as Smillie put it. "It wasn't so much the partying and the female population. That was a nice benefit."

———

These carefree years came to an end very suddenly. On November 13, 1998, tragedy struck the Trudeau family. While skiing in the Kootenay mountains of British Columbia, Michel was swept away by an avalanche and carried by the weight of his equipment down to the bottom of Kokanee Lake. Three of his buddies managed to swim to the shore, but Michel's body was never recovered. He was twenty-three years old.

At Michel's funeral in St-Viateur d'Outremont church, Justin and Alexandre could be seen supporting their frail father Pierre, who was crushed with grief. Margaret looked utterly devastated. She fell into a deep depression. The former prime minister never recovered.

All Justin would say is that it had "been hard for the whole family."

A little over a year after the accident, Justin and his mother started a fundraising campaign for the Canadian Avalanche Foundation. He gave speeches, organized fundraising activities, and joined his mother and brother in building a cabin in memory of Michel and other skiers who had lost their lives in the Kootenay region of British Columbia. The three-storey cabin was inaugurated on July 12, 2003, replacing the one where Michel had spent his last night before losing his life in the avalanche.[13]

Life gradually came back to normal. Justin took up his work as a snowboard instructor on the ski slopes, although he and Sean now wore helmets. Two years later, when his father was dying, Justin took leave from the high school where he was teaching and returned to Montreal. Pierre's death from prostate cancer unleashed a real tsunami of emotions among Canadians. Many people asked CBC Television to rebroadcast the eulogy given at the funeral by Justin.

Justin stayed in Quebec long enough to take care of family matters and then returned to teach in Vancouver. But everything had changed for him on the West Coast. The hardships of the last few years bore down on him, and he missed Montreal, the city of his teenage years. People around him could see how restless he was. "I am a Québécois. Montreal is my home. That's where I'm going," he later told his friend Thomas Panos.

CHAPTER 3

RUNNING IN PAPINEAU

The Liberal Party of Canada was impressed by the eulogy Justin Trudeau gave at his father's funeral, and saw the young man as a rising star. Justin felt drawn toward politics, but he was in no hurry. He knew his record was slim and that he needed more experience before going into public life. Shortly after the funeral, Gerald Butts, a close friend from the English program at McGill, asked him whether he was ready to go into politics. Justin replied that he had no burning desire. He was twenty-eight years old, and just didn't feel ready.

"I haven't done anything. I haven't accomplished anything," he would tell *Maclean's* magazine two years later, with his trademark frankness. "My father was 20 years older than me when he got into politics. I won't be rushed."[1]

Justin was well travelled. He had obtained a bachelor's degree in English literature at McGill University, and then another bachelor's in education at the University of British Columbia. He loved teaching, but once he got back to Montreal he realized it was time to move on to something new. So he left teaching to become an advocate for youth movements, joining the Board of Directors of Katimavik, an organization offering young Canadians opportunities for volunteering, which had been founded by his father's close friend Jacques Hébert in 1977. Justin loved nature just the way his father Pierre had, so he also became an environmental advocate.

He was never far from the spotlight. He attended the Juno Awards gala in Ottawa in 2003 and was a judge on CBC's literary competition *Canada Reads*. He introduced the Dalai Lama to a crowd of 30,000 at Toronto's SkyDome in April 2004. In a public talk called "The Power of Compassion," the Buddhist monk lit up the crowd, telling them, "The 20th century was the century of violence.... The 21st century should be the century of dialogue." Justin Trudeau introduced the Dalai Lama as a man "who gets along with just about everyone" in a world of violence, mistrust, and hatred.[2] The Dalai Lama put his arms around the former prime minister's eldest son, pressing his cheek against Justin's for a long moment.

That same year, Justin Trudeau was hired by CKAC Radio in Montreal as a commentator. He was sent to cover the Olympic Games in Athens. Although he was a novice at broadcasting, as in everything he did he was not afraid to leave his comfort zone and take up something new. His assignment was to provide listeners with the historical, cultural, and human context of the Games.

"I know people are going to criticize me," the budding broadcaster said. "They are going to criticize my French for sure. But I just consider this a new challenge. I want to learn, and I hope that people will let me learn along with them."[3]

Justin was swept up in the euphoria of the Olympics, but he was also swept off his feet by Sophie Grégoire, who joined him in Athens. She had been a friend of his late brother, Michel, and they had already met at Brébeuf. He could hardly fail to notice this beautiful young woman with chestnut hair and blue eyes. They met up again when co-hosting a benefit event for the Starlight Children's Foundation. The next day, Sophie sent him an email, but he never answered. Catherine Clark asked him why he hesitated when he already seemed to be smitten by Sophie, a former model and a star of the CTV show *eTalk*. "Because I knew that the day I went for coffee with her was the last day I would ever have as a single man," he replied candidly.

When Justin declared to Sophie on their first date that he wanted to spend the rest of his life with her, she didn't know how to respond. After two or three weeks, she realized he was serious. Then a few weeks later, she realized he was right. They were practically inseparable. They moved in together three months later.

His friend Thomas Panos was passing through Athens and saw that Justin had found the woman of his dreams. "You could tell they were madly in love with each other."

After the Olympics, the young couple holidayed in the Greek islands. Things moved on quickly from there. The "royal" couple got married in Montreal the following year, on May 28, 2005. The Canadian public was treated to a fairy-tale wedding. Ben Mulroney, the son of Brian Mulroney, was there. The newlyweds left the party behind the wheel of Pierre Elliott Trudeau's pride and joy — the old silver Mercedes convertible. They spent their honeymoon in Morocco.

Once back in Canada, there was increasing buzz about Justin's political future. Justin himself asked Gerald Butts a thousand and one questions. He was particularly concerned about the impact politics could have on his private life.

In 2005, he started a master's degree in environmental geography at McGill, but withdrew from the program in the fall of 2006. He grew a moustache to play the role of Talbot Papineau in the CBC/Radio-Canada mini-series *The Great War*. Young Trudeau was lucky to be able to jump from one activity to another. His father had left him an inheritance of $1.2 million and Justin drew rich fees as a keynote speaker on behalf of charitable organizations and school boards: his publicity agency paid him fees of $290,000 in 2006 and $462,000 in 2007. A few years later, these generous fees would prove controversial.

Justin was much in demand. He realized he appealed to crowds. Little by little, he was being drawn to politics.

———

In 2006, the Liberal Party of Canada was in a shambles. Prime Minister Paul Martin, who had succeeded Jean Chrétien three years earlier, resigned after a humiliating defeat that resulted in Stephen Harper's Conservatives forming a minority government.

The Liberal Party held its leadership convention from November 28 to December 2. Bob Rae, former New Democratic premier of Ontario, and Michael Ignatieff, an intellectual and prolific author based at Harvard University, led the field of eight contenders.

Justin Trudeau had been seen off and on since his father's funeral. He now made an entrance at Montreal's Palais des Congrès, where the convention was being held. There he would play an important role in choosing the next Liberal leader. When journalists asked which candidate he favoured, Justin replied that he didn't have a lot in common with Michael Ignatieff. He was wavering between Stéphane Dion and Gerard Kennedy, the former minister of education in Dalton McGuinty's Liberal government in Ontario. Justin was introduced to Kennedy by his friend Gerald Butts, who had served as McGuinty's principal secretary.

In his mid-forties, Kennedy was a star of the Ontario government. His French was wooden and he was a relative unknown in Quebec, but the positions he took on renewing the Liberal Party resonated with Trudeau, who had gone through the same exercise when running the youth program for the Liberal Party Renewal Commission. The report Trudeau published in the fall of 2006 impressed Tom Axworthy, who had been one of Pierre Elliott Trudeau's close colleagues.[4]

Delegates at the convention realized the Liberal Party was at a crossroads. The Gomery Commission of Inquiry into the sponsorship scandal had made damaging and highly publicized revelations. Voters were disgruntled with the Liberals and had given them a severe drubbing in the 2006 election. They won just 103 out of 308 seats in the federal Parliament, and got only 13 seats in Quebec. This amounted to a net loss of 32 seats across Canada and 8 within Quebec.

The Liberals had immediately started looking for a new leader who could bring the party back to power. But this was a daunting task. Prime Minister Stephen Harper had established himself right across the political landscape. The Conservatives obtained 40.3 percent of the popular vote, and won 123 seats. In Quebec, they had gone from no seats at all to 10.

In the House of Commons, Harper launched a charm offensive, shifting the spotlight away from the Liberal leadership race. On November 22, 2006, the prime minister stunned Canadians by tabling a surprise motion in the Commons that read: "That this House recognize that the Québécois form a nation within a united Canada." The motion was adopted five days later by a vote of 265 to 16. Prime Minister Harper lost his intergovernmental affairs minister Michael Chong, who resigned dramatically. Chong considered Canada "an indivisible nation"[5] and preferred to resign from office rather than simply abstain from a vote that, he feared, would strengthen the hand of Quebec sovereignists. The pro-sovereignty Bloc Québécois was still going strong, with 51 seats in the federal Parliament, but Harper's stratagem left the Bloc no choice but to support the motion.[6] The New Democrats supported it as well.

Harper's gesture was well received in Quebec, although many people were left wondering what it actually meant. In other parts of Canada, the motion proved more controversial.

Stéphane Dion and Michael Ignatieff voted in favour of the Conservative motion, but fifteen Liberals voted against, including several candidates for the leadership. Two Toronto-area MPs, the former hockey star Ken Dryden and Joe Volpe, voted against it. Gerard Kennedy — who did not hold a federal seat at the time — also came out against it, since he feared the word "nation" was ambiguous and therefore subject to interpretation. Bob Rae, who also did not sit in the Commons, was lukewarm about the motion, and said the party should focus on more pressing issues.

The Liberal leadership convention in Montreal thus unfolded with Harper's motion as its backdrop. The different camps made their moves, but the first ballot proved frustrating. No single candidate had enough support to stand out above the crowd. So when Kennedy decided to drop out of the race after the second ballot, his supporters (including Justin Trudeau) moved their block of votes to Stéphane Dion, attracted by his social policies and also his Green Shift plan, which proposed a carbon tax to reduce greenhouse gas emissions. Dion was also the second choice of another three hundred delegates, MPs, and senators: Eleni Bakopanos, a faithful party organizer and former MP whose riding was next to Dion's riding, lined up their support.

The pro-Dion camp was increasing its advantage. Stéphane Dion came first on the third ballot. His team realized the tide was turning in their favour when delegates started sporting green scarves. "Everyone wants to be with a winner," recalls Eleni Bakopanos.

The first contender to rally to Dion was the Ontario businesswoman Martha Hall Findlay, who dropped out of the race. Bob Rae was both disappointed and astonished by the turn of events — after all, he had the backing of Jean Chrétien, and he thought he had a good chance of winning. He angrily released his supporters, few of whom went to the Dion camp.

On the fourth ballot, Stéphane Dion, the candidate nobody could picture as leader, finally came out on top. Party faithful and MPs gathered around him, sporting their green scarves. Michael Ignatieff had stood a good chance; he was the only candidate to have supported the motion of the Quebec wing of the party recognizing the Quebec nation. But his turn would have to wait. Dion had served under Jean Chrétien as inter-governmental affairs minister and father of the *Clarity Act*. He had also been minister of the environment under Paul Martin. He appreciated Justin Trudeau's support but didn't set aside a riding for him to run in.

This leadership race marked a turning point for Justin Trudeau. He was no longer merely the son of his father: he was now assuming an important role of his own, on a larger field. The party faithful at the convention were all over him. It wasn't clear just yet *why* he was going into politics. He would later say he was motivated by "a sense of duty" and the desire to make the world a better place for his children.[7]

But he was going to take his time, and keep his cards close to his chest.

He lived in the chic Montreal riding of Outremont, and would have liked running there. But the party had other plans and he was advised to look for another riding. Stéphane Dion was keeping Outremont for Jocelyn Coulon, former international news editor at *Le Devoir*. This choice proved to be a blessing in disguise for Justin because New Democrat Thomas Mulcair won the riding in a by-election on September 17, 2007, and was re-elected there in 2008, 2011, and 2015.

Justin Trudeau still had other options. The party offered him a riding on the South Shore of Montreal, but he preferred to continue looking on the island. Then, out of the blue, he announced on February 22, 2007, that he would seek the Liberal nomination to run in the Montreal riding of Papineau.

As he explained to his rivals, the riding appealed to him because it was like a microcosm of Canada. Papineau was an urban riding full of halal markets, little shops, and designer boutiques, with a French-speaking majority and a diverse minority of 113 cultural communities or ethnic groups. Issues were complex in the riding. For Justin Trudeau, under-standing Papineau was like understanding Canada as a whole.

So this was the riding where he decided to make his mark. He liked competition, and he believed he "could win back the riding," as he told a local newspaper. Vivian Barbot, a competent candidate for the Bloc Québécois, had snatched Papineau during the 2006 election, beating the federal Liberal minister Pierre Pettigrew by just 990 votes. Pettigrew had been recruited by Jean Chrétien and had represented the riding for a decade, succeeding André Ouellet, who had dominated the riding for twenty-eight years. In fact, Papineau had been a Liberal stronghold since the beginning of the twentieth century.

By 2006, however, the Liberals were at a low ebb. Pierre Pettigrew, former minister of foreign affairs, was devastated by the defeat, and had already publicly announced he would not be running again. He left politics for good, returning to the business world.

Trudeau was cautious. He had grown up in the political universe and was used to double-talk. He wanted to sound out Pierre Pettigrew in person before doing anything, so he flew to Toronto to seek advice from the former MP for Papineau.

"Justin had the courtesy to come visit me in person, to ask my true intentions," Pierre Pettigrew recalls. "Did my public statements reflect what I really planned to do?" Pettigrew's answer was categorical: "I won't be coming back. I have done my time."

The former minister was not at all surprised by Justin's interest in politics. He had known Justin as a child. Before entering politics himself in 1996, Pettigrew had often attended meetings at 24 Sussex Drive as a representative of the Privy Council and former adviser to Pierre Trudeau. He had often seen "the Trudeau boys chasing up and down the stairs in slippers before the VIPs arrived."

Pettigrew had lost sight of Justin when the young man had headed out to Vancouver. But now here Justin was, in person, looking for information. Pettigrew confirmed that Papineau would provide him with an excellent political base, although winning the riding would take a lot of patience and hard work at the grassroots level. Justin would have to adapt to the different realities of Park Extension with its multi-ethnic character, Villeray with its French-speaking majority, and Saint-Michel, the core of Montreal's Haitian community. The former minister explained to Justin how difficult it was to sound out the citizens in the riding, since the immigrant population was in a constant state of flux: July 1, Quebec's statutory day for lease renewals, saw tenants moving in and out in droves.

Despite these words of caution, Pierre Pettigrew had one message for Justin: "Go for it!"

Justin Trudeau took him at his word. In the months leading up to the nomination contest in Papineau, he criss-crossed the riding, getting to know each neighbourhood, holding meetings, and going door to door two or three hours a day. According to veteran organizer Reine Hébert, who came to work for him, he kept up this pace at least five days a week. He gained the support of the Haitian community, starting with Emmanuel Dubourg, the Quebec provincial member for Viau. Trudeau had an army of volunteers working for him.

Justin Trudeau's two rivals in the nomination contest were lagging behind. Both Basilio Giordano, former city councillor for Saint-Léonard and publisher of Canada's oldest Italian newspaper, *Il Cittadino Canadese*, and Mary Deros, city councillor for Park Extension since 1998, had a good standing in the community. But neither of them had seen young Trudeau coming.

Mary Deros had a lot of experience and she felt her chances were good. Hadn't Pettigrew himself told her the previous year, at the Liberal leadership convention, that the way was clear? She threw herself into the race, wooing the riding's ethnic groups, attending many community events, making herself available. Then she discovered to her great surprise that Justin was doing exactly the same thing.

Of Greek and Armenian ancestry, she had great visibility in the community and knew the riding inside out. But she had a shoestring organization. Her "team" consisted of just two people — herself and an organizer, who did everything by hand. He hated computers and manually drew up lists of members and groups to meet. "That was really unusual," Deros recalls with a touch of irony.

Justin Trudeau meanwhile, backed by a young and dynamic machine, worked tirelessly. He was good at connecting with people. He held meetings as often as he could in restaurants and coffeehouses, at least five times a week. He sat down with leaders of the Pakistani, Italian, and Greek communities, for example. He was becoming an increasingly recognizable presence in the district. He was seen at community centres and golden age clubs, where he laughed, laid on the charm, and showed how accessible he was.

His manner was pure Justin Trudeau, and it was contagious.

"You sit down with ten people," his organizer Reine Hébert recalls with a chuckle, "and those ten then speak to twenty more, who in turn reach forty more. It's like the multiplication of the loaves." Hébert had been director-general of the party, Senator Pietro Rizzuto's right-hand woman, and Jean Chrétien's chief organizer. She had organized Chrétien's successful campaign in Quebec when he ran for the Liberal leadership.

When she learned that Trudeau was planning to run in Papineau, she called before dropping by to see him. She explained she had known his father and she had a lot of experience as an organizer. She offered to work for him. Justin knew her by reputation but not in person, and accepted her offer. Reine Hébert wanted to understand first of all what was motivating him to run for the Liberal Party.

"I want to move this country forward, and I want to serve," he answered. According to Hébert, Pierre Elliott Trudeau's son did not have higher ambitions for the moment. He still had no idea of becoming prime minister: he knew he had to learn politics from the ground up. In future years he would often explain that he went into politics out of a sense of duty.

Hébert was convinced that Trudeau was "the candidate of the future," at a time when the Liberal Party badly needed renewal. She got to work in Papineau, a riding she found interesting but hard to figure out. From the beginning, she knew Trudeau would face serious obstacles because his family name rubbed part of the Quebec population the wrong way. The Trudeau name reminded people of a turbulent period in Quebec history. The October Crisis, the *War Measures Act*, the patriation of the Canadian Constitution without Quebec's consent — many Quebeckers reacted in bitterness at the mere mention of Pierre Elliott Trudeau's name.

Justin knew this only too well. When canvassing door to door, he would introduce himself as Justin. "We didn't run the campaign on the Trudeau name," recalls Reine Hébert. On the positive side, though, the family name was respected by ethnic groups committed to the idea of a united Canada. The eulogy Justin had given at his father's funeral doubtless played in his favour. "I am sure it had an impact on people," says Hébert.

The day of the Liberal riding nomination, April 29, 2007, was nonetheless nerve-wracking. The Trudeau team left nothing to chance. Area captains had been appointed to get the francophone vote out in

Saint-Michel, Villeray, and Park Extension. The team was targeting ethnic groups, community organizations, and golden age clubs.

Reine Hébert got a young Liberal, Louis-Alexandre Lanthier, to help her organize press coverage on the day of the vote. Pablo Rodríguez, the Liberal MP for Honoré-Mercier, knew Justin well and was called on to introduce him.

Trudeau addressed the party faithful gathered at the Collège André-Grasset, describing his roots, his devotion to the riding (which incorporated some of his father's former riding of Mount Royal), and his admiration for the *Canadian Charter of Rights and Freedoms*. But, he announced loud and clear, he was his own man.

"My name is Justin Trudeau," he said enthusiastically. "I am Justin Trudeau! A man with a dream. I want to work with you. Share your challenges and your successes."

Clearly, the crowd in the packed hall was favourable to him. The Italian and Greek communities in particular had always been devoted to the Trudeau family.

The suspense didn't last very long. Trudeau won on the first ballot. Evidently, the party faithful preferred a novice to two experienced candidates. He got 690 of the 1,260 votes, Mary Deros got 350, and Basilio Giordano received 220. Reine Hébert believes several Liberal supporters changed camps "because of the father." Justin's family name and his celebrity status played a role. The strength of his organization too. At the end of the evening, Louis-Alexandre Lanthier wished the future MP for Papineau good luck before returning to Ottawa.

"An immigrant's daughter in Montreal against Pierre Elliott Trudeau's son? I never thought I had a chance," recalls Mary Deros with regret. She nonetheless concedes that her rival, who has since become a friend, worked extremely hard to win the Liberal nomination in Papineau. "Justin Trudeau's strength is that he works his territory so well: he gets out a lot." Justin definitely benefited from his spontaneity and ability to connect with people.

———

Justin Trudeau had won the first round. He was now assured of being on the ballot as Liberal Party candidate in the next federal election, which would take place on October 14, 2008. He set out to devote all his energy to beating the Bloc Québécois MP Vivian Barbot.

A former teacher and former president of the Quebec Federation of Women, Barbot was an energetic, intelligent woman. She wasn't afraid to speak her mind and she was never shy about slamming her opponents. She could see the upcoming campaign in the former Liberal stronghold would be a tough one — she had only barely snatched victory from Pierre Pettigrew.

From the outset, she found her rival hard to grasp. She echoed an increasingly common criticism of Justin Trudeau: that he cuts a handsome appearance but his ideas are unclear.

"He's all image: his tie is straight, his hair is well groomed, he has a winning smile, but that's about it," she says. "I would like to see beyond all that." He's a nice young man, she adds, but he was "surfing" on the Trudeau name in order to dazzle ethnic voters, without taking any personal risks of his own.

During the campaign, she met the Liberal candidate more than once. She says he never revealed his true self.

"I never got through to the real person deep down. In any case, he only gives you a half-handshake with his finger-tips," she says with conviction. "It's really unpleasant."

On the ground, the Liberal candidate in Papineau seemed deft at handling whatever situation arose, although he sometimes made gaffes.

For example, on May 4, 2007, just a week after winning the Liberal nomination, he unleashed a storm of protest among his Liberal supporters because of his slippery language about bilingualism, one of the pillars of his father's political legacy.

During his first public appearance as the Liberal candidate for Papineau, Justin Trudeau questioned whether the system of distinct French-language and English-language schools should be maintained. Wouldn't it be "cheaper" to have a single bilingual school system, he said nonchalantly before some 2,000 elementary school teachers in Saint John, New Brunswick.

"The segregation of French and English in separate schools is something that deserves serious re-evaluation. People are being divided and assigned different labels."[8]

What he didn't say, however, was that bilingual schools were a hotbed of assimilation for French-speaking minorities. His statement landed with a resonating thud in New Brunswick, Canada's only officially bilingual province! It had taken the French-speaking Acadians of New Brunswick epic legal battles, sometimes even in a climate of violence, to rid the province of bilingual schools where English became the dominant language, and to obtain French-language schools of their own.

In answering a question from the audience, Justin Trudeau said he was not in favour of bilingualism, but preferred "trilingualism" or even "quadrilingualism."

The Société des Acadiens du Nouveau-Brunswick came out slamming the thirty-five-year-old candidate for "his total ignorance of the cultural and linguistic reality of Canada." Louise Landry, president of the Association des enseignants francophones (the association of French-speaking teachers), said she was simply "trembling" with rage.

The Liberal candidate's sensational remarks also outraged Liza Frulla, a former Liberal minister in Paul Martin's Cabinet. She couldn't stand the attitude of this "young upstart" playing "the rock star" who knew nothing about the founding principles of Canada as a country.[9] While some attributed this blunder to the candidate's lack of experience, others felt it did not augur well for the federal Liberal Party, which had been torn apart a few months earlier by the issue of recognizing Quebec as a nation.

"Justin and I are going to have a talk," said the Liberal MP and former minister Denis Coderre, who reaffirmed unhesitatingly the Liberal Party's recognition of Quebec as a nation.[10]

Justin Trudeau's remarks were even taken up by the English-language media. The conservative *National Post* ran an editorial on May 9, 2007, under the title "Read the Charter, Justin," saying out loud what others were thinking to themselves: Prime Minister Trudeau would have yelped with indignation over his son's ill-considered statement.

Stung to the quick, Liberal leader Stéphane Dion gave his star candidate a serious warning: "Everybody is bound to make statements that require clarification, and he shouldn't be judged on the basis of a single statement."

Justin Trudeau apologized for offending Acadians and francophone minorities, stressing that francophone institutions "are essential to their development." He said he was proud of the legacy of his father, who had succeeded in enshrining Canada's linguistic duality in the Constitution.

On December 15, 2007, Trudeau added fuel to the fire by reiterating his opposition to Stephen Harper's motion in the House of Commons recognizing the Québécois as a nation, to the dismay of the Liberal Party faithful in Quebec. "I have a problem with this whole idea of a special status for Quebec and with the recognition of Quebec as a distinct society in the Constitution and also with the recognition of the Québécois as a nation: it simply creates divisions, and separates people into groups within other groups," he told *Nouvelles Parc-Extension News*. "Who are *les Québécois* that they should be recognized as a nation?"

A few days later, on December 20, the same man who, a year earlier, had denounced the "Quebec nation" as an idea of the nineteenth century, now said during a fundraiser in Toronto that the Quebec nation undeniably existed. Justin Trudeau added that he was proud of his Québécois and Canadian identity, and that he supported his leader's position on the matter.

It was now clear to everyone that Justin Trudeau wasn't given to doublespeak. No, he lacked proper judgment on several sensitive issues. And yet, his public statements seemed refreshing to some observers. In any case, in the end he apologized!

The powers that be in the Liberal Party could see the young candidate in Papineau was a rising star, but he needed supervision. Reine Hébert recommended that Justin Trudeau recruit Louis-Alexandre Lanthier as his campaign manager. Lanthier had worked for several Liberal ministers and MPs in Ottawa: Sheila Copps, Pierre Pettigrew, Mauril Bélanger, Hélène Scherrer, and Ken Dryden. He had supported Dryden at the Liberal leadership convention in 2006.

Lanthier sought various assurances. He wanted first of all to be completely free to run the campaign as he saw fit, a campaign on the ground where he could limit what the candidate said to the media.

The candidate was in a hurry, but the manager he had chosen still wanted to take the time to get to know him before coming to a decision. In May 2007, Justin Trudeau met Lanthier in a restaurant in Ottawa, where he was visiting for Mother's Day. They talked for three hours. The conversation wasn't about vision, but about strategy. For the Liberal organizer, what really mattered in a campaign was establishing contact with the voters. But the way things were going, Lanthier regretted that candidates, particularly in Quebec, were skipping door-to-door campaigns to focus on walkabouts and media interviews instead. He said it was time to come back to the old style of campaigning.

Justin Trudeau had no prior hands-on experience in politics and accepted this advice. Louis-Alexandre Lanthier in turn agreed to manage his campaign. He moved from Ottawa to a small apartment in the centre of Papineau riding. His living room became the Trudeau campaign headquarters. His team deliberately deprived Justin of a personal office. His office would be the street, community halls, associations, and coffeehouses where he could shake hands and be seen in public.

———

The campaign was well organized but got off to a bad start. On the day of the launch — September 24, 2008 — a hundred pro-independence protesters answered the call of the Jeunes patriotes du Québec, a radical faction of the sovereignty movement, and marched to the Liberal candidate's campaign office, brandishing signs, drums, banners, and whistles.

"No Trudeau in Papineau," they chanted. They were indignant about "absurd remarks he had made, such as treating unilingual francophones as lazy."

They were referring to an address Trudeau had given in February 2008 at a language conference in Edmonton, before a group of four hundred teachers, when he said: "People who sit around waiting for others to learn their language are not only lazy — they are shooting themselves in the foot, because they are limiting their ability to communicate with the rest of the world."[11]

The protesters were met by Liberal campaign workers who broke into a spontaneous rendering of "O Canada." The police finally had to create a security perimeter in front of the Liberal candidate's campaign office on rue Saint-Denis. Things cooled off fairly quickly. Bloc Québécois leader Gilles Duceppe said he dissociated himself from the fringe group of protesters. He had nothing in common with them.

But the incident meant that Justin had once again to offer public apologies. "I am young," he told *Le Devoir*. "I am not always going to say the right things the right way. But it's true that I believe bilingualism is better than unilingualism. I believe a society that doesn't promote bilingualism is being a bit lazy. But I never accused individuals of being lazy."[12]

Things calmed down and Justin Trudeau went back to the approach he had taken during the Liberal nomination contest in Papineau. He met increasing numbers of people in the riding, and visited multicultural associations and community centres. His team got him to walk more slowly in the streets of the riding, and to remove his sunglasses. He went door to door in the predominantly pro–Bloc Québécois district of Villeray where he wasn't always welcome. People sometimes asked what this rich guy could possibly have to offer to the poor people in the riding.

Trudeau was tireless. To show he was already working hard, his campaign team put together a minister's timetable for him, even though he still hadn't been elected an MP. The campaign lasted one and a half years, and he attended eight to ten events per week, giving his support to different projects and making himself available to everyone.

"We had an open house party at Christmas," one member of the campaign team recalls. "We put ads in the local papers and we invited the population to come see us."

The Liberal Party of Canada liked the way things were going.

Justin Trudeau had a way of getting people to talk about him, even if they didn't always have good things to say. In some federal ridings where the Liberals stood a chance, they requested that he appear on stage. But the campaign was hard going in Papineau, and his campaign manager often turned these requests down. In fact, Louis-Alexandre Lanthier laid down the law: he would not allow Trudeau "to be outside the riding for more than three days in a row."

His opponents weren't sure what to make of young Trudeau. He made awkward remarks that were sometimes over the top. He had never written anything substantive. "I didn't agree with his father," recalls Gilles Duceppe, "although I have to say he was an intellectual of a high calibre. As for the son, does he actually have any ideas?"

The Liberal candidate nevertheless had name recognition, so the Bloc Québécois brought out its heavy artillery. Four days before the election, the Bloc issued a press release urging Quebeckers to defeat Justin Trudeau "out of respect for the (French) language." Duceppe accused Trudeau of wanting to "take up his father's old battles" in order to "impose bilingualism in Quebec." Duceppe also slammed Trudeau for ripping into "lazy" unilingual people, "as if there was something abnormal about speaking one's language, living in one's language, and wanting to work in one's language."[13]

The Trudeau team wasn't particularly concerned about the Bloc's characterization of the Liberal candidate. They took Duceppe's words as an indication that the former prime minister's son was making a difference. Late in the evening of October 14, 2008, Justin Trudeau heaved a sigh of relief: things worked out well for him on election night. With a total of 17,724 votes against Vivian Barbot's 16,535, the new MP for Papineau had a majority of 1,189 votes, or 2.8 percent. The Liberals were ecstatic!

Trudeau likes to consider this victory as a great achievement. But there was nothing miraculous about his breakthrough in Papineau. The riding had been a Liberal stronghold since the beginning of the twentieth century. The way Vivian Barbot sees it, Justin Trudeau doesn't deserve much credit because he was "riding on the glory associated with his father."

But many people who followed the campaign closely believe Trudeau was the unavoidable choice in Papineau. "There had been the sponsorship scandal and all that," recalls Jean-Ernest Pierre, the owner of CPAM, the Haitian radio station in the Saint-Michel district of the riding. "Vivian Barbot actually rode the resulting wave of dissatisfaction, and when the Liberal Party got reorganized, and Trudeau's name became more widely known in the riding, voters in Papineau found they simply couldn't resist."

———

It had taken some time, but Justin Trudeau had reached his objective. The MP for Papineau settled into his office, but he didn't want to isolate himself. He enjoyed a wide range of riding activities, helping build a community centre, taking part in a round table on poverty, and attending popular festivals. He took a real interest in community action.

Jean-Ernest Pierre, owner of the Haitian radio station, considered Trudeau awkward. The young MP had a lot to learn. On official occasions he was sometimes brusque. During a ceremony honouring the radio-station owner, Trudeau ticked off the honouree.

"He thrust the trophy in my hands as if he was getting rid of a package. Bam, just like that!" Pierre recalls with a laugh. "Maybe he was angry, I really can't say, there must be an explanation…. It was so awkward. I wanted to slap young Trudeau on the wrist and tell him that's not the way things were done!"

Over time, the radio-station owner saw Trudeau grow with experience. "I interviewed him shortly afterwards, and I could gradually see changes in him to the point where I can now say he is ready to assume the true role of a politician."

On November 20, 2008, Justin Trudeau gave his inaugural speech in the House of Commons without attracting much attention. Responding to the Throne Speech, he took a few shots at the Harper government, accusing it of plunging Canada into budget deficits whereas the Liberals had maintained a socially responsible economy with sound practices and principles.[14]

Trudeau applied himself to learning how to be a backbench MP in Ottawa. He was not happy, though, to be away so often from his family in Montreal. He wondered every day whether it was all worth it, but he admitted to TV host Catherine Clark that he enjoyed his new role, the intellectual stimulation he derived from it, and the strategic side of politics. On the other hand, he had less freedom than before and his income had taken a hit.

Justin Trudeau had often been seen with his father in the hallways of Parliament, but he was now having a little difficulty finding his way around Parliament Hill. Other people recognized him, though. "The security guards remember me," he joked.

He was familiar up to a point with the setting, but he wasn't yet in his element. When he entered the House of Commons where his father had spent nineteen years, he was conscious of being part of a family tradition. His father had served in the House, and so had his grandfather James Sinclair, but "there was nothing automatic" in his becoming an MP. As he proudly told Catherine Clark on CPAC, he got elected through his own hard work and not because of the Trudeau family name. After taking up many different things, Justin Trudeau now seemed finally to have found his own path.

———

Three years later, in 2011, Stephen Harper called an election in the hopes of landing a majority. The MP for Papineau was ready to do battle. And although he was re-elected in the riding, the 2008 election proved a disaster for the federal Liberals. Stéphane Dion faced a possible mutiny and resigned. Michael Ignatieff, the man from Harvard, took his place.

Justin Trudeau had his share of run-ins with the Bloc Québécois. In March, Gilles Duceppe went to the Jean-Talon Market along with his candidate Vivian Barbot, who was trying to win back her seat. TV cameras followed the two of them when suddenly Justin appeared. Duceppe found the incident extremely disagreeable. "Trudeau seemed to have turned up at the market just to attract attention to himself," recalls Duceppe. "He was there to take advantage of the coverage we had been offered, taunting us with an 'I wanted to say hello, and welcome to my riding!' So what if he was the MP. People with the least bit of class don't do things like that."

According to the Trudeau team, there had been no question of seeking a personal confrontation with the Bloc. Actually, Trudeau had been sent out to buy some fruit and had run into Gilles Duceppe purely by chance.

The race in Papineau attracted media attention. Barbot told the media her opponent was angling to become Liberal Party leader instead of taking care of constituents in the riding. She went straight for the jugular and told Trudeau to stop hiding behind his father's name and take part in real debates.

This clash between two campaign organizations and two different ideologies didn't come as a surprise. What did surprise people, however, was the spectacular rise of the New Democratic Party in Quebec. NDP leader Jack Layton maintained his optimism and smile despite his debilitating illness, and he was hugely popular — something opinion polls hadn't predicted. On election day, May 2, 2011, the NDP "Orange Wave" resulted in 59 MPs elected in Quebec and 103 across Canada. The Bloc's support vanished, and the party shrank from 49 MPs in 2008 to just 4. Gilles Duceppe resigned after being defeated in his riding. Michael

Ignatieff suffered the same fate and also stepped down. From one day to the next, the Liberal Party of Canada was once again without a leader.

Justin Trudeau managed to withstand the Orange Wave unleashed by Jack, although the majority of his fellow Liberal MPs were defeated. He got 38.4 percent of the popular vote in Papineau, which translated into 4,327 votes more than the next candidate, the virtually unknown New Democrat Marcos Radhames Tejada. The election marked the end of Vivian Barbot's political career for the Bloc Québécois.

Justin Trudeau had stumbled now and then, but he was proving himself. He still didn't know how to speak in bite-sized clips for radio and TV news, but he had shown he was a formidable opponent on the ground, and that he was always ready to don his boxing gloves.

CHAPTER 4

THE FIGHT

In politics, image is everything. When Justin Trudeau stepped literally into the boxing ring in March 2012 to square off against a tough Conservative opponent, he knew his political future was at stake. Even though the bout was a fundraiser for cancer research, he knew he would lose face if he didn't do well.

As it happened, his family name and the way his father's policies had shaped the contemporary Canadian landscape put Stephen Harper's Conservatives into a cold sweat. There was something visceral about the way Harper made it his mission to destroy the Liberal Party of Canada and everything it stood for in order to bring about the triumph of Conservative values.

Justin Trudeau's opponent in the ring was the Conservative Senator Patrick Brazeau, an Algonquin from the Kitigan Zibi reserve near Maniwaki, Quebec. Brazeau had served as a reservist in the Canadian Armed Forces, and was a black belt in karate. Stephen Harper had named him to the Senate in January 2009.

From the outset, Brazeau made no bones about his plan to demolish his Liberal opponent. His plan seemed credible. His bulging biceps were the envy of other boxers. The tattooed Brazeau had long black hair, penetrating blue eyes, and rippling muscles. Most observers expected him to win. In Trudeau's entourage, the Conservative was described with some apprehension as "strong as an ox."

Organized by Final Round Boxing, a private boxing club in Ottawa, the match was held on March 31, 2012, in a hotel in the federal capital. The two opponents had no title to defend, so their contest had no real standing in the world of boxing, but it would go down in Canadian political history.

Publicity for the fundraising bout highlighted how different the two star boxers looked. Posters showed a ferocious Brazeau ready to devour his opponent, while Trudeau had the well-groomed look of a fashion model. The two men had agreed to fight in order to raise money for cancer research: Brazeau's mother had died of lung cancer, while Trudeau's father had succumbed to prostate cancer.

The event was well attended. Tickets sold for $250 apiece, and tables around the ring went for $3,000. The event raked in $230,000. The Brazeau clan spread through the hall. Federal Conservative ministers Leona Aglukkaq, Rona Ambrose, and James Moore took their places, along with the Ottawa Tory MP Pierre Poilievre. When Trudeau made his appearance, the Conservative supporters went wild, taunting him, jeering him, doing everything they could to dishearten him.

They weren't just attacking an MP: they were going for the Trudeau name and Justin's rising popularity. The MP for Papineau hadn't yet entered the Liberal Party of Canada's leadership race, but his name was being floated and he was perceived as a real threat. Even an aggressive threat: Hadn't he insulted Environment Minister Peter Kent in the House of Commons, accusing him of being "full of shit"? Trudeau had even said Stephen Harper's right-wing shift on abortion and gay marriage was making Canada unrecognizable, to the point he would prefer living in an independent Quebec — although he later backed off from that statement.

Sporting a helmet, gloves, and shorts in the traditional red of the Liberal Party, the forty-year-old boxer knew he couldn't afford to lose. He left nothing to chance. His boxing coach was none other than Ali Nestor Charles, flyweight champion, Chinese boxing champion, and 2012 world champion of the Universal Boxing Organization in the super middleweight class. Charles was a tough former street gang member who had done a lot of soul-searching after one of his buddies was killed in a random shooting. Martial arts had proved to be his salvation.

A little over one year after being elected MP for Papineau, Justin Trudeau had visited Académie Ness Martial for the first time, on Crémazie

Boulevard East in Montreal. This was where Ali Nestor Charles ran his training gym as well as "Ali et les princes de la rue," a youth refuge. The premises were well appointed and brightly lit. Trudeau had taken an appointment to find out more about the place and its curriculum of sports studies for young people at risk.

This sports-studies program is the only one of its kind in North America. It has received accreditation from the Quebec Ministry of Education and enables students to spend half of the day on their studies and the other half on martial arts. As a former teacher, Justin couldn't resist walking between the rows of desks on the second floor and helping teenagers train in the ring. It came naturally to him, since his own father had initiated him into boxing when he was twenty years old.

When the MP for Papineau finally found out he was going to face Senator Brazeau, he ramped up his training. And Ali did nothing by halves. Justin Trudeau ended up training in Ali's gym from two to three hours a day, three to four days per week over a six-month period. He also occasionally trained at the Final Round Boxing club in Ottawa, along with his brother Alexandre, bringing along toys in his boxing bag for his children Ella-Grace and Xavier.

His Montreal coach knew he would be boxing in enemy territory in Ottawa. So part of Justin's training was psychological. When he turned up for a boxing session in Montreal, a hundred pairs of eyes glared at him during his sparring. Why?

"People were there to jeer him, shout abuse, do everything they could to throw him off his stride," Ali explains. He filled the place up with spectators ready to torment the would-be champion. Justin had to be mentally ready to withstand the pressures and the insults that would surely rain down on him. This experience was repeated a few times. Ali wanted his protegé to go through the toughest training possible, to avoid humiliation in the final boxing match, and this meant exposing him to "tough people with real attitude."

"If he hadn't taken the fight seriously, I would never have trained him," Ali recalls with an air of determination. "He was under-estimated in the lead-up to the boxing match. And being under-estimated is his strength, his motivation. He never lets anyone discourage him."

———

The Conservatives expected Trudeau to wipe out in the ring, and they were doubtless hoping to use the shock appeal of images of Trudeau's defeat in their campaign ads. But the Conservatives were counting their chickens before they were hatched.

The bell rang. A few friendly voices yelled out, "Trudeau, Trudeau," but most eyes were riveted on Brazeau. The thirty-seven-year-old senator, sporting the traditional blue of his party, started off well, showering his taller but less imposing opponent with blows. But in the second round, Trudeau surprised everyone by mounting a counterattack, hammering away at the Conservative, who was getting unsteady on his feet.

The bout didn't last long. Brazeau seemed overwhelmed. The referee stopped the action for eight seconds during the second round to give him a breather. Then in the third round, Brazeau got a second standing eight count. Trudeau looked like the winner. Brazeau was completely powerless to fend off Trudeau's storm of repeated punches, and the referee ruled Trudeau the winner by technical knockout. Ali's fighting strategy paid off. He had urged Justin to take the least punches he could while holding Brazeau off with his longer reach, and then tire him out to score points. Brazeau gave everything in the first round and held nothing in reserve. Ali says that the outcome was a foregone conclusion: "Before the match, Brazeau had gone around blabbing that his strategy was to run Justin over like a locomotive. So we knew he was planning a stupid strategy of brute force, like some Cro-Magnon."

Ali, all dressed in Liberal red, paraded the winner triumphantly on his shoulders. Trudeau was all smiles and lifted his arms in the air. His mother and his wife were there to cheer him on. They were seated at a table surrounded by pink boxing gloves.

The Conservatives stood glaring in icy silence. They had undoubtedly been hoping for a huge public relations coup on the federal political scene. As for Brazeau, he wearily admitted he had made a mistake by "coming out like a madman."

Trudeau couldn't refrain from a little boasting. How could he explain his victory in the ring?

"It isn't really because of the training I did. It's just the way I am," the Liberal champion said. "I can take a lot of punches and stay on my feet. That's a lesson Pat learned this evening, and maybe a few others have learned as well." But he admitted Brazeau could throw a hard punch, and at times he had felt his own legs sagging.

Liberal supporters were ecstatic about Trudeau taking a long shot and winning. They couldn't help thinking that the Liberals — the party of Laurier — had taken a beating during the federal election on May 2, 2011, but were still standing.

The champion was obviously pleased with his performance. He compared his boxing bout with political struggles in the House of Commons, and said he was proud to be fighting for Canada. He almost sounded like Jean Chrétien!

This contest also had a distinctly personal meaning for Justin. He had always loved boxing, so finding himself in the ring was like fulfilling "a childhood dream."

"This was a present he wanted to offer himself for his fortieth birthday," his boxing coach says. Ali is full of admiration for this politician in boxing gloves, who grew up in his father's shadow and wanted to prove to himself that he was his own man. "We knew this was not just a boxing match. Sure, he's called Trudeau, but that doesn't tell the whole story. He's a person in his own right, he has proven himself, he has proved he has what it takes to be where he is."

Ali adds that Trudeau has a calculating side, and it has served him well in the boxing ring and in politics.

———

As the loser, Brazeau had to go through an excruciating ritual, with the cameras rolling. He had his ponytail cut off in the lobby of the House of Commons, and he had to wear a hockey sweater in very Liberal red for an entire week, a torment he accepted with good grace. On the back of his sweater featured the name "Trudeau" in block letters, along with the number "1."

Brazeau wasn't too keen on having his hair sheared. For the First Nations, long hair has deep cultural significance — which is why Justin Trudeau proposed the wager before the match, with a cunning smile: "When a *warrior* cuts his hair, it's a sign of shame, so it's very apropos."

When Brazeau was asked what had hurt him the most during the bout, he answered, without missing a beat, "My ego." His nose all swollen, he readily admitted he had been taken aback by the determination of his Liberal opponent.

Brazeau proposed a rematch, but Trudeau turned the offer down, saying he was a parliamentarian, not a boxer. In any case, the rematch would be the federal election in October 2015.

Anything can happen in the world of boxing. But according to Éric Bélanger, head coach at the Final Round Boxing club, Trudeau put the odds on his side. Seeing him in the ring that evening, Bélanger could tell the MP for Papineau was "an advanced intermediate" boxer who had been training for some time already and was confident. Brazeau, on the other hand, had failed to take the boxing match seriously.

Brazeau "thought that Justin was all curls and nothing more. He tried to clobber Justin, then tired out after the first thirty seconds. Justin is very intelligent. He came to the boxing match with a game plan, and given his ability, he brought that plan to execution."

————

Opinion was divided as to whether the contest should be taken seriously. But one thing was clear: the public got to see Justin Trudeau in a new light. Which suited the federal Liberals, who were increasingly impatient to find a permanent leader.

Even so, by entering the ring in the first place, the MP for Papineau had taken a huge risk. What if the Liberal Party's greatest hope had lost?

"Let's just say that if Justin had been knocked out, Canadians from coast to coast would have seen the TV clip of Justin tumbling to the ground, over and over again for an entire week," says Pablo Rodríguez with a chuckle — Rodríguez would become Trudeau's campaign manager during the Liberal leadership race. "I think it would have been a fatal blow. Any chance he had of becoming party leader would have been wiped out."

But the bet paid off for Trudeau. Sipping a coffee in a noisy Ottawa restaurant, Rodríguez says, "The boxing match was important because physical courage is not something you see very often. Everyone can flex his muscles, but it is rare to see real displays of physical courage, and when people do show that, they don't necessarily carry it off that well. Justin clearly demonstrated real physical courage, which is part of his nature as a person. It is rare for people with physical courage to wipe out completely."

Trudeau's victory in the ring gave ammunition to the weakened team of interim Liberal leader Bob Rae, holding the fort in the House of Commons.

Buoyed by the victory, the Liberal MP for Saint-Léonard Saint-Michel, Massimo Pacetti, rose the following Monday in the House of Commons. He remarked that the political arena had moved to the boxing arena on a memorable Saturday night at the Hampton Inn. The Conservatives failed to take into account the Liberal's ability to stand up to repeated blows and come back even stronger, he said. Pacetti concluded with pride: "Let this fight be a sign that Liberal strength is returning."

Justin Trudeau, a backbencher who practically went unnoticed in the House of Commons despite his pedigree, gained incredible visibility. The boxing match, broadcast live on the English-language Sun News network late at night, and shown later on the French-language TVA Nouvelles network, reached hundreds of thousands of TV viewers. Footage of the match reached (and continues to reach) a far greater audience on the Internet, where it went viral, according to Pablo Rodríguez. The people most impressed by the match are young people — the primary segment of the population targeted by the Trudeau team.

Some press reactions were favourable, others were negative. Justin had often been seen as his mother's son, emotional, vulnerable, and without much intellectual calibre. For the time being, he was being described as "the hero of the evening."

Le Devoir wrote that Trudeau got on the nerves of a lot of people in Quebec "with his princely manner. But some people must have been overjoyed to see him deliver a technical knock-out to Senator Brazeau. He may not have the same intellectual calibre as his father, but the fact is, he has real courage, as well as remarkable flair for showmanship. Showbiz-politics is here to stay, so it might as well be done in style."

Some English-speaking editorial writers saw in Trudeau's fifteen minutes of glory the launch of a new political career at the national level. They recalled how his father had been deadly serious in facing down the rowdy sovereignists in Montreal who were pelting him with debris on the reviewing stand. Justin "trained hard for the match. And, as with his father, that training and discipline paid off."[1]

The fight would go down in history, said one popular columnist in the influential *Globe and Mail*, adding that Justin Trudeau was nevertheless *not* the man of the hour and should go into another line of work, since he was so completely innocent of the qualities necessary to revive the fortunes of the Liberal Party.[2]

Meanwhile, the rabble-rouser Ezra Levant, co-host on Sun News of the boxing event, had been rooting for the Conservatives. By the end of the bout he was eating crow. He had called Trudeau "a shiny pony" while predicting an easy victory for Brazeau. Levant was stupefied by the outcome of the evening, which he admitted had turned into a one-man show dominated by Trudeau.

For the time being, Justin Trudeau didn't worry about what critics were saying in the press. He had scored a victory so spectacular it almost made people forget his moments of immaturity, his hesitations, his poorly considered remarks, and his lack of experience. Trudeau was now starting to look like a player to be contended with on the federal political scene. He showed he was a risk-taker like his father, and he could surprise people. He had more going for him than the Trudeau name: he had appearance, dynamism, charisma, and star quality. And, as everyone knows, celebrities have an edge at the starting line.

CHAPTER 5

THE PARTY'S GREAT NEW HOPE

In the aftermath of the Liberal Party of Canada's disastrous performance in the May 2, 2011, federal election, it was time to look for a new leader. All eyes turned to Justin Trudeau. He didn't have much of a track record and he lacked experience as a parliamentarian. But he was used to dealing with crowds, he knew how to work a room, and his boxing victory over Patrick Brazeau had given his profile a boost.

The Liberals had been in power during most of the twentieth century, so losing a third election in a row had come as a withering blow. The party was in a shambles. And that wasn't all: the New Democratic Party's Orange Wave now put the Liberals in third place in the House of Commons. This was simply unprecedented.

The Liberals had dropped from 103 seats in 2006 to a disappointing 77 in 2008, and then a paltry 34 in 2011. The party now seemed light years from the era of Pierre Elliott Trudeau, not to mention Jean Chrétien's three back-to-back victories. With 103 seats in the House of Commons, the New Democratic Party now formed the Official Opposition — quite an accomplishment for a party that had previously seen itself as the conscience of Parliament (and were considered the perennial also-rans). Stephen Harper had led two minority governments since 2006, but now headed a majority government, although with minimal representation from Quebec, where he was deeply unpopular.

The morning after the election rout, Liberal leader Michael Ignatieff announced his intention of stepping down. He submitted his letter of resignation to the Liberal National Board of Directors on May 11 to leave the party some time to pick up the pieces. According to party regulations, the Liberals had to choose a new leader five months after the incumbent leader resigned. This put the date for a leadership convention in October 2011 at the latest.

But several MPs hotly contested the idea of holding a fourth leadership race in the space of just eight years, so the party board of directors decided to change the regulations, announcing in June 2011 that the leadership race would be launched in the spring of 2013, sometime between March 1 and June 30. And so began the longest leadership race in the history of the Liberal Party of Canada.

Michael Ignatieff took the election results hard. He had been recruited by the Liberals and hyped as the great hope of the party. But he hadn't delivered. Not only had he led the party to its most resounding defeat of all time, but he had lost his own seat in the Toronto riding of Etobicoke-Lakeshore. So he headed back to academia, taking up a teaching appointment at the University of Toronto before returning to Harvard in 2014.[1]

Liberal supporters were downcast. Many defeated MPs packed up and left Ottawa. First Dion and now Ignatieff had failed miserably. It wasn't clear who could assume the leadership. Pessimists felt it was game over for the Liberal Party, now apparently on the verge of extinction.

During this gloomy period, activity slowed to a snail's pace. It was only in June 2012 — more than a year after the electoral defeat — that the date of April 14, 2013, was finally set for the party convention to replace Michael Ignatieff. Meanwhile, Bob Rae assumed the interim leadership in the House of Commons. According to party regulations, the interim leader had to be bilingual. Moreover, the interim leader had to accept not to run for the permanent party leader's position to ensure that no single candidate had an undue advantage during the race. Rae was an experienced parliamentarian who knew his files well and understood the inner workings of Parliament Hill. The Liberal caucus had chosen Rae as interim leader over Marc Garneau in a vote on May 25.

Bob Rae would hold the fort for two years. He started off by dismissing the idea of a merger with his old party, the NDP, which some people saw as a way to get progressives back into power. The Liberal Party was far from dead, he told anyone willing to listen. Canadians had not suddenly turned into "members of the Tea Party." Rae, a Toronto-area MP, played a lead role during Question Period. As a former premier of Ontario, he handled press briefings well, responding with gusto to Conservative attacks. He would later say that his greatest achievements as interim leader were keeping the Liberal Party from falling by the wayside and raising new funds to fill party coffers. Rae enjoyed being interim leader and he made no bones about it.

By late spring 2012, things started heating up. Still, candidates weren't exactly lining up at the door. A month after his boxing match of March 31, Justin Trudeau once again refused, officially, to run. He preferred taking care of his young family and his riding, he said. In fact, he had a thousand and one reasons not to run, the race would involve many challenges, and his chances of winning seemed slim. But at the same time, he told *Maclean's*, "Those are the very reasons that make the whole idea tremendously exciting to me."

For his part, Bob Rae was now taking a serious look at running. For several months, the MP for Toronto Centre had people wondering about his true intentions, and this was stirring up controversy in the caucus. Hadn't he committed to not entering the race? If he went back on this commitment, he would have a considerable advance on rival candidates. Some members of the party executive, close to Michael Ignatieff, let it be known they didn't want Bob Rae as leader. Some of Justin Trudeau's close supporters meanwhile worked behind the scenes, sounding out their man's chances. Rae wanted to know what his unofficial rival's intentions were, but when the two men discussed the matter, Trudeau left Rae dangling in suspense. "It was extremely disappointing for Bob," says a credible Liberal source.

And then on June 13, out of the blue, Bob Rae announced he was not running after all. The sixty-three-year-old MP from Toronto hadn't waited for the Liberal Party board of directors to announce its decision on his candidacy: apparently, that very evening they were preparing to free him from the commitment not to run. "The way in which I can serve my party best," Rae said, "is by not running for the permanent leadership."

His supporters were devastated. Even his closest colleagues hadn't seen this decision coming. In the end he never offered a public explanation for why he had changed his mind. Perhaps he realized the Liberals wanted to reinvigorate the party with new blood. Justin Trudeau was clearly thinking about running, and even if Rae won — which Trudeau considered possible — there was a good chance Rae would serve only one term as party leader.

Many observers felt Rae would have been a credible candidate. But doubts surfaced about the potential liability for the Liberals of Rae's unpopular term as NDP premier of Ontario during a recession. Many Ontarians still nourished bitter memories of the austerity measures he had introduced as premier, particularly the way he had slapped civil servants with a salary freeze as well as forced leave without pay. Bob Rae would have had a hard time delivering seats in Ontario. And the Liberal Party could not realistically hope to rebuild without strengthening its power base in Ontario, which represented over a hundred seats in the House of Commons — one-third of the national total. Rae was torn but clear-headed enough to realize it was "in the best interest of the party" that he stay out of the race, as he had promised to do.

Bob Rae had already run twice for the Liberal leadership, in 2006 and again in 2009. But his timing was off. "Bob waited too long to get into the game," says Peter Donolo, Jean Chrétien's former director of communications. "He should have run in 2000 or in 2004." By 2012 it was too late. Beyond tactical considerations, Rae knew that his candidacy would create divisions in the party. "He was reaching the end of his career," says a well-informed source, "and this wasn't the way he wanted to be remembered." The Trudeau faction concluded Rae had sacrificed himself for the good of the party. "Bob has an incredible sense of self-abnegation," says Pablo Rodríguez. "He has played a central role, he is an unsung hero."

Rae's departure set the scene for many potential candidates to step forward. On June 27, 2012, the constitutional lawyer Deborah Coyne became the first to enter the fray. A former adviser to Newfoundland premier Clyde Wells and the mother of Justin's half-sister Sarah, she wasn't considered a serious candidate.

But now the last obstacle barring the way to Justin Trudeau's candidacy had been removed. The media followed the undeclared candidate everywhere. He took all the new attention with a grain of salt. "Being under pressure doesn't affect him that much," said one of his close colleagues.

———

Liberal supporters knew as little about Justin Trudeau as the public did. But people knew how determined he was. They quickly forgot gaffes such as the furor over his saying Stephen Harper had taken Canada so far to the right that "maybe I would think about wanting to make Quebec a country." In Quebec, what impressed people most was the way he had survived the collapse of the party, which now counted a meagre 7 seats in the entire province.

But officially Justin Trudeau repeated the claim that he was not in the race. Three days before Bob Rae threw in the towel, Trudeau told an audience in Winnipeg: "I am under a lot of pressure to reconsider. For now, I haven't."[2]

Even so, Trudeau crossed the country to assess public perceptions. In early July 2012 he attended the Calgary Stampede wearing a white Stetson, blue jeans, and cowboy boots. He continued to deny he was running, but his denials didn't ring true. He was seen chatting up Liberal supporters as they feasted on pancakes at a party breakfast, and he posed for photographs.

He said this Stampede didn't seem all that different from the previous ones he had attended, but he admitted the Liberal leadership race was much on his mind. Before entering the race, Trudeau said, he wanted to know whether he could be "a good father, and maybe a good prime minister." He also told journalists he was at the Stampede to congratulate Calgary Liberals: "Someone who chooses to be a Liberal in Calgary isn't doing it because it makes them popular," he joked.

Things started to speed up at the end of the month. Even if Trudeau continued to say he wasn't running, he actually was giving it serious thought. Gerald Butts, who was working at the time as president of World Wildlife Fund Canada, set up a committee to explore the question. Trudeau held a three-day meeting at Mont-Tremblant at the end of July, bringing together his close confidants: Katie Telford, Louis-Alexandre Lanthier, Dominic LeBlanc, Luc Cousineau (head of his riding organization), Richard Maksymetz (chief of staff for the British Columbia finance minister), his brother Alexandre, Tom Pitfield, and the pollster David Herle. They were accompanied by their families. A dozen colleagues and assistants were invited to the meeting to get a good sense of the situation. Did Justin have a chance of winning? Was this really the right time to run?

Some were for, others were against, but there was general agreement about one thing: the Liberals should dismiss any idea of merging with the NDP. Justin told the group he opposed the idea because the two parties disagreed on fundamental issues. He added he would never support repealing the *Clarity Act*, "a move that would effectively make it easier to break up the country."[3] Justin's advisers handed him and his wife Sophie a report; the first theme that stood out was protecting the middle class. Rather than making any definite recommendation, the report analyzed the Canadian political landscape, laying out several different scenarios for him as a potential candidate. Once again, Justin Trudeau was being presented with a crushing schedule, but he knew this was the price required for victory.

The MP for Papineau hesitated. He knew he lacked experience. Besides, he enjoyed being an MP. Bob Rae's decision, however, was forcing him to think seriously about his future. Was destiny knocking on his door? According to Professor Robert Asselin, who would soon join Justin's team, Pierre Trudeau had once said that in politics, "you don't always control which way the current takes you." Asselin adds: "As soon as Rae bowed out of the race, the search was on to find someone truly capable of leading the party. There wasn't that much choice. It wouldn't be an exaggeration to say the party was down to a handful of names — perhaps two or three."

Still, it was a big step. As the son of a prime minister, Justin knew better than anyone how challenging it was to balance politics and family life. His children were still young, and according to historian John English, if life at 24 Sussex Drive was more enjoyable for Pierre Trudeau's children than it seemed at first sight, it was "not perfect." The Trudeau brothers had witnessed their parents' fights, they had grown up separated from their mother, "and that wasn't easy for them." Justin had seen first-hand what a political career could do to a couple. He knew his mother had presented Pierre with an ultimatum, demanding that he get out of politics. But English says political circumstances didn't leave the prime minister any choice — he was a federalist by conviction: "Pierre wouldn't leave, because the separatists had just been elected" in Quebec.

There had been several dangerous episodes in the Trudeau family history — episodes Justin simply couldn't ignore: the epic battles with the Quebec sovereignty movement, the virulent attacks and threats. Pierre Elliott Trudeau himself had his life directly threatened by the FLQ in 1968.[4]

This was on the personal level. But on another level, Justin could see the Liberal Party was teetering on the brink. If he didn't run, his father's party might disappear altogether, meaning there might be no second chance for him to run at a later date. As Robert Asselin recalls, "Many people told him — the way people told Obama in the United States — that if he waited, he might not get that second chance."

Justin and Sophie took the summer of 2012 to think it over. By early September they had decided: Trudeau would run. "He felt the time was ripe," says Asselin. "He could run for leader, or he could do something completely different — but if he stayed in politics, he had to accept that running might just prove to be his destiny."

———

For the movers and shakers of the Liberal Party, Justin Trudeau was not a natural choice. But after the failures of Stéphane Dion and Michael Ignatieff — two intellectuals who did not appeal to voters — the party needed to find a leader who could rebuild the Liberal brand. After wiping out at the polls three times in a row, the party needed a saviour.

The party rank and file still dreamed of getting back into power. But the political context was challenging. The May 2 election results were like a tsunami, changing the dynamics of Parliament and polarizing federal politics as never before. The NDP Orange Wave had dramatically weakened Liberal support. The Bloc Québécois had been nearly wiped off the electoral map. Jack Layton had won over the hearts of Quebeckers, but he was no longer there to direct the destinies of his party. Jack had been an inspiration during the election campaign, braving storms in rubber boots and supporting himself on a cane. But he died of cancer on August 22, 2011. His death was deeply moving for Canadians right across the country. Thomas Mulcair, the former provincial Liberal Quebec minister who had snatched the riding of Outremont from the federal Liberals, took Jack's place as NDP leader. Stephen Harper meanwhile had a comfortable majority of seats in the House of Commons, and therefore a free hand to promote the Conservative legislative agenda.

The Liberal Party of Canada had been searching for itself ever since the reign of Jean Chrétien. The Liberals seemed a spent force, weakened by circumstances, their own incompetence, and the bold merger in 2003 of the Canadian Alliance with the Progressive Conservative Party. The Liberals could no longer profit from electoral divisions on the right to gain power.

The reasons for the federal Liberal Party's decline were many. Internecine warfare between the Martin and Chrétien factions had torn the party apart and undermined public confidence. Paul Martin had for many years aspired to take over the leadership of the party, but as things turned out, on finally replacing Chrétien as leader on December 12, 2003, Martin was to have only a short time in power — too short to allow for any significant long-term policy innovations. Moreover, Martin's minority government disregarded Jean Chrétien's advice and launched the Gomery Commission into the sponsorship scandal. The Commission hearings received an enormous amount of media coverage, gave ammunition to the opposition parties, and led directly to the downfall of the Liberals. The Liberal brand was discredited, particularly in Quebec where the party would have a hard time regaining lost ground.

Then in December 2005, the Liberal minority government lost a confidence motion in the House of Commons tabled by Stephen Harper with Jack Layton's support. Paul Martin handed over power to the Conservative leader after the general election held on January 23, 2006. Harper, MP for Calgary Southwest, formed a minority Conservative government. Martin now had no choice but to step down as Liberal leader.

This defeat sent the Liberals out into the political wilderness. To make matters worse, there was no clear candidate to take Martin's place as leader. "The Martin faction made sure of that," says Peter Donolo, Jean Chrétien's communications director and later Michael Ignatieff's chief of staff. In fact, "Martin's people got rid of all the star candidates," Donolo adds blandly. "I don't think it was really a war between rival factions. It was more of a putsch. The people around Paul Martin became impatient and didn't want to wait any longer. At the time, Paul was very popular across the country. He had been an incredibly popular minister of finance. So his people got impatient, and perhaps he did as well."

As soon as the Martin faction seized power, adds Donolo, it got rid of "a generation" of potential successors, possibly believing them to be a threat. Frank McKenna, Brian Tobin, and several other high-profile Liberals were swept aside. So when the Martin government lost power in January 2006, "there was no obvious heir or obvious cadre of potential leadership candidates the way there was in 1984 or in 1968."

The Liberals now found themselves in a power vacuum. They ended up opting for less experienced leaders who were simply no match for Harper and his powerful machine. Delegates at the 2006 leadership convention faced an unsatisfactory choice between Michael Ignatieff, an outstanding intellectual perceived nonetheless as a foreign import, and Bob Rae, a career politician lacking real Liberal roots.

Delegates faced a choice "between someone who wasn't Canadian and someone who wasn't Liberal," Donolo adds with a chuckle. "That's the way a lot of people saw it. It's not fair, but that's the way a lot of people saw it."

Jean Chrétien's former communications director doesn't mince words: delegates settled for Stéphane Dion for want of a better alternative. He became "the accidental leader" because "he was the one people disliked the least."

———

Stéphane Dion, the man who was chosen out of the blue in 2006, would struggle as party leader, and he did not hold the position for long. His speech at the leadership convention was short, just like his term as leader. Dion was the only candidate from Quebec and had served as a fine minister of the environment under Paul Martin. But he was a virtual unknown outside of Quebec, whether among party faithful or the public at large. In his home province, the fact that he had piloted the adoption of the *Clarity Act* made him seem like the spiritual son of Pierre Elliott Trudeau: this hardly endeared him to Quebec nationalists.

Dion was serious, slender, a hard worker, and a ferocious debater. A former professor of constitutional law at the Université de Montréal, he could quote sections of the *Canadian Charter of Rights and Freedoms* by heart. But he was a novice at the art of politics, which sometimes proved an advantage since he could claim in all honesty not to have been drawn into the battles between the Chrétien and Martin factions. Besides, Dion didn't have a good command of English, something the Conservatives and the English-language media criticized.

As soon as Dion became Liberal leader, the Conservatives pounced on his environmental plan, the Green Shift. And they did a good job. The plan was too complex to explain, and it was easy to misrepresent. Stéphane Dion couldn't get his message across. As a way of reducing greenhouse gas emissions, Dion proposed taxing fossil fuels, an idea that didn't go over well with Stephen Harper's electoral base in western Canada. Conservative attack ads portrayed Dion as a weak leader with a single goal: increasing taxes.

The disappointing results of the October 14, 2008, election weakened his position further. Stéphane Dion barely received a round of applause from his own troops. Nobody could imagine at the time that the Liberals were actually *not* at their lowest ebb — not just yet. Several people openly called on him to resign, but he refused, preferring to remain in place until the next party convention scheduled for the following May. Michael Ignatieff's team[5] was still in leadership race mode, and believed the Liberals could have done better in 2008. They feared the Liberals were likely to collapse in Quebec where Dion was seen as someone who had taken a hard line on the Quebec sovereignty movement during the 1995 referendum and then had been the architect of Plan B.[6]

This was the least of Stéphane Dion's problems, however. He had formed an ultra-secret alliance with Jack Layton's NDP, unbeknownst to Ignatieff, in order to bring down the Harper government and take power as a coalition. Bloc Québécois leader Gilles Duceppe had also agreed to support the other two parties for eighteen months. This took place in December 2008, just seven weeks after the federal election in October in which Stephen Harper had won another minority government and gained 19 seats, while the NDP had picked up 8 and the Liberals had lost another 26.

The opposition parties were outraged at the Conservative fiscal update of November 27, which provided no concrete measures to counter the worst economic recession since the Great Depression. It did, however, propose to eliminate state subsidies for political parties. In other words, the Conservatives were proposing to cut the financial lifeline of the opposition parties. The opposition took this as a direct affront.

The Liberals and New Democrats considered the Harper government had lost the confidence of the House of Commons, and therefore, the Tories should hand over power to a coalition government led by Stéphane Dion.

The idea of a coalition was quite well received in Quebec but was extremely unpopular in the rest of the country. According to the written agreement between the three parties, the Bloc Québécois would support the coalition without getting any seats in the federal Cabinet. This condition was far from reassuring Canadians outside Quebec, who could not tolerate any alliance whatever with sovereignists. The alliance led to a "public furor" across Canada, says Louis Massicotte, a political scientist at l'Université Laval. "People underestimated just how toxic Bloc Québécois support for the alliance was."

Stéphane Dion's Liberal MPs were meanwhile pressured by the party whip to consent to the agreement, whether they wanted to or not.

Justin Trudeau, now a freshly elected MP, seemed to favour the idea. He even congratulated the Bloc Québécois for having "set aside the issue of sovereignty."

"We witnessed a historic moment when a coalition was formed," he said in one of his first speeches in the House of Commons. "The Bloc Québécois agreed, in the interest of the economy and in the interest of Quebeckers and Canadians, to set aside the issue of sovereignty to take care of the economy, just as we, the Liberals and the NDP, will set aside the national question to some extent to focus on the economy. That is what is important. It is a historic agreement."[7]

Bloc MP Paul Crête had to do something of a balancing act: while defending the proposal to form a coalition, he vowed that "this will never stop the Bloc Québécois from continuing to promote sovereignty."

Stephen Harper counterattacked, saying that the proposed Dion-Layton coalition had no popular mandate to take power in Ottawa. He denounced the alliance with "separatists" as undemocratic, calling it no less than a coup d'état. In an effort to sound reassuring, Stéphane Dion quickly retorted that the Conservatives had lost the confidence of the House. They had lost the right to govern. In their place, the coalition government would take measures to address the economic crisis, he claimed.

But Dion's message still didn't get across. His pre-recorded statement to the nation was so badly recorded, many people compared it to a home video. The statement destroyed the little credibility he had left. The image of Dion was blurry and was tinged slightly red. By the end of the statement, the camera had zoomed in so closely on his face that he seemed to have no neck. The Conservatives and the media had a field day mocking the statement. Even among Liberals, many saw it was an amateurish piece of work.

In the House of Commons, the Harper government managed to delay the date for the non-confidence vote to December 8, but in the end, the vote never took place. On December 4, to get the country out of a constitutional crisis, Governor General Michaëlle Jean prorogued Parliament at Stephen Harper's request until January 26. Harper ended up dodging the non-confidence vote he would most likely have lost. The plan of forming a Liberal-NDP coalition backed by the Bloc Québécois was buried once and for all.

"The coalition plan was a great idea on paper," says a long-standing Liberal supporter who found the episode extremely discouraging, "but the plan was not properly sold to the people of Canada or to the caucus." Stéphane Dion never discussed the plan "with anyone." "It was a failure of leadership."

The plan may originally have been Jack Layton's idea, but as leader of the Official Opposition, Dion was the one facing the backlash. At the time, few Liberal MPs were willing to say a kind word about him. Dion could see he had lost the support of his own party, so he announced on December 8 he would step down as leader as soon as a replacement could be found. It came as no surprise that Michael Ignatieff was named interim leader.

Peter Donolo believes the idea of a multi-party coalition was perceived as illegitimate because the Conservatives had only just been elected. It was a colossal error in judgment, he says, that would have disastrous consequences for the federal Liberals outside of Quebec.

And there were more errors to come.

———

On May 2, 2009, Michael Ignatieff was crowned leader of the Liberal Party of Canada at the party convention in Vancouver. This was the second time he had run for the position. The victory was a foregone conclusion.

Dominic LeBlanc, a young bilingual MP from New Brunswick and childhood friend of Justin Trudeau's, withdrew from the race on December 8, 2008, to throw his support behind the former Harvard professor. Bob Rae, who had shared a residence room with Ignatieff at the University of Toronto, withdrew the next day. Rae was bitter about this turn of events: Ignatieff would later say Rae felt Ignatieff didn't deserve to win. Their friendship never recovered.

Ignatieff, famous as a champion of human rights, was parachuted in to his new position. He would never succeed in affirming his leadership. In his book *Fire and Ashes*, he would later recount that he was quite naive when he became leader: he knew little about the nitty-gritty of politics and he knew even less about the Liberal Party. As a student, he had supported Pierre Elliott Trudeau's leadership campaign in 1968, but he had been far removed from active politics since then. Moreover, while pursuing his career as an academic and writer, he had been living abroad for the past thirty-five years.

At first, when Liberal organizers Alfred Apps, Dan Brock, and Ian Davey presented Ignatieff with an offer on a silver platter to lead the party in October 2004, he found the idea "absurd." But "politics ran in his blood,"[8] and he allowed himself to be persuaded to go from observer to actor on the political stage. Even so, he leaves the distinct impression in his book that he never really wanted to be leader. He even thought of resigning in the fall of 2009. He dreaded the drudgery of Question Period and also the anxious expressions of his employees, who "avoided looking him in the eyes" as Liberal support continued to decline in the opinion polls.

One thing was definite: Michael Ignatieff hadn't done the necessary groundwork. He admitted he had overestimated his own abilities as a politician. He had underestimated the "ferocity" not just of negative Conservative attacks but also of dissent within Liberal ranks. Even when Stéphane Dion warned him of the devastating impact of attack ads, Ignatieff didn't go on the offensive.

In fact, Ignatieff had taken over a party that was both weak and impossible to lead. The agreement to form a Liberal-NDP coalition and replace the Harper government was dead in the water, yet it came back to haunt him. He saw the plan concocted by his predecessor as the action of "a desperate leader, clinging to power by any means, resorting to a *coup de théâtre* to survive."[9] So in January 2009, Ignatieff disavowed the agreement, even though it bore his own signature. People in his inner circle maintain that he was forced to sign it, like other Liberal MPs. This about-face damaged his credibility and spread doubt in the public mind.

Michael Ignatieff thought that by disavowing the coalition scenario, he had negotiated some sort of ceasefire with the Harper government. But the Conservative machine took no prisoners. He was subjected to negative attack ads that had a direct impact on public support for the Liberals. The Harvard professor had a hard time adapting to the Conservatives' permanent election campaign and the negative attack ads questioning "my attachment to the country, my patriotism."[10]

The Conservatives quickly transformed Michael Ignatieff's strengths into weaknesses. He was presented as a great intellectual just passing through Canada as a visiting professor.

The Liberal leader only began to take these negative attack ads seriously when he realized how they were demolishing his credibility. Crowds turned out to hear his speeches, but nobody really listened, because deep down they took him for a dilettante.

The Liberal Party was heavily in debt, and had neither the means nor even the instinct to respond in kind to this "unprecedented" advertising blitz, Ignatieff later wrote.

In March 2011, the Liberal leader dropped his gloves, announcing he would overthrow Stephen Harper's government for "contempt of Parliament." A first in Canadian political history, the showdown started when a parliamentary committee found the Harper government in contempt after it refused to reveal to parliamentarians the true costs of its law and order bills, the F-35 fighter jets it planned to order, and the net impact of corporate taxes. By doing so, the government impeded the ability of MPs to carry out their duties, concluded the opposition-dominated Procedure and House Affairs Committee. In other words, parliamentarians were being asked to adopt legislation without being given sufficient information. (This finding was rejected by the Conservative MPs on the committee who issued a dissenting report.)

Ignatieff denounced the Conservative's secret ways as an attack on democracy. Parliament was not in the business of issuing "blank cheques," he said. With the support of the other opposition parties, he set the wheels in motion on March 25 to topple the 40th Parliament, censuring the Conservatives with a non-confidence vote of 156 votes to 145. Stephen Harper's second minority government bit the dust. But the subsequent election of May 2 didn't turn out the way the Liberal leader had expected.

During the campaign, Harper proved to be a cunning opponent. He warned Canadians about this "dangerous coalition," the "improvised coalition" that the Liberal Party would try to put in place again if voters didn't give him a majority government. He even talked about a "coalition of losers." Stephen Harper created a powerful image in the minds of voters, particularly in English Canada, where people were dead set against any alliance with Quebec sovereignists.

The Liberal leader stuck to his guns. Michael Ignatieff denounced the way the Conservatives had prorogued Parliament and then had been found in contempt of Parliament. From day one of the campaign he formally excluded any coalition with the NDP and the Bloc. But this only reminded voters of the way the Liberals had previously flirted with the Bloc. Ignatieff would later acknowledge that flatly turning down the idea of a coalition destroyed his last chance to become prime minister.

The Conservatives also had fun portraying the Harvard professor as an aristocrat. On a Conservative-funded website, Ignatieff was attacked for "his considerable wealth" and the life of privilege the Ignatieff family enjoyed. This was nothing like what most immigrants experienced on arriving in Canada.

The Liberal leader attacked the Conservatives on CTV for this undemocratic campaign of lies that went beyond any acceptable limit, because it directly attacked his family and his patriotism. Ignatieff explained that his family had lost everything during the Russian Revolution. His family had arrived in Canada without a dollar to its name. His father had laid railway tracks in British Columbia to earn a living and pay for his studies. "He lived the life many immigrants live." Unwittingly, Ignatieff reinforced the Conservative Party message by going on the defensive, saying, "A Canadian is a Canadian is a Canadian. I am a proud Canadian."

The Liberal leader never threw off the negative image of being a "visiting professor."

With these events still fresh in mind, Justin Trudeau took his decision and set his team in marching order. The target date was April 14, 2013. They had to start from scratch. Rebuilding the party would be challenging. Liberal riding associations either had disappeared or were teetering on the brink.

In general, party veterans had no part in Trudeau's organization, and some were offended not to be consulted. But Jean Chrétien — still nicknamed "the boss" — was always somewhere nearby. The leadership candidate gathered a team of friends and colleagues in their early forties or younger. Some had young children. The joke went around that Trudeau's inner circle might just open a daycare centre.

Gerald Butts was the key player. He was Justin's friend and confidant, and played the role of power broker. Tall, slender, with small eyeglasses, he stayed mostly in the shadows, except that he was very active on social media where he vigorously defended his candidate against all comers. Butts was the leading strategist of the campaign. He was the one to approve all important initiatives and decisions. "He's the boss," says a former member of the Liberal caucus.

Butts was originally from Glace Bay, Cape Breton, where his father had been a coal miner. He did a bachelor's degree and then in 1996 got a master's in English literature at McGill University. He and Trudeau took part in debating tournaments together. He was a phenomenal debater himself, and served as president of the McGill Debating Club and was twice Canadian intercollegiate debating champion. After serving as principal secretary to Ontario Liberal Premier Dalton McGuinty, Butts became president of World Wildlife Fund Canada. He stepped down from that job in order to run his friend's leadership campaign.

The inner circle included Katie Telford, who had also worked for the McGuinty government. She kept up to date on voting trends and moods by analyzing tables and figures, and by following social media closely. She had managed Gerard Kennedy's leadership campaign in 2006, and when Kennedy stepped aside, ensuring the victory of Stéphane Dion, she worked as Dion's assistant chief of staff in Ottawa. Louis-Alexandre Lanthier had been at Justin Trudeau's side from his very first days in politics, and was in charge of press relations. Mike McNair had worked for both Dion and Ignatieff, and now served as a political adviser to Trudeau.

Another recruit was Robert Asselin, professor and associate director of the Graduate School of Public and International Affairs at the University of Ottawa. He joined the team in August as a political adviser. Asselin was attracted by the way Justin Trudeau's campaign was signalling generational renewal. He had long been close to the Liberal Party, having written speeches for Paul Martin, Stéphane Dion, and Michael Ignatieff, among others, and having worked for several ministers. Recruited by Gerald Butts, Asselin did not know Justin Trudeau, but he was interested in helping him run for the leadership.

According to Asselin, "the most successful Canadian prime ministers have been from Quebec, since they have been able to build bridges between anglophones and francophones. It's possible to win an election without Quebec, the way Mr. Harper did, but let's say this results in less of a national party, and as the years go by, a party that's harder to hold together." Asselin was often the one writing French-language speeches and passages for Trudeau. He sometimes had to call the young MP to order, warning him, for example, to stop repeating poorly considered comments that stirred up controversy.

It was easy for Justin Trudeau to build a team. He had grown up in a family environment filled with countless advisers and experts, which meant he had an almost ready-made network of contacts the minute he decided to run for leader. And he wasn't the only member of the team to have a prominent father. Long-standing friend and Montreal entrepreneur Tom Pitfield was the son of Michael Pitfield, clerk of the Privy Council under Pierre Elliott Trudeau. Tom's wife, Anna Gainey, was the daughter of the former captain of the Montreal Canadiens, Bob Gainey. A long-standing friend of Justin's, she had been the right-hand woman of ministers Bill Graham and John McCallum in the Martin government, and then became president of the Liberal Party of Canada in February 2014 at the age of thirty-six.

In Ontario, Trudeau recruited Navdeep Bains, the former MP for Mississauga-Brampton South, who had supported Gerard Kennedy's leadership bid. Bains had known Trudeau from the time he first set foot in the House of Commons in 2008. Bain was at first surprised to see his colleague aspiring to become party leader, but he quickly came out in support of Trudeau because he "knew his character" and believed he had what it took to lead the party to victory. Justin told Bains he was running because he wasn't satisfied with the quality of the other candidates. He thought he was the best person to lead the party, and he would take the time needed to put things right.

Another team member was Cyrus Reporter, who had been the right-hand man of former justice minister Allan Rock as well as a member of Paul Martin's election war room in 2005.

In the Atlantic region, the leading team member was the MP for Beauséjour, Dominic LeBlanc, a childhood friend of Justin's as well as the son of former governor general Roméo LeBlanc, who had been a close friend of his father's. Justin had often spent seaside holidays with the LeBlancs in southeast New Brunswick.

In western Canada, a key team member was Bruce Young, former organizer for Paul Martin and the provincial Liberals in British Columbia. Young and Trudeau had first met during the Liberal leadership race in 2006, when they had both supported Gerard Kennedy.

In Quebec, Justin Trudeau sought to recruit Pablo Rodríguez, working through his brother Alexandre to sound him out. A former Montreal-area MP, Rodríguez had witnessed his friend Justin's first days in politics. Alexandre met him several times to convey his brother's interest in running. Then, at the end of August, Justin put through a call to Pablo, greeting him informally with a "Hey, it's Justin!"

Pablo Rodríguez couldn't resist Trudeau's overture. The two men had known each other for a long time and had friends in common, particularly Jacques Hébert, founder of Katimavik and one of Pierre Elliott Trudeau's closest friends. Shortly before dying, Hébert had gone door to door to help Rodríguez get elected, knocking on two hundred doors in a single day. He and Justin had also taken part in environmental protest marches in the streets of Montreal.

"There has always been a very good synergy between the two of us," says Rodríguez, who had been swept out of office in the disastrous 2011 election, and who dreamed of returning to active politics. Pablo was originally from Argentina. Politics was his passion. He gathered a team of volunteers in Quebec to support Trudeau's leadership, building a formidable organization on a shoestring budget.

The team only had one month to get everything ready. Trudeau wanted to launch his leadership campaign on October 2 in his home riding of Papineau. Gerald Butts provided what needed to be said in broad brushstrokes. Robert Asselin and Alexandre added the idea of building bridges with Quebec.

There just wasn't enough time. The organizers wanted to delay the campaign launch, but Justin Trudeau flatly refused. He insisted on October 2, which was his brother Michel's birthday, and moreover, he didn't like "waffling" the way he had been doing for the past month when journalists asked about his political ambitions. According to one of his advisers, "he likes when things are clear, when things are direct."

The day of decision finally came. On the evening of October 2, 2012, Justin Trudeau confirmed the least well-kept political secret in the country. In a speech that was widely covered by the media, he announced at the William Hingston Community Centre that he was running for leader of the Liberal Party of Canada. The room was overflowing with supporters, brandishing red placards bearing a single name: *Justin*. The Trudeau family name was practically nowhere to be seen. People crammed the aisles and even the staircases. Over five hundred people from a multitude of nationalities were in attendance reflecting the image of the very multicultural riding of Papineau.

Justin Trudeau appeared in a grey suit and silver silk tie, his hair rather long. He seemed nervous. He wasn't using a teleprompter. During a fairly mundane thirty-minute speech about continuity and renewal, he kept his comments to generalities. "I love Montreal. I love Quebec. And I am in love with Canada," he said with his typically theatrical air. "I love this country, and I want to spend my life serving it. That's why I'm so happy to announce here, tonight, my candidacy for the leadership of the Liberal Party of Canada."

The crowd cheered. Before this friendly audience, Pierre Elliott Trudeau's son laid out the big political directions that mattered the most to him: education, protection of the middle class, striking a balance between economic development and the environment, redressing historic injustices faced by the First Nations, the empowerment of young people — "an essential resource for society."

He reminded his listeners of the great achievements of the Liberal Party and the values that have been its inspiration: medicare, an independent foreign policy, immigration, the inalienable rights and freedoms inscribed in the Charter. It was clear he aimed to make the middle class the keystone of his program. But Trudeau was still vague about the details. He didn't have much to say about his economic vision, either. The key to growth and progress was a thriving middle class, Trudeau said, which provided realistic hope for the future. But the news on Canada's economic front was "not so good," he added: incomes were stagnating, costs were going up, and debts were exploding.

The candidate made a commitment to do politics in a new way, to remain positive and to avoid resorting to personal attacks. Which didn't prevent him from taking on his political opponents: the NDP sowed regional resentment, he said, while the Conservatives privileged one sector over others with the promise that "wealth would trickle down, eventually."

As for the Liberal Party itself, he was brutally frank. The party had a strong foundation, but, he said, it was time to face the facts: the party was out of touch with its base and with the expectations of Canadians. "I've too often heard it said in Liberal circles that the Liberal Party created Canada. This, my friends, is wrong. The Liberal Party did not create Canada. Canada created the Liberal Party. Canadians created the Liberal Party," he said. "When we were at our best, we were in touch, open to our fellow citizens and confident enough in them to take their ideas and work with them to build a successful country," he added, inviting Liberals "to write a new chapter in the history of the Liberal Party."

He said he wanted the Liberal Party "to be once again the party that promotes and cherishes the francophone reality of this country.... And I want the Liberal Party to be once again the vehicle for Quebeckers to contribute to the future of Canada.

"We know some Quebeckers want their own country. A country that reflects our values, that protects our language and our culture, that respects our identity. My friends, I want to build a country too. A country worthy of my dreams. Of your dreams. But for me, that country reaches from the Atlantic to the Pacific, from the Great Lakes to the Great North," he said over wild applause. "Quebeckers have always chosen Canada because we know it is the land of our ancestors.... Will we put this history aside now because people of other languages came after us with the same dream of building a better country? Of course not. Our contribution to Canada is far from over."

He acknowledged his candidacy might put the Liberal Party in the spotlight again. But he wanted to lower expectations. There would be ups and down, the star candidate admitted, because a change of leader in itself wouldn't solve problems, and he wouldn't have all the answers. He had strengths and weaknesses, but he felt sure he could "convince a new generation of Canadians that their country needs them."

Justin then took a more personal tone. He described his unusual life experience, from growing up at 24 Sussex Drive to crossing the country as a little boy. "I feel so privileged to have had the relationship I've had, all my life, with this country, with its land, and with its people. From my first, determined steps as a toddler to my first, determined steps as a politician: we've travelled many miles together," he added. What other candidate could make this claim? He had an intimate relationship with Canadians who had witnessed him growing up. He knew this gave him an undeniable advantage and he played on it.

The young MP only mentioned the name of Pierre Elliott Trudeau once, when recalling what his father had said at Michel's funeral.

Justin Trudeau said the patriation of the Constitution in 1982 without the Quebec government's consent was "a debate for another era." It was not something current, he added during a press briefing after his speech. "People are talking about the future, about building together. In my opinion, that's the way people want to go, but it is one of the accomplishments that enabled us to create a better country in the past."

In the months to come, Trudeau intended to show Liberals he had the right stuff to be their leader, he wasn't just his father's son. He came out against the idea of a merger with the NDP, saying he hoped the Liberal leadership campaign would help people see him as his own man — as "Justin."

After this short press briefing, he set out on the campaign trail.

————

His first stop was Calgary, Stephen Harper's Conservative bastion and hostile territory for the Liberals. Albertans had long resented Pierre Elliott Trudeau for introducing the National Energy Program in the 1980s,[11] a series of measures that had greatly reduced Alberta's oil revenues.

Albertans might transfer their resentment from Pierre Elliott Trudeau to his son, so Justin Trudeau decided to take the bull by the horns.

From the outset, he said the National Energy Program had been poorly conceived and had divided the country. This was the first time he had ever distanced himself publicly from this father's controversial legacy. He added it was "wrong to use our natural wealth to divide Canadians against one another.... It was the wrong way to govern in the past. It is the wrong way today. It will be the wrong way in the future." He promised that he would "never use the wealth of the West as a wedge to gain votes in the East."[12]

The MP for Papineau added he wasn't even ten years old when the NEP was adopted. It was time to move on.

The campaign trail included stops in Richmond, British Columbia, and Mississauga, Ontario. At the end of the tour, Trudeau stopped in Dieppe, a little French-speaking town in New Brunswick on the outskirts of Moncton. Luck was on his side. Three days after launching his campaign in Montreal, his childhood friend Dominic LeBlanc confirmed a persistent rumour. He came to the microphone to announce he was stepping aside from the Liberal leadership race to support his friend. This was in the best interests of the party, LeBlanc added, praising Trudeau for his tireless work as an MP. Nobody found the announcement surprising. It was hard to compete with Trudeau. An unknown candidate from Manitoba, the ambulance technician Shane Geschiere, was also dropping out of the race to support Trudeau.

But then, was taking over the leadership of a weakened party in the House of Commons really that attractive a proposition? High-profile candidates were not rushing to grasp the chance. Bank of Canada Governor Mark Carney decided to accept the top position at the Bank of England instead, while Denis Coderre set his sights on becoming the mayor of Montreal.

The official launch date of the Liberal leadership campaign was November 14, 2012. Little by little, candidates made their intentions known. At the starting gate were twelve candidates. Apart from Justin Trudeau, four other candidates stood out from the pack: Martha Hall Findlay, former MP for the Toronto riding of Willowdale and a business-woman, was taking a second run at the leadership; Marc Garneau, the first

Canadian astronaut, had been re-elected in 2011 in the Montreal riding of Westmount-Ville-Marie; Joyce Murray was MP for Vancouver Quadra; and Martin Cauchon, Jean Chrétien's former minister of justice, entered the race at the last minute.

The other candidates were the businessman George Takah; Karen McCrimmon, the first woman to command a Canadian air force squadron; Ottawa lawyer David Bertschi; Vancouver Crown prosecutor Alex Breton; David Merner, former president of the British Columbia wing of the Liberal Party of Canada; Jonathan Mousley, an economist and former assistant to the minister David Collenette; and Deborah Coyne, former adviser to Clyde Wells and a staunch opponent of the Meech Lake Accord.

———

The strategy of the Trudeau team consisted of reaching out to a newly created category of Liberal supporters and focusing on many regions where they could get votes, since each of the 308 federal ridings had an equal weight in the vote. The team wasted no time selling new party membership cards, given that this was a complicated process and sometimes resulted in bargaining and never-ending discussions. New members often wanted to trade their support for some advantage, whether specific party resolutions, items on the legislative agenda, or promises. The other disadvantage was that membership cards came with an expiry date, which meant the whole process of recruitment would have to be repeated at a later date!

The supporter category, which became effective on May 2, 2012, offered much more flexibility, and the Trudeau team decided early on to zero in on this new class of voters. It was a way for the party to bring in new people after the election fiasco of 2011. Criteria were loose: supporters did not pay anything and had to be Canadian residents at least eighteen years of age, and not be members of any other federal party.

These non-member supporters could help choose the next Liberal leader by sending in their votes. This was quite a change for the party. At the Montreal convention in 2006, when Stéphane Dion won the leadership race, about five thousand delegates had voted in the fourth and final ballot. But those days were gone. There would be no actual delegates at the 2013 convention. Instead, it was expected that tens of thousands of supporters would cast their votes for the next Liberal leader from the comfort of the homes, whether online or by telephone.

The reason for creating this new category of party supporters was to bring about the renewal of the party by increasing its base. The Liberals wanted a new kind of supporter — the citizen interested in politics who nonetheless did not necessarily want to join a party. They wanted to bring in support from all spheres of society, throughout the Canadian population, without relying solely on long-standing members of the Liberal family.

Recruiting these supporters was a valuable tool for the Trudeau team. They simply had to put their email address on the application form and then check a box if they wanted to volunteer for their candidate or make a donation. This provided a mine of information to the Liberal Party, making it possible to enlist the help of supporters in organizing events and to approach them directly for a modest contribution to the campaign.

In fact, this recruitment method suited the Trudeau camp very well, since it could draw on "a very large number of volunteers who were completely familiar with new platforms," says Pablo Rodríguez. "New technologies would enable us to recruit people with just a few clicks."

On the other hand, these new supporters were not as engaged as full members, with the result that they were less loyal and reliable. It was all very well to apply online as a supporter, but it was another matter altogether to get these supporters to register to vote in a leadership race.

The Trudeau team sought to boost the number of supporters streaming in by creating a direct link between them and the leadership candidate. The website www.justin.ca covered every move he made, as well as the consistently positive reaction of the crowds he met. The site included photographs of Justin with his wife Sophie and their children Xavier James and Ella-Grace. The team also kept the MP's Twitter and Facebook accounts updated and lively.

This approach could be the launching pad for the rebuilding of the Liberal Party, Trudeau told the *Globe and Mail* in an interview.[13]

On the campaign trail, young volunteers accompanying Trudeau were called on to patrol Liberal events. Once the candidate finished speaking, they made their way down the aisle, brandishing iPads and inviting people to become Liberal supporters on the spot. Sometimes Trudeau laid on the charm and did the inviting himself. He was very good at attracting crowds. Events usually resulted in dozens of signatures, sometimes more.

"I sent Justin to give speeches at McGill, Concordia, and the Université de Montréal," Pablo Rodríguez recalls. "We set young people up at a table, and equipped them with iPads. We took in supporters by the shovel. It was just incredible!" The same thing happened in community centres and golden age clubs, where volunteers helped sign up people online.

Whenever Trudeau met someone in the street or spoke to people in a restaurant, his campaign workers were at the ready with application forms, and quickly asked if they wanted to support the star candidate's campaign. Call centres were also kept busy recruiting supporters and lining up votes for Trudeau. One call centre in Old Montreal was just buzzing with activity.

In Ontario, Navdeep Bains was on the front lines. Elected MP at the age of twenty-six but defeated in the 2011 election, he knew what back-breaking work it was to get the party out of the doldrums. He put in place a "particularly aggressive" strategy for recruiting the maximum number of supporters in the suburbs surrounding Toronto. He led a relatively unstructured recruitment campaign, but the results were what mattered most. His role was essentially to identify potential supporters, contact them, follow up by email, reach them by phone, and get them to attend public meetings to meet Justin.

The message was always the same: "Hope and change." Pierre Trudeau's eldest son was presented as a man who detested Stephen Harper's political direction and who was ready to do whatever was needed to reverse the trend.

Between events, Justin Trudeau himself often took the time to get on the phone to drum up support.

CHAPTER 6

A LEADER IN WAITING

Once the Liberal leadership race got underway on November 14, 2012, Justin Trudeau was practically the only candidate. Jean Chrétien had been hounded by Paul Martin, and Pierre Elliott Trudeau had had to fend off John Turner. But Justin had no real opponent running against him.

Rae's sudden withdrawal had left well-known figures on the national scene little time to get organized. The Liberals had long maintained themselves in power by masterfully orchestrating the transition from one leader to another, although the process had often been a bitter one. But now they were thrown into confusion. Clan warfare had burned good potential candidates, like Frank McKenna, Brian Tobin, and a few others who were now into their fifties and didn't feel up to the task of assuming the leadership of the third party in Parliament and then rebuilding it from sea to sea.

Many had expected Paul Martin to remain in the saddle long enough for Michael Ignatieff to grow into his new role, to "Canadianize" himself, and to build his power base within the party. But this proved a miscalculation. First, Ignatieff lost to Stéphane Dion in the leadership race, then Dion resigned after a failed attempt to oust Stephen Harper. But when Ignatieff picked up the torch, he didn't last long either, losing to Harper in 2011. Ignatieff's departure left a vacuum. Nobody was waiting in the wings, ready to step in. In fact, Liberal supporters were leaving the party in droves and didn't even turn up for meetings.

In the aftermath of the 2011 election — the worst Liberal defeat in history — the first priority was rebuilding the party. It would be a huge task, requiring enormous patience. This time, the Liberals wanted to reverse the downward spiral and choose a leader who would stay on for more than one mandate. This time, the party would give the new leader a chance.

Justin Trudeau was not everybody's favourite candidate, but he seemed the best hope for the party. He was a champion of the *Canadian Charter of Rights and Freedoms,* he adroitly positioned himself as heir to his father's legacy, he clearly defended Liberal values, and he reinforced the ideals of the party faithful.

The fact he was a backbencher with no government experience didn't really matter. Most party faithful were interested in his ability to win the next election and become the next prime minister. The "blue" Liberals of Bay Street, however, who had remained close to Paul Martin and Michael Ignatieff, had their doubts. Yet Justin Trudeau was better than anyone else in the party at raising funds. Riding associations eagerly sought him out.

Opinion polls too showed that he had what it took to be a winner. The young Trudeau was giving a huge boost to the Liberal Party, which had bolted ahead of the NDP (now ranked third) to 31 percent of voter intentions and was tied with the Conservatives.[1] Many Liberals were now looking ahead to the 2015 elections with confidence.

"They don't know who to reach out to, and he's got the [Trudeau] name," says historian Michael Behiels at the University of Ottawa. "And they discover slowly that there's much more to him than they thought. Everyone was surprised really by his skills, especially his people skills, his ability to reach out."

People were starting to say it was time for a change of the guard. The millennials were the up and coming generation. Society was undergoing profound change, and there was a pressing need to bring together this new generation of Canadians under the Liberal banner.

At forty-one, Justin Trudeau seemed younger than his age and was bursting with energy. He was a precocious child of the Internet generation. He had never been involved in the Martin-Chrétien wars or the sponsorship scandal, which meant he had no baggage that could compromise his chances of appealing to party veterans. Above all, he didn't owe anybody anything, whether in his immediate entourage, in the party, or in the business community.

Trudeau kept his organizers happy. He was like a retail politician from another era, with a real flair for informal contact with the voters. And he was backed by a solid organization and an army of twelve thousand volunteers, according to his own calculations.[2] He readily accepted having his photo taken with strangers and he liked shaking hands.

Out in public, Trudeau was simply in his element. A politician who had never made a single memorable speech in the House of Commons, he preferred being seen outside of the "Ottawa bubble." There he was free to interact with people in their normal environment, from shopping centres to organized events. This appealed to the Canadian public.

As a strategy, this made sense: he wanted to draw in people who didn't necessarily find politics that attractive — young people, women, the middle class.

Wherever he went, rooms filled up to the rafters. So did party coffers. After three months, Justin Trudeau could take pride in having raised $600,000.[3] He could afford the luxury of holding five to six events per day, criss-crossing the country from east to west. His goal was to meet a thousand people per day.[4] He often met this target.

The MP from Papineau made a notable appearance in a popular bistro in Pickering, Ontario, where he deplored stagnating incomes, the rising cost of living, and the explosive debt load of many Canadians, while insisting on the importance of advancing the middle class. He added that the Liberal Party needed to fight public cynicism about the political class and earn public trust by listening to the population instead of indulging in navel gazing.[5]

He also made appearances in western Canada, in Calgary and Edmonton, and also in British Columbia, where the Sinclair name still meant something.

Then it was off to Prince Edward Island and New Brunswick, where the Liberal leader Brian Gallant, a friend he had made through Dominic LeBlanc, accompanied him during a frenzied tour of the province. This sprint brought in $150,000 for the Trudeau camp. It was such a frenzy of activity that Gallant, who would become premier of New Brunswick a year and a half later, nicknamed Trudeau "the tornado." "I impressed many people when I visited fifty-five ridings in fifty-five days," according to Gallant. "Justin toured almost the whole province in just two days, and he kept smiling all the way through."

No man is a prophet in his own land. Quebeckers have a long memory, and they weren't about to forget the sponsorship scandal. Justin Trudeau attracted a certain curiosity, but he wasn't always taken seriously. People in Quebec hadn't followed the ups and downs of his career the way people had in English Canada. In any event, all eyes in Quebec were riveted on the Charbonneau Commission investigating corruption in the construction industry, unfolding like a soap opera with a new episode every day. By the fall of 2012, not a single Quebec pollster had bothered to devote a single poll to Trudeau, as if he didn't really have a place in the political landscape.

In December, Pablo Rodríguez took his protegé to Le Barillet, a restaurant in Jonquière — an institution in the nationalist bastion of the Saguenay region. This would be the first test of the Quebec campaign. Would he be able to make a breakthrough here? Once Justin reached the restaurant, people recognized him as the son of Pierre Elliott Trudeau, and they wanted to chat with him. But the meeting turned into a bit of a scene when about twenty young girls gathered around him to catch the moment on camera.

"They rushed in to see if they could have their picture taken with him," remembers Pablo Rodríguez. "People went gangbusters. He is a handsome man, and whether you like it or not, a politician's physical appearance counts for a lot. Justin's charisma and appearance attract a lot of people."

The test proved to be a success: Justin Trudeau's team signed up twenty-five supporters at Le Barillet.

———

Trudeau had another string to his bow: he had gained the support of a majority of Liberal MPs. This was an important signal for the party faithful, who liked voting for a winner. Given the general slump of party fortunes, he couldn't count on the backing of the Big Red Machine put in place by the late Keith Davey, the Liberal master organizer who had helped many a federal candidate get elected. But he could count on his social media skills. By the opening of the campaign, Trudeau had

150,000 followers on his Twitter feed — an indication of the massive interest he generated as a candidate, even if there was no way to know whether these people would vote for him. The MP for Papineau had regular exchanges over the Internet, he tweeted all the time, and he posted his photos on social media. At this early point in the campaign he wrote his own tweets, attracting a mass of followers. His fan base grew exponentially.

Although there was no wave of support for him building in Quebec, the first opinion polls suggested that nothing could put a dent in the image of the most popular Liberal in the country. Justin's game plan was disciplined. He was both politician and boxer, and he knew he was comfortably ahead of the pack and needed to be cautious. There was no place for bluff and thunder or sweeping statements that his opponents could turn to their advantage.

Even if everything seemed to be going well, running for the leadership was still a risky venture, as Justin Trudeau admitted shortly after launching his campaign in an address to an enthusiastic crowd in Winnipeg. Nobody doubted he was confident about his chances, but he had never met this kind of challenge before. Expectations were sky-high, and according to his adviser Robert Asselin, many people felt "if the party still had a future, it was with Justin."

Justin Trudeau's organizers, meanwhile, wanted a real leadership race, even if they knew he was ahead. A real race would help them convince the naysayers that the MP for Papineau had won the leadership because he earned it. And Trudeau liked a challenge. As his main adviser Gerald Butts put it, Trudeau is at his best when he's facing competition.

———

As soon as Marc Garneau entered the race, the Trudeau camp began to keep a close eye on him. Who could match Garneau's impressive CV and his brilliant career as an astronaut? The Trudeau camp also kept watch on Joyce Murray and particularly on Martha Hall Findlay, who was considered Justin's most aggressive opponent, since she wanted to improve on her previous performance. She had come last in the 2006 leadership race and then lost her seat in the House of Commons in 2011.

Martin Cauchon, former MP for Outremont, was not considered a threat, because "his support was above all based in Quebec." Clearly, the former minister of justice still nourished political ambitions, but he had come late to the leadership race, and he had rarely shown up at recent party gatherings. "Martin has always had his own convictions," people said with a shrug.

There were twelve candidates in the race, which made things somewhat chaotic. Trudeau didn't devote much time to the lesser-known candidates. Their presence on social media gave them a visibility they would otherwise never have had, but they had little chance of winning. David Merner, Jonathan Mousley, and Alex Burton dropped out of the race rather than pay the full $75,000 leadership entry fee.

Even with nine candidates in the running, it was all too easy. The race was leading up to a coronation, something the party had vowed to avoid after Michael Ignatieff's "aborted leadership." According to a well-placed Liberal, Ignatieff had been parachuted into the leadership position by "non-elected party officials, a disgusting process." Was Justin Trudeau also being offered the leadership of the Liberal Party on a silver platter?

The first two campaign debates, in Vancouver and Winnipeg, didn't attract much attention: the candidates spoke one after the other to a Liberal moderator. The format of the debates was awkward, and there were few direct exchanges, making it hard to assess the strengths and weaknesses of each candidate. Most candidates came out swinging at Stephen Harper rather than at Justin Trudeau, whom they apparently wanted to spare. The general tone of these debates was restrained, as the candidates sought to avoid confrontations and the kind of very public family squabbling and divisions that had characterized the Liberals over the past few years. Those squabbles had only helped the Conservatives. People remembered how the Conservatives had lifted clips from the candidates' debates during the 2006 leadership race, only to use them in attack ads to weaken Stéphane Dion's image as new leader.

Marc Garneau, however, was not a man for half-measures. He decided to shake things up. There was an air of frustration about Garneau as he struggled to catch up to the leading candidate. He was a man who rarely raised his voice, so when he lashed out at Trudeau at an Ottawa press conference in mid-February 2013, he was clearly not in his comfort zone.

Garneau demanded that instead of merely making fine-sounding but shallow statements, the front-runner should clearly articulate his vision for the country and define his policies, particularly where the middle class and young Canadians were concerned. Otherwise, the Conservatives would have a field day launching their attacks on the next Liberal leader, the way they had done with Michael Ignatieff and Stéphane Dion.

Garneau cast himself as the candidate of substance and called on Trudeau to explain his priorities before the race was over. The former astronaut pointed out he had clearly articulated his own vision, the foundations of which were the knowledge economy, employment, and financial security. It was time for Trudeau to lay his cards on the table.

The Trudeau team took Garneau's angry words in stride, seeing in them less a show of strength than the reaction of a candidate falling by the wayside and eager to attract attention to himself. Trudeau's advisers turned down Garneau's offer of a one-on-one debate. Why risk a duel when Trudeau's campaign was doing so well?

They hoped people would rally to a candidate who remained positive, so they stuck to their game plan, which was to remain silent and avoid responding to attacks.

Justin Trudeau also had no interest in getting drawn into acrimonious conflicts. In fact, nothing seemed to be able to throw his campaign off the rails. He was extremely cautious, and only released his policy positions in small doses over the weeks and months that followed. He came out in favour of foreign investment in the oil sands and in favour of the Keystone XL pipeline, which would channel Alberta oil to refineries in Texas. But on environmental grounds he came out against the Northern Gateway pipeline project, which would send diluted bitumen down to the British Columbia coast.

He came out for the legalization of marijuana, a policy that worried many people, whether for feigned or real reasons. He also wanted to implement democratic reforms to give more power to MPs. He proposed raising the post-secondary attainment rates from 50 percent to 70 percent without laying out a schedule or explaining how he would bring about this change. Since education is a provincial jurisdiction, his team added that this proposal would involve working closely with the provinces to fix targets. Trudeau also said the federal government could intervene in the areas of student loans and research councils, and noted that it holds the responsibility for the First Nations education system.

Trudeau stirred up a storm by coming out in favour of scrapping the long-gun registry, a position Marc Garneau thought it was wisest not to contradict. But in general, Garneau labelled Trudeau's policy statements as small announcements that only addressed "the subject of the day."

Scott Brison, who had run for the leadership in 2006, says it was at this point that Marc Garneau started to show his desperation. You only have to glance at the financial reports the candidates had to file with Elections Canada to see how much more successful Trudeau was in raising funds: he brought in almost $700,000, while Martha Hall Findlay raised $150,000, and Marc Garneau, $122,000. It would be hard to turn things around.

On February 16, during the third of five debates held in Mississauga, Ontario, Garneau went on the offensive again. This was his last chance to make a good impression before the March 3 deadline for signing up supporters. He needed to make a big impact. As the first Canadian astronaut and a former naval officer, his leadership abilities spoke for themselves, he said. Could Justin Trudeau, the star candidate who had said practically nothing substantial so far, say as much? Garneau accused his rival of lacking both vision and experience.

"What in your resumé qualifies you to be the leader of the country?" asked the former astronaut. "It's not enough to be a good speaker," he added with a touch of irony.

For once, Justin Trudeau was on the defensive. "Leadership," he said, "is about drawing people in, and about involving Canadians in the kinds of conversations we have" on key issues. He had won twice in Papineau, he pointed out, and then fired directly back at Garneau over the applause of the audience: "You can't lead from a podium in a press conference, you can't win over Canadians with a five-point plan, you have to connect with them."

Garneau wasn't satisfied. The real test of leadership, the sixty-three-year-old told his forty-one-year-old rival, is to be able to take difficult decisions, something that a leader often has to do alone. A leader needs to be able to draw on a store of experience. "You've spoken in generalities," he said.

Trudeau came back to his theme of campaigning at the grassroots level. He had won the Liberal nomination in Papineau, beating the Bloc Québécois incumbent in 2008, and then survived the Orange Wave in 2011 — and it was all because he had succeeded in convincing people to come together under his leadership in a riding that was not particularly open either to the Liberal Party or to himself personally. But he got the most approval from the audience when he said what many Liberals wanted to hear: "You have to have a record of winning, Marc."

In this exchange between the two rivals, Pierre Trudeau's son seemed to lose a bit of his aura of standing above any possible attack. The exchanges that followed were polite, but now they were starting to bring out the weaker points of the leadership candidate from Papineau.

But it was Martha Hall Findlay who hit the hardest. She was a personal friend of Justin Trudeau's, and she had sat next to him on the Liberal benches in the House of Commons. This fifty-three-year-old former Ontario MP hit Trudeau where it hurt the most: his personal fortune.

She mentioned a recent article by a journalist from the *Ottawa Citizen*, who had asked Trudeau to reveal the extent of his personal fortune. For the sake of transparency, he admitted he had "won the lottery" by inheriting $1.2 million from his father. That was an enviable amount of money to inherit, but a bigger problem lay in the rich speaker's fees Trudeau raked in. He admitted he had been paid handsomely for giving speeches in schools and libraries and for non-profit organizations. In his best year, he had earned more than $450,000. Once he was elected to Parliament, his speaker's fees dropped to a total of $277,000 over four years, although during this time he was often conspicuously absent from the House of Commons.

Martha Hall Findlay said it was hard for Justin Trudeau to claim to be speaking for ordinary people: "You keep referring to the middle class but you yourself have admitted you don't belong to the middle class. I find it a little challenging to understand how you would understand the challenges facing real Canadians."

A member of Trudeau's inner circle says "this attack really shook him up. He was disappointed. A good friend had deliberately set out to hurt him."

But the Toronto businesswoman hadn't finished yet. Hall Findlay said the supply management system should be dismantled, and she questioned

Trudeau's ability to lead. Was Justin Trudeau really up to taking on Stephen Harper, or was the party simply going to go for a celebrity lacking experience as well as substance?

The former MP for Willowdale was booed at times, but she also met with some applause. Trudeau had often heard recriminations like this, ever since he made his entry into politics, pounding the pavement in the Papineau riding. People often asked how he, as the son of a prime minister, could possibly understand the daily concerns of people in the riding.

"I've been lucky in my life," said Trudeau, "to have been given an opportunity to go to great schools, to travel around the world, and what is important for me is to put everything that I have received … in the service of my community. And that is what my identity is all about."

Deborah Coyne, meanwhile, who had had a daughter with Pierre Trudeau, wanted to avoid getting sucked into this party infighting, and said she would take no part in this particular exchange.

Marc Garneau intervened to calm things down, coming to Justin Trudeau's defence. A candidate aspiring to high public office should not be discredited because of his income, he said. Garneau's words were well received.

As for Joyce Murray, she opposed the notion of "class," since it was so divisive.

Martha Hall Findlay had wanted to strike a devastating blow; in the end, though, she had to apologize. But in an editorial meeting with the *Ottawa Citizen*, she nevertheless hammered home the same message, explaining that the Liberal Party was at a crossroads and needed a leader capable of taking on Stephen Harper. The choice the Liberals made should be dictated by substance and experience, not by celebrity. She pointed out she was from a family of six children, and had been raised "in comfort," but she could never have gone to university without obtaining a student loan. It wasn't the circumstances of one's birth that mattered, she said — obviously referring to Justin Trudeau — but what one made of one's life.

The attacks over his personal finances put Trudeau on the defensive. He explained on the campaign trail in Ontario that MPs were allowed to have supplementary income from other sources, and "in my disclosure I've been more transparent than any politician ever has."

Whatever he said, it was clear he had fared poorly during the exchange. Several of his parliamentary colleagues wanted to know how he could accept $277,000 in fees to give speeches in schools and for non-profit organizations, whereas appearances like that were a natural part of his work as an MP, a full-time job for which he was already drawing a good salary. Given a groundswell of opinion against this practice, he offered to refund his fees to any group that felt it had been wronged.

———

All eyes were focused on Justin Trudeau. Marc Garneau was widely admired, but the party faithful didn't know him as well. Schools were named after him, he had performed brilliantly in space, but he often seemed lacklustre in the House of Commons. He was more a scientist than a political animal; he sometimes appeared too rational, and he didn't show his emotions. He had to fight the perception that he was the candidate being held in reserve in case Justin Trudeau wiped out. Worst of all, as both a gentleman and a former astronaut, he lacked the killer instinct that was needed to take on Harper.

"I am nice," Garneau told the Canadian Press in an interview. "But if people don't think that I'm tough, they've got something coming to them. You don't get to where I am today without being tough. You can be nice about it but I'm tough. Inside, I'm tough."[6]

The party was talking renewal, so as a sixty-three-year-old leadership candidate, Garneau could hardly play the youth card. People liked him for his composed and serious manner. Ontario MP Ted Hsu, who was campaigning for Garneau, praised his intelligence, integrity, and discipline. Was this a way of saying Garneau lacked charisma?

Canadians wanted "a steady hand they can trust to make decisions," Hsu added. "I don't think Stephen Harper is particularly exciting either."

But the majority of Liberals saw this leadership race as the last chance to rebuild the party, and they couldn't picture Marc Garneau as leader. According to pollster Darrell Bricker, "Garneau is just another guy with grey hair and a red tie. Liberals were looking for someone who could catapult them into power."

Garneau had to face the facts: despite all his hard work, Trudeau was maintaining a commanding lead. On March 13, one month before the next leader of the Liberal Party of Canada was to be chosen, Garneau withdrew from the race. The candidate who had made it seem as if the sky was the limit had to come back down to Earth.

"I cannot mathematically win," Garneau told journalists. "Justin Trudeau will win the Liberal leadership in a resounding victory," he predicted.

And he was right. According to an internal survey of six thousand Liberal members and supporters, Trudeau enjoyed 72 percent support, and with just 15 percent, Garneau had no way of catching up. Joyce Murray had the support of 7.4 percent of those surveyed, and Martha Hall Findlay, 5.2 percent. Cauchon, Bertschi, Coyne, and McCrimmon did not feature in the survey.

Overnight, Garneau turned into the good soldier ready to support the adversary he had just accused of lacking substance. The MP for Westmount-Ville-Marie didn't regret the harsh language he had used. It was normal during a leadership race to criticize one's rival, he said. Did that mean Justin Trudeau now had the experience needed to become prime minister of Canada? Garneau wouldn't say, although he admitted that Trudeau had "surprised a lot of people" during the campaign and that he was "the best choice."

By withdrawing from the race, it was Garneau who surprised people. Martin Cauchon was flabbergasted. He felt nothing had yet been decided and there remained many stages in the campaign before the votes crystallized. Then on February 25, Toronto lawyer George Takach withdrew from the race to support "Prime Minister" Trudeau. This meant that remaining contenders had a greater chance to make their mark.

Joyce Murray, a fifty-one-year-old candidate, jumped at the opportunity. Her team claimed that Garneau had quit the race because he didn't want to come third, behind Joyce!

Did this mean Trudeau now had an insurmountable lead? His Quebec campaign director Pablo Rodríguez believed it was too soon to tell. His candidate was "making a breakthrough in Quebec and elsewhere." But it wasn't a done deal, since "many supporters still had to sign up in order to vote, and the deadline was March 14."

The Trudeau team, meanwhile, pressured the party establishment to postpone the deadline by one week. The Liberal Party executive didn't resist Justin Trudeau's request; on the contrary, it went all-out to accommodate him. A rival candidate found this grotesque: the party claimed the delay ensured greater public participation, whereas the real goal was to help Trudeau recruit new supporters. "Do I look like an idiot?" asked the defeated candidate. "They were just making fun of us."

Joyce Murray's team had also asked the party to postpone the deadline by one week, but the left-wing Liberal candidate was met with frosty silence. "That's the way it was," said one of Murray's close advisers, referring to Trudeau's advantage over the other candidates. "If things didn't work out his way …"

Joyce Murray had tried positioning herself in the race as a candidate ready to debate on substantive issues and avoid personal attacks. She used her skills as a former British Columbia minister of the environment, seeking to corner Justin Trudeau with tough questions during the televised debates. One of her advisers says with a touch of sarcasm that Murray wanted to see whether Justin — a "thoroughbred" — had what it takes to cross the finish line. The idea was to test Justin, who gave every sign of being an inexperienced "young colt."

Joyce Murray raised the idea during the very first candidates' debate of forging a strategic alliance between the Liberals, New Democrats, and Greens, so the three parties would co-operate on fielding just one candidate per riding in order to beat the Conservatives. But the other leadership candidates, including Trudeau, saw this as a defeatist strategy. Murray turned to Trudeau and asked him point-blank what his plan was to defeat Stephen Harper.

He answered rather awkwardly that it was important to reach out to people across the country — which was a way of saying that policies would come later on. He said the only way to get rid of old-style politics in the Liberal Party was to stop imposing policy directives from the top down, and to draw on the energy and ideas of party supporters at the base.

By championing environmental issues and a proportional electoral system, Joyce Murray thought she had lined up impressive support. The noted environmentalist David Suzuki endorsed her, and groups favouring electoral reform promised to recruit supporters for her. At one point, she even believed she had recruited more registered supporters than the presumptive front-runner Justin Trudeau.[7] But it wouldn't be enough to catch up.

The last debate took place on March 23 in Montreal. This was Martin Cauchon's last chance to score some points. National unity and Quebec's place within Canada were not on the agenda, but the former minister of justice didn't see how the subject could be avoided. "Not talking about it is surrealistic," he said. He saw this as an opportunity for tripping up Trudeau, who had often crossed swords with Quebec nationalists.

The squabbles and quarrels had gone on long enough, the former prime minister's son interjected: "For far too long we've tried to buy Quebec, to buy them off rather than to get them involved in building a prosperous, strong and united country." He invited Quebeckers to take a greater interest in debates on the federal scene. But during a leadership debate receiving scant media coverage, this statement didn't have much impact.

———

Nobody doubted that Justin Trudeau had rock star appeal, a rare ability to charm people. But his judgment was often questioned, as well as his lack of substance. In a column entitled "Monsieur Trudeau's Resumé,"[8] André Pratte of *La Presse* wrote that nothing in Justin Trudeau's background indicated he had what it took to lead the Liberal Party, and he definitely lacked the mettle of previous leaders. Peter Worthington wrote in a column for the *Sun* chain that Justin was his father's son but he "has his mother's brains."

Justin Trudeau's leadership campaign was driven by image-makers and did nothing to dispel this impression. He talked in generalities and invited the public to submit their own ideas, to share their concerns, and to take a greater interest in the federal political system. "This campaign is about conversations, not one-way monologues," he explained.[9]

The cautious assessment of his advisers was that it would be suicidal for Justin Trudeau to unveil his election platform a full year and a half before the federal elections slated for October 2015. If he made any premature policy announcements, rival parties would steal his ideas while turning him into an easy target.

His original plan for the leadership campaign had been to unveil a big part of his program at least every three months, but as time went on he changed his mind. "You can't believably commit to a new, more open way of doing policy, then publish a full platform before you have had a chance to get people's input!" he wrote in *Common Ground*.[10]

———

Trudeau may have been doing his best to be careful, but some of his statements proved controversial. For example, Quebec Premier Pauline Marois slammed him for saying during a Quebec stopover that there was no need to strengthen Bill 101, Quebec's Charter of the French Language. And when he said in Saint-Jérôme there was no need to bring Quebec into the Canadian Constitution since that was an issue from a previous era, he came off sounding like Jean Chrétien.[11] He couldn't detect any interest in the population to reopen the issue: it was time to move on to more pressing concerns such as employment, the economy, and foreign policy. Then, speaking on the French-language television network TVA, Trudeau said he wouldn't close the door definitively on constitutional discussions. First, the premier of Quebec would have to ask him to open such discussions, and second, it would have to be done in a way that didn't create divisions.

During a campaign tour of eastern Ontario in November, Justin Trudeau mentioned that the long-gun registry had been a "failure," and he didn't plan to bring it back once he gained power. Former justice minister Martin Cauchon reminded him scornfully that the Liberals were the ones who started the registry in the first place, and it was one of Jean Chrétien's more important legacies. Like most Liberals, Trudeau had voted several times against scrapping the registry. But now, the same young man who had grown up under the police protection of the RCMP at 24 Sussex Drive, surrounded by long guns, pistols, and shotguns, said that owning a firearm was part of Canadian culture. He later had to explain he meant the registry was a failure because it continued to prove divisive. Whatever the case, several Liberals MPs agreed with him, adding that the registry had been poorly conceived and should be dropped.

There was no mystery in the fact that Justin Trudeau as a former schoolteacher was in favour of raising the post-secondary attainment rate from the current 50 percent to 70 percent. But in practical terms, this proposal didn't make a lot of sense. When it was pointed out to him that education was a provincial jurisdiction, he had to issue a clarification in an opinion piece in *La Presse*.

He had sketched out some of his priorities but still hadn't given any clear indication of his economic vision for the country. Trudeau came out in favour of the takeover of the Alberta oil company Nexen by the Chinese state-owned company CNOOC (China National Offshore Oil Corporation) because he considered this takeover would create thousands of jobs for the Canadian middle class, which had been falling behind over the past few years. By 2025, China was expected to have more than 220 cities with over a million inhabitants each, and seemed a gold mine of opportunity for Canadian business. "What if our goal was to become Asia's designers and builders of livable cities?" he asked in an op-ed piece in the *Vancouver Sun*.

So he congratulated the Harper government for approving CNOOC's takeover of Nexen, but was taken aback by Ottawa's decision to authorize future acquisitions in the petroleum sector only "under exceptional circumstances." Vague restrictions did nothing to encourage foreign investment, he said, while promising to create a healthier investment climate.

On a campaign visit to Prince Edward Island, the leadership hopeful came out in favour of eliminating the new employment insurance measures introduced by the Harper government. These measures penalized the frequently unemployed and pressured them to accept work an hour away from their homes. This was proof, he said, that the Harper government had no concept of the reality of workers in the Maritimes. This position was well received in the region.

Justin Trudeau also laid out a detailed five-point plan for democratic reform: he proposed relaxing party discipline so MPs could vote according to their conscience, with two exceptions: the first was money bills, since any vote against a budget could be construed as a non-confidence vote; the second was any measure contrary to provisions of the *Canadian Charter of Rights and Freedoms*.

He said that candidates who wanted to run for the Liberals would have to earn the privilege, and this included incumbent MPs. Nomination meetings would be free from outside interference: the party leader would not intervene to impose a particular candidate. This position irritated several long-standing MPs, who didn't see why they would no longer have the leader's backing when the time came to choose the next candidate in a riding they already represented.

———

Justin Trudeau's most important commitment — and one that set him apart from the other leadership hopefuls — was to improve the prospects of the middle class. Without making concrete promises, he said a Liberal government would help families that were struggling to make ends meet. He wasn't particularly impressed by studies showing that the middle class was better off in Canada than in other countries. "For people experiencing it on a day-to-day basis, the stagnation of the middle class doesn't need any explaining."

Justin Trudeau acknowledged that "average family incomes have increased, with the arrival of a new generation of educated women into the labour market. But the weakening of the middle class is a reality stemming from an undeniable fact: the individual incomes of people making up the middle class have been stagnating over the last few decades."[12]

Meanwhile, he added, the size of the Canadian economy had doubled over the past thirty years, and the people benefiting from this growth were the wealthy. If economic success wasn't shared equitably, then people in the middle class could end up questioning the political system and values underlying this growth.

Apart from this statement, Justin Trudeau made no memorable speech or policy announcement during the entire leadership campaign. There was one possible exception: his position on legalizing marijuana, which in any case had been lifted word for word from Joyce Murray's platform, as one of her advisers pointed out. Trudeau's campaign was based above all on his magnetic appeal, which left his rivals scrambling. He articulated no big ideas; his program was about Justin.

———

One week before the Liberal leadership convention was held, the candidates gathered one last time before the party faithful for an evening of speeches. Things were just buzzing in Mississauga on Saturday, April

6, 2013. Cameras were in position, last-minute preparations were made, discussions were going on behind the scenes. Every detail counted: the tie, the hair, the clothes. Even if the format had changed, Trudeau and his team felt they were taking part in a real convention, just like the old days.

For once, Justin seemed somewhat nervous, and Sophie seemed even more so. Louis-Alexandre Lanthier broke the ice by dancing behind the stage. A few minutes before giving his speech, Justin let off steam by dancing with his wife. A Liberal Party photographer caught the moment on camera. Sophie wore high heels and a dress in Liberal red, and Justin wore a dark grey suit. The royal couple looked as though they were having fun at some evening gala.

The next day, Justin Trudeau posted the photograph on his Twitter feed, asking people to be sure to vote. The photo captured his youthful vigour and went viral. There couldn't have been a better ad for the end of the leadership campaign. Trudeau was a master at using social media to his advantage. At the beginning of April, he welcomed his two hundred thousandth follower on his Twitter feed.

The moment of truth was nigh. There would be no surprises this time.

———

In Ottawa on April 14, the reception hall at the Westin Hotel was full. In a few hours, Justin Trudeau's fate would be sealed.

People were waving placards. The supporters of the six surviving candidates shook hands and slapped one another on the back. After an evening off in the federal capital, Justin was there with his family. He no longer felt nervous the way he had in Mississauga. "He was pretty calm," says a friend. "He's a confident guy, and he likes winning."

As one speech followed the other, there was a kind of fever in the air, but there was really no suspense. This was not like traditional Liberal leadership conventions, where sudden reversals had taken place in real time. This time, supporters had already cast their secret ballots electronically, so there would be no sudden movements of delegates across the convention floor: unlike the convention in 2006, there would be no negotiations on the sidelines or last-minute horse-trading between factions. Competition for newly created supporters had replaced competition for delegates, and here there was simply no way to beat Trudeau.

Former leaders of the Liberal Party followed one another to the micro-phone. Jean Chrétien warmed up the convention hall, reminding Liberal supporters better than anyone else could of the glory years of the party. Chrétien, the old lion, roared that the leadership convention marked the "beginning of the end of the Conservative government."

Justin Trudeau's team kept a close eye on the situation. Gerald Butts, the architect of the campaign, was more visibly nervous than any other team member. The convention was, after all, the culmination of months of relentless work. "He had spent so much time building the movement," Robert Asselin recalls. "You could feel he was bringing a chapter to a close." On the morning of the vote, the friends on the team got together to capture the moment in a photograph.

There was no particular suspense when party president Mike Crawley began reading out the results of the vote. Justin's victory was no more than a formality. "The only thing we didn't know was the margin of the victory," says Pablo Rodríguez.

So Justin Trudeau, the prodigal son, had taken a gamble, and he had won. He got 24,688 points — more than 80 percent of the total points represented by the votes of supporters and party members.[13]

Joyce Murray was devastated by the results. She had expected a stron-ger showing, but her second-place tally was just 3,130 points. Martha Hall Findlay came third with 1,760 points, followed by Martin Cauchon with 815, Deborah Coyne with 214, and Karen McCrimmon with 210. The Ottawa lawyer David Bertschi had withdrawn from the race shortly after Marc Garneau dropped out.

This was a moment for Justin Trudeau to savour. He had won the lead-ership of the Liberal Party of Canada on April 14, 2013, almost forty-five years day for day after his father Pierre Elliott Trudeau had won the lead-ership on the fourth ballot on April 6, 1968. Justin sat with his wife Sophie and his children on his knees, listening with a smile as the results came in. Then, to wild applause, he rose to greet the party faithful.

The new leader knew how partisan conflicts had torn the Liberals apart in the past. He wanted to bring the party together. One of his close advisers even says that in the event Justin had lost the race, he didn't intend to come out in support of any other candidate, for fear of opening old wounds in the party or "creating new ones." His victory speech set out to smooth over divisions.

"Canadians turned away from us because we turned away from them," he said, "because Liberals became more focused on fighting with each other than fighting for Canadians… Well, I don't care if you thought my father was great or arrogant. It doesn't matter to me if you were a Chrétien-Liberal, a Turner-Liberal, a Martin-Liberal or any other kind of Liberal. The era of hyphenated Liberals ends right here, tonight. We welcome all Liberals as Canadian Liberals. United in our dedication to serve and lead Canadians!"

Trudeau also considered he needed to give voters a reason to vote again for the Liberal Party. He promised to champion the cause of the middle class. "The purpose of the Liberal Party of Canada will be for you."

Trudeau wanted to put an end to negativity, cynicism, and fear. He rejected the divisive and negative politics waged by Stephen Harper's Conservatives. He added, with a touch of sarcasm, that the New Democrats had found nothing better to do than imitate the divisive approach taken by the Conservatives.

He reserved a special place in his speech for Quebeckers, whom he invited to come back to the Liberals, to build Canada, "a grand, yet unfinished project."

"The time has come for us to write a new chapter in the history of our country. Let's leave to others the old quarrels and old debates that lead nowhere. Let's leave to others the ultra-partisan rhetoric and the old ways of doing politics. Let's leave the personal attacks to them. "Quebeckers, let us be, together, once again, builders of Canada," he said, promising to work hard to deserve their trust.

The new leader didn't devote much attention to economic issues, but he warned that the road would be a long one and they could expect Conservative attacks to be ferocious.

In fact, immediately after Justin Trudeau won the Liberal leadership, the Conservatives issued a press statement saying Trudeau might have a famous last name, but in a time of global economic uncertainty he didn't have the judgment or experience to be prime minister.

This would prove to be the beginning of a new Conservative offensive, but as things worked out, it would not deliver the results the Tories were hoping for.

Justin Trudeau had thought long and hard before taking the leap into politics, but once he decided to make his move, it had seemed a foregone conclusion that he would win the leadership of the Liberal Party, according to John English: "For the first time, people who thought the party was maybe on the way out, saw that perhaps it wouldn't be the case. So very quickly, from a very early stage, it became clear that Justin was going to win and if he did, the party had a chance to do much better."

As leaders, Dion and Ignatieff had both turned out to be flops. Many Liberals felt it was time for a new long-term approach, time to dispense with repeated leadership races that exhausted and demoralized the party base, time to support a strong candidate capable of pulling off a compelling victory. For many Liberals, Justin Trudeau was the party's insurance policy. He wouldn't drop everything and wander off, the way Paul Martin had done after losing the 2006 election.

According to Gordon Ashworth, who had run Pierre Elliott Trudeau's national campaign in 1979–80, Justin was sure to win because of the political context in 2012–13. Once Bob Rae dropped out of the race, the way was clear for Trudeau. He had few serious opponents. This made it easier for party supporters to make up their minds.

Ashworth says the 1968 leadership campaign had featured strong and well-known candidates who had played key roles in the Liberal Party for some time. Pierre Elliott Trudeau was minister of justice and an anti-establishment candidate. There was no guarantee he would win. He was closely trailed by high-calibre, experienced rivals, eight of whom were ministers, and he won only on the fourth ballot. Twelve thousand Liberal delegates had flooded Ottawa to attend the leadership convention, with a great deal of enthusiasm. The Liberal machine just hummed away. Besides, the party was in power, which gave a significant advantage to candidates as they formed alliances, recruited volunteers, and built their networks of supporters.

This was not at all the case in 2012, however. When Justin Trudeau entered the race as a backbencher, the party had been out of power since 2006. The other candidates included just two MPs and one former minister. The Liberal machine was at a standstill. The party had to face the wrath of supporters now abandoning the party in droves. In other words, it was back to the drawing board.

According to Ashworth, after the "Liberal non-race" that had resulted in Michael Ignatieff being crowned leader, the party faithful wanted a leader worthy of their support. Justin Trudeau offered unique advantages: he had a well-known name, he was active in the House of Commons and had interesting ideas (granted, few agreed with Ashworth on this point), and he had the backing of a talented team of advisers.

Many supporters considered it was time to bury the hatchet and rebuild the party, banking on a front-running name rather than the ideas of a second-rung candidate. "Who the hell is Joyce Murray?" asked many Liberals — even ones in her own camp.

So Justin Trudeau was viewed positively: his more awkward public statements were quickly forgiven, given his power to draw crowds and his effectiveness in raising money. By mid-April 2013, he had succeeded in raising $2 million in contributions.

During this long leadership race, Justin actually faced very little opposition from his rivals. "We didn't want to shake things up too much," admits a member of Joyce Murray's team. "It was important that Justin win big," to convince people the Liberals had a future.

Marc Garneau had portrayed Trudeau as a risky bet but ultimately admitted the Liberals made the right choice: "I was a possible choice," he says, "but I was the choice of a minority." Politics had become a bit like show business, and people wanted "a certain tone, an attitude." The former astronaut understands finally that "a candidate could only win over the hearts of the rank and file by showing his personality, and not just his ideas."

But Garneau isn't ready to say the Liberals chose celebrity over substance. "Mr. Trudeau decided to campaign on his personality, which turned out to be a good decision. Even if he didn't regularly articulate a series of policy statements during the leadership campaign, he articulated a few positions. Finally, people made a wise choice," Garneau concludes modestly.

After following a somewhat tortuous course, the new leader of the Liberal Party settled into the position he had worked so hard for. The party had wanted to avoid a coronation — but in the end, the party faithful shrugged it off with a smile of satisfaction.

CHAPTER 7

ENTERING THE FRAY

When he burst onto the federal political scene, Justin Trudeau created a whole new challenge for Stephen Harper's team. The new Liberal leader blew onto the stage like a breath of fresh air. He spoke in a way that broke with the conventions of old-style politicians. He definitely radiated charisma.

To counter the popularity of the young Liberal leader, the Conservative electoral machine switched into high gear. The Tories scrutinized his every move: they dug into his past and brought to light embarrassing or provocative statements he had made. In short, they sought to define him for the electorate before he had the chance to define himself. They began their offensive the day after he won the Liberal leadership.

The Conservatives posted an attack ad on YouTube showing Justin Trudeau in Ottawa in 2011 taking off his shirt in a fake striptease act, and they added burlesque music to the video clip. The message was clear: he was an intellectual lightweight, a man entirely out of his depth and unfit to become prime minister. But the Tory message bombed. The video images had been filmed during a fundraiser for the Canadian Liver Foundation, a charitable organization. The foundation swiftly came to Trudeau's defence, recalling he had generously offered to auction himself off for a sit-down meal with the highest bidder — which brought the charity $1,900. The whole event drew $128,000 in donations.

Another Conservative attack ad made fun of Trudeau's previous jobs as a whitewater rafting instructor and drama teacher (ignoring other subjects he taught), asking how he could possibly be expected to manage the economy.

The Conservatives were going with a strategy that had helped destroy the public images of Stéphane Dion and Michael Ignatieff, two poorly known personalities who had never succeeded in leaving their mark. Dion had been better at defending ideas than at cutting ribbons. Little known outside of Quebec, Dion was very direct — too direct at times. He didn't have Justin Trudeau's social graces. Worse, once the Harper camp's attack ads started pummelling and degrading Dion, the Liberal Party simply lacked the means to respond, or to explain his Green Shift policy. Don Boudria, Dion's former campaign manager, says Dion had been warned that his Green Shift "could not be sold to the public," but Dion went ahead with it anyway. He believed the strength of his arguments would win out over the attacks the Tories were directing at him.

Stéphane Dion's inner circle hoped the same kind of backlash would occur as with Jean Chrétien, whose partial facial paralysis was mocked in a Conservative ad. Chrétien benefited from a strong public reaction against the Tories' ad. "We thought Canadians would not go for this, we thought these American-style attack ads would fall flat here," says Boudria. "If they hadn't worked against Jean Chrétien, then surely they wouldn't work this time."

Michael Ignatieff had been no more successful in appealing to the Canadian public. The Liberal power brokers wanted people to believe Ignatieff was a globe-trotting academic cast in the mould of Pierre Elliott Trudeau. But Ignatieff had a glaring popularity deficit. It made no difference that people called him by his nickname "Iggy" or that he donned a hockey sweater while skating on the Rideau Canal; he was barely recognized in public. The party realized this was going to be an uphill battle.

"Who the heck knew who he was? He hadn't even lived here," recalls a disheartened former director of the Liberal Party.

Ignatieff was the first leader of the party who had never done an "apprenticeship," recalls Peter Donolo, as he had never served as a minister in a government portfolio. He quickly became an easy target for the attack ad campaign waged by the Harper machine. Canadians had the impression Ignatieff was standoffish. According to the former Liberal MP Eleni Bakopanos, Ignatieff's "intellectual arrogance" meant "he didn't know how to talk to people." He didn't seem credible to Liberal supporters and the general public, and eventually he met with the same fate as his predecessor.

The attack ads defined Dion and Ignatieff because "there was no history with the public," says Peter Donolo. In Ignatieff's case, the Conservative commercials "used clips of him saying things I'm sure he regretted saying," he adds. Ignatieff was the opposite of Jean Chrétien, who had served as minister in at least twenty different portfolios and was a very well-known public personality, and therefore had an image that couldn't be manipulated as easily.

Moreover, Justin Trudeau's predecessors had become leaders in a very unfavourable environment. In the aftermath of the sponsorship scandal, the Canadian public wanted nothing better than to punish the Liberals. Once the Conservative attack ads were unleashed, Dion and Ignatieff both made the fatal mistake of giving free rein to the Conservatives.

Pollsters all agreed that attack ads were effective when they contained a shred of truth and when the person under attack confirmed the message.

"So when the Conservatives attacked Stéphane Dion as not being up to the job, as soon as unfortunately Dion had a misstep, he validated the Conservative attack ads," says Nik Nanos, head of the public opinion firm Nanos Research. "The same with Michael Ignatieff. He never responded to the 'just visiting' [message] and as a result, it was perceived as being acceptance. "

But with Justin Trudeau, labels simply didn't stick. So far, the new Liberal leader had stood up to Conservative attacks. On the one hand, he showed he was not a soft touch: he promised to respond to each and every one, without descending into personal attacks. On the other hand, he was so good at filling party coffers with contributions that the Liberals could now afford to respond, which hadn't been the case with Stéphane Dion or Michael Ignatieff. Dion had weak support in the caucus and lacked a national organization. Neither he nor Ignatieff knew the people in their own party.

Trudeau's biggest advantage, meanwhile, was the way he had an intimate relationship with the public and the Liberal Party. This rapport went back to his early childhood. In terms of political opportunity it was solid gold. A famous photograph shows his father Pierre Elliott Trudeau on the steps of Rideau Hall, the governor general's residence, holding little Justin under his arm like a package. He had also appeared on the prime minister's Christmas card in 1972, squeezed in between his parents with a bootie on just one foot. By the age of eleven, he was attending Leonid Brezhnev's funeral. These images were etched in the collective memory of many Canadians.

People meeting him for the first time naturally called him Justin, and his entire leadership campaign had focused on his first name. "He was like everybody's brother or cousin," says Don Boudria. "And he made no bones about it. You have seen his campaign T-shirts? The name 'Trudeau' doesn't appear on them."

Justin Trudeau has always received greeting cards and letters from people across the country: messages from grandmothers, Canadians young and old, men and women. His friend Mathieu Walker realized this when he was helping Justin move from Old Montreal to a new address and came across a box full of correspondence. "Oh, I get these letters all the time," said Justin, who had never mentioned it to anyone before.

In fact, the Justin Trudeau brand went back a very long way, and was strengthened in the public mind by the funeral eulogy he gave for his father. There is no comparison to the painstaking work Stephen Harper had to put into creating his public image from scratch, because he was still relatively unknown when he made it to 24 Sussex Drive.

"People remember Justin Trudeau as a little kid," says pollster Nik Nanos, "an asset no other politician has. No one remembers Tom Mulcair as a kid or Stephen Harper as a kid. So Trudeau has that equity he can draw on."

Typically, most Canadians couldn't name the prime minister's wife or say how many children he had. But people always remember Justin as "the little kid at 24 Sussex" and even his birth on Christmas Day, says the pollster. This familiarity makes people feel empathy toward him. "So it makes it harder to attack that little kid."

This had become clear in Papineau as soon as Trudeau began meeting people on the street. Many voters were attached to the Trudeau family name. These were people like Bernard Toussaint, a constituent in Papineau and a long-standing Liberal supporter. He had a good impression of Justin Trudeau even though he didn't know much about him. Toussaint said he was ready "to give young Trudeau a chance," because the other leaders were old and his father had done a good job, although he was often in conflict with Quebec.

"If Justin Trudeau went by another name, then things would be different," he added. "It's natural. When a family has done something good, people are always going to remember that."

It was almost instinctive. To some extent, some Canadians feel protective about Pierre Elliott Trudeau's son, as if he were their own son, says Wayne Easter, a Liberal MP from Prince Edward Island. "They know him, they've seen him in diapers.... I've seen him since he was born on Christmas day. And if you're attacking Justin, it's like attacking your kid. You know, you all get mad at your kids, what did they do that for? But we love them just the same, you do not like to see them attacked."

Trudeau was comfortable with people. He noticed them and he effortlessly struck up conversations with them. Anecdotes about his father often broke the ice. "When he speaks to you, it is you he is speaking to. His eyes are not wandering off somewhere else," says Mary Deros, the municipal councillor he beat for the Liberal nomination in Papineau riding.

Justin Trudeau grew up under the spotlight. According to his friend Mathieu Walker, being in public was normal for him. That's the way he was raised. Walker remembers going to a hockey game with Justin and his father. Fans started following them just to get the former prime minister's autograph. He also remembers going to a restaurant with them and being astonished when the owner delivered a giant platter to their table, saying how honoured he was to welcome Pierre Elliott Trudeau and his son. Justin had a lifestyle where he was "the focus of attention," says Walker. "That's just part of his being, that's standard for him."

This intimacy with the public helped Trudeau fend off the Conservative attack ads in the months after he became Liberal leader. "Because he is known, it is hard to redefine him," says his adviser Pablo Rodríguez. "Right off the top, people already have an idea who he is."

A little over a week after the Conservative attack ad campaign started, Trudeau brought out his own TV ads. He was sitting at a teacher's desk, a chalkboard covered with mathematical calculations behind him. He picked up a remote and used it to turn off the Conservative ad showing him doing a striptease. Wearing a suit and white shirt open at the collar, he was showing himself as he was — a teacher — which, his advisers say, made him appear like regular folks.

In the ad, the Liberal leader denounced the undesirable effects of negative politics. He said Canadians could continue distrusting one another, or they could stand shoulder to shoulder and get to work. He said his two victories in Papineau riding and his election as Liberal leader testified to his ability to lead. Without alluding directly to Pierre Elliott Trudeau, he presented himself as a son, a father, and a leader promising to work hard to earn the trust of Canadians.

With this reply, the young leader was right on target. By playing the simplicity and spontaneity card, he positioned himself "as someone who was not a professional politician," says Luc Dupont, professor of communications at the University of Ottawa.

The image of the teacher was a familiar image, not a threatening one. Justin seemed close to people, more down to earth than his father, who had come across as an intellectual. This helped build Justin's brand, says Nanos.

The Tories had missed the mark. They targeted the Liberal leader with ads that were possibly too exaggerated to be credible. And perhaps the public was now immune to attack ads. Besides, after seven years of Conservative rule there was doubtless a greater appetite in the population for change — and for a rejuvenated Liberal Party under a new leader.

However, Justin Trudeau was no ordinary politician: he had an easy rapport with Canadians, and this was an advantage he turned to good effect and intended to continue putting to good use. Which sometimes enraged his opponents: "People always give him a second chance," sighed a strategist for the NDP.

———

Canada is not used to political dynasties, but the public's reaction to Justin Trudeau suggests that nostalgia for the Trudeau years was also at work. Pierre Elliott Trudeau revelled in controversy. He had given the finger in Salmon Arm, British Columbia, invoked the *War Measures Act*, introduced unpopular wage and price controls, and imposed the National Energy Program. Nonetheless, he had grown in public stature over the years. In fact, according to Professor Alex Marland at Memorial University of Newfoundland, he had become a mythical figure.

It was hard to call to mind Pierre Trudeau without recalling his great intellectual ability, which was acknowledged by opponents and admirers alike. People noticed his son's good looks, but Justin Trudeau is credited above all with emotional intelligence. He is a warm person, and he speaks with emotion. That is what enables him to reach out to people. While running for the Liberal leadership in 2012–13, his campaign slogan was "hope and hard work," which reminded people of Jack Layton's message of hope during the 2011 federal election campaign. Justin did nothing to discourage the comparison.

Pierre and Justin both stand as charismatic leaders. Historian John English, who knew Pierre well and also knows his son, said that "something extraordinary" happened whenever Pierre Elliott Trudeau entered a room, even if he didn't say much and seemed shy. Justin, meanwhile, is not as shy, but he is equally able to light up a room.

But in other respects the son is unlike the father: their professional careers could not have been more different, and they do not bear much resemblance to each other, whether temperamentally or physically.

By the time Pierre Elliott Trudeau entered the political arena he was already fully formed. He had written widely and had become well known through *Cité libre*, a magazine he co-founded. When Prime Minister Lester B. Pearson recruited Trudeau in 1965, he, along with Jean Marchand and Gérard Pelletier, were "the three wise men" who gave such momentum to the federal Liberals in Quebec.

By 2013, Justin was still in the learning phase. He had worked mostly with young people. He had been chair of the board of Katimavik, had taught in high school, given speeches in school settings and on behalf of civil society groups, and had been elected twice in Papineau. He was a man of the people, and his team tried to show him in the best light possible. But it was hard to picture him leading the country. His charisma drew people but didn't unleash the kind of frenzy associated with his father. In 1968, the Trudeaumania phenomenon "was practically sexual," recalls Richard Gwyn, a journalist who wrote a biography of Pierre Elliott Trudeau.

Marc Lalonde, who served as Pierre Trudeau's principal secretary and then minister of finance, has never understood the public craze for the former prime minister. But it was tangible, hard to control, and at times frankly "troubling." Trudeaumania seemed more like the excited mood of the crowd at a Beatles concert than the sort of response one would find in a political gathering.

Pierre Trudeau had been one of those rare politicians who brought style to politics. Here was an intellectual who could quote Plato just as easily as he could do somersault dives into his swimming pool. The public was captivated by this man with a rose in his lapel, zipping around Ottawa in a convertible, constantly surrounded by celebrities, and sometimes departing for long canoe trips in the wilderness.

Crowds surged around this man who "had suddenly become a rock star." The best example Marc Lalonde can give is an event organized at the last minute on the outdoor esplanade of Place Ville-Marie in Montreal, on a lovely spring day in 1968:

> Mr. Trudeau was supposed to turn up at lunchtime when suddenly five thousand people were pressing around him. All the employees working in Place Ville-Marie came down to have their lunch outdoors, just to hear Trudeau greet them with a few words. At the time, Pierre Trudeau was a phenomenon. For the young generation, he represented hope for change, for renewal. He stood for the rising aspirations within Canadian society. And this just snowballed. It was closely related to the fever for change raging among young people across Western countries at the time. But the older generations joined in as well. He was just as popular in golden age clubs.

There was something surrealistic about Trudeaumania. Women would throw themselves at this bachelor approaching fifty, with his sporty look and progressive ideas. Wherever he went, a bevy of young women in miniskirts and go-go boots seemed to be bobbing around him.

Marc Lalonde says that public enthusiasm for Justin is nothing compared to the euphoria of crowds over Pierre Trudeau, although this euphoria did not stand the test of time:

The first wave of Trudeaumania was more exuberant than what I would call "Trudeaumania 2.0." I believe even Mr. Trudeau himself was surprised by the phenomenon. It reflected a moment in time at the end of the sixties when a new generation got interested in politics and was deeply committed to social issues.

According to Marc Lalonde, the exciting and turbulent sixties included ultranationalism in Quebec, the events of May 1968 in France, the protest movement against the Vietnam War in the United States, the shootings at Kent State, and terrorism in Europe. But there was also a feeling of excitement surrounding the centennial year in Canada as well as Expo 67 in Montreal, which drew fifty million visitors.

In this whirlwind atmosphere, Trudeau was "the spark that lit a spontaneous explosion of enthusiasm, which had never really been planned in advance," says Lalonde. "Nobody was being bused in by force!" Even before Pierre Trudeau became Liberal leader, he adds, people found "his great intelligence and personal charisma" fascinating, since they enabled him "to challenge a whole series of concepts and policies."

As minister of justice in 1968, Pierre Elliott Trudeau struck an emotional chord in the country by modernizing the *Divorce Act* and softening provisions in the Criminal Code regarding homosexuality and abortion. And he did it with flair, famously saying, "There's no place for the state in the bedrooms of the nation."

Lalonde recalls:

> When he spoke of building a just society, or a more just one, he spoke from deep personal conviction, and he had already written extensively about the matter, so he wasn't just positioning himself on the short-term during an election campaign. There was something deeply authentic about Pierre which people identified with.

Like his father, Justin was known for progressive ideas, but few people knew his personal convictions on a wide range of issues. Marc Lalonde had only seen Justin on and off over the years, and had never followed his career closely, but he believes Justin has a natural flair for politics. Of Pierre Trudeau's three sons, Justin is the most extroverted, and seemed the likeliest to follow in his father's footsteps. Sacha, "a thinker and a more reserved man," has less interest in political life. And those who knew Michel all agree he had absolutely no inclination for politics.

Justin has the most obvious talent for politics, Lalonde says. "He likes communicating with people," unlike his father, who didn't willingly reach out to other people. "Let's just say that grassroots politics was not Pierre's strong point — far from it — whereas Justin is like a fish in water" when it comes to meeting new people.

"There is no doubt that Justin is better at retail politics than his father," says Lalonde, Pierre Trudeau's former adviser. "He also belongs to a whole new political generation that is tech-savvy. The whole nature of politics nowadays has changed, whether because of Twitter or other innovations. Getting Pierre Trudeau to make a telephone call was like pulling teeth, whereas for Justin I have the impression he spends his time tweeting as soon as he gets a free moment. I think he has a personality that matches our age."

Patrick Gossage, Pierre Trudeau's former press secretary, agrees with this assessment. The former prime minister was a man of ideas with an "aristocratic" bearing, who loved diving into his files but felt public appearances should come second. His advisers made a very revealing study about the way he used his time.

The study "showed he only spent like 5 percent of his time strictly on politics," such as public meetings and walkabouts in public, adds Gossage. "When I had to lead his father through a crowd, he was very, very charming, you would be totally taken with him, but he'd give [them] forty seconds and then he'd want to be moved on."

As a politician, Justin devotes practically all his time to public appearances. Patrick Gossage says he criss-crosses the country, meeting every possible group he could imagine, shaking hands, greeting people, kissing babies, hugging girls, "yakking people up endlessly."

In this respect, Justin Trudeau is like his mother, a very outgoing woman, and like his grandfather James Sinclair. The grandfather was an institution in Vancouver, and has a building named after him. In his own day he was considered to be "an incredible organizer" who worked day and night to help his constituents and to make sure his riding in the North Vancouver suburbs remained securely in Liberal hands.[1] Justin has confirmed that his grandfather Jimmy had "the charisma and outsized personality of a true old-school retail politician," and that when he himself ran as the Liberal candidate in Papineau, "I took as my model … Jimmy's door-to-door style of campaigning."[2]

Despite their differences, Justin shares one feature with his late father: he is not afraid to stand out, and even to shock people. Pierre would do the occasional clownish pirouette or pull on his necktie and pretend he was being strangled. Justin, meanwhile, has fun tumbling down the stairs.

"It's something my father taught me," Justin explained during a 2010 Télé-Québec interview, adding that a few weeks beforehand, while lugging some suitcases, he had simulated a fall on the stairway of the elegant Fairmount Royal York Hotel in Toronto.[3] The TV host interviewing him, Patrick Lagacé, was stunned to hear this, and asked his guest to provide a demonstration down the stairs of the TV studio. Trudeau performed the stunt to perfection, to the host's amazement. "You were really worried," joked the MP as he got up again. But Justin had mastered the art of falling when studying judo.

People had also seen Justin suddenly throw himself face-down on the ground and pretend to be dead. Some people said this was childish behaviour. "He was criticized strongly for this," John English says. "Guess where he learned this from? From his father. His father used to do that at parties all the time."

Pierre Elliott Trudeau liked to be unique when it came to the way he dressed, the books he read, and the art he liked.[4] People remembered his silk scarves, his leather sandals, and the iconic fringed buckskin jacket his son was shown wearing in an article in *Maclean's*. Justin has turned up in blue jeans and sandals at meetings with the Liberal caucus or with his inner circle of advisers. In December 2011, the MP for Papineau was called to order in the House of Commons for turning up without a necktie, which was against regulations. An adviser said this was nothing more than an oversight: he had taken off his tie between two events and had forgotten to put it back on again. Back in 1967, his father had been called to order for the same reason. He had been wearing a silk scarf at the time, and the head of the Official Opposition, the Conservative John Diefenbaker, had drawn attention to the "bizarre" clothing of Lester B. Pearson's minister of justice, calling on him "to abide by the rules of decorum of the House."

Like Pierre, Justin doesn't fit the traditional mould of the Liberal Party. The establishment felt his father was too far to the left and too unpredictable. Even so, Prime Minister Pearson offered him Mount Royal, a safe seat in Montreal. Justin, on the other hand, had to beat a charismatic Bloc Québécois incumbent in the Papineau riding, at a time when the federal Liberals were in free fall. As Justin has remarked, despite his father's accomplishments he had never been forced to rebuild the Liberal Party of Canada and revive the once-powerful Big Red Machine. As Pierre's son, Justin found that public expectations of his performance were sky-high.

———

In the Liberal family there has always been a vague feeling deep down that Justin Trudeau was destined one day to become prime minister. Justin maintained a public presence, introducing the Dalai Lama at an event in Toronto, for example. He never quite closed the door on a role in public life. But he took his time.

Following his election in 2008, the MP for Papineau didn't draw attention to himself at caucus meetings, but he didn't go unnoticed either. He said he was there to learn. Whenever he entered a meeting, he struck up brief conversations with people here and there. "He wasn't a dominating presence," a participant in these meetings recalls, "but people knew he was there. The others were merely faces in a crowd, whereas he created a buzz, and he knew it."

So when Trudeau made his entrance into the caucus meeting room five years later as the new Liberal leader, he was welcomed warmly. The MPs had seen the promising numbers in the opinion polls, like everybody else. The party was weaker than it had ever been, and they knew that the son of one of their historic leaders could be their "ticket to an electoral victory, so they clung to that," says a source close to the caucus.

Some party faithful expressed private doubts about the new leader's intellect, but they took solace in the hope he could lead them to the promised land. They had something to cheer about when they found out in December 2013 that he had raised $500,000 for the party in just ten days. And nobody could claim Justin Trudeau didn't work hard. In short, he was starting to make his mark. "I thought he was flaky and light," says a Liberal MP speaking on condition of anonymity. "What I saw was a guy who rolls up his sleeves and gets to work."

In any event, the Liberal Party had spent ten years crossing the desert, and had to make a show of unity. All in all, Trudeau's transition from MP to leader was a smooth one.

"Put your iPads away," he announced at the first caucus meeting on April 17, 2013, with the air of a schoolteacher. This meeting coincided with the thirty-first anniversary of the *Canadian Charter of Rights and Freedoms,* which Justin liked to hold up as one of his father's greatest achievements. The MPs were treated to a fine speech in which their new leader called for party unity. The Liberal Party of Canada was at a crossroads, he told them, and rebuilding it would demand a great deal of effort from everyone.

With the cameras rolling and rounds of applause erupting from time to time, Justin Trudeau told them the Charter was at the centre of what it means to be a Liberal. He couldn't help knocking the federal Conservatives for mistrusting the Charter: they had even refused to mark the thirtieth anniversary of its adoption in 2012.[5]

As for the NDP, Trudeau said they were "deeply conflicted about the Charter largely because of a political calculation they've made, pandering to a tremendous number of very vocal sovereigntist Quebecers who find it unacceptable that Quebec be excluded from the Canadian Constitution." He concluded by saying no document is more broadly supported "by all Canadians, including the vast majority of Quebecers."[6] It was easy to see that Trudeau wanted to position the Liberals as the party of the Charter.

He had long kept his distance from the Liberal Party and from politics in general, but now he would rarely miss a caucus meeting.[7] And when he was present, according to MP Wayne Easter, he wasn't off somewhere else: "He's not signing Christmas cards or doing other work when caucus is on. He's paying very close attention."

Easter was one of the first Liberal MPs to come out supporting Justin Trudeau; he felt it was time for a generational change in the leadership. He was surprised that Justin had decided to run given the burden it would place on his young family, and also because he seemed to enjoy the personal aspects of being MP for Papineau. "He likes helping people deal with disability problems related to the Canadian Pension Plan," remarks Easter.

During the weekly caucus meetings, Justin's "black humour" would sometimes take over when he should have kept quiet. He had to retract remarks a number of times at these meetings. "He's got a good sense of humour and will say some things that aren't politically correct, [things] that you can say amongst friends, but in the political environment …" Easter didn't complete the sentence, leaving the impression the new Liberal leader could be impulsive and say things that got him in hot water.

He "needs to talk less.… It's what got him in trouble a few times. He doesn't need to explain all the *A*s, *B*s, and *C*s, he needs to show his position in terms of principle," says the MP from Prince Edward Island, before jumping to his leader's defence.

"But this guy is a young guy, he's the leader, he's going to make mistakes, and that's fine: at least he's making mistakes in a very honest and open way" — without distorting the message the way the Conservatives do, he adds.

People say Justin Trudeau brings people together more than Paul Martin or Jean Chrétien ever did. MPs feel that "they have a right to speak their mind. And you're not going to be snapped at as a result," says Easter, carefully choosing his words. "I don't think 'conciliatory' is the right word, it's more a willingness to hear all points of view.… But when the decision is made, he's very firm in the decision. And the expectation is that we should all be on the same page."

This is nothing like Jean Chrétien's hands-on leadership style. Chrétien would say right off the bat: "I don't agree. End of discussion." "Chrétien had a lot more wide-ranging discussions than people really think, but when people went against him, there were consequences," Easter says, laughing out loud. "I felt them!" That's as much as the MP says about the respective management styles of the two Liberal leaders. He would not add anything else about Paul Martin's management style, because "his little minions" would react by "knifing him" in the back, he continues, with an air of disgust.

Easter made a wry face when he heard Justin Trudeau promising a different kind of politics. Others have tried and failed. In 1993, Prime Minister Kim Campbell shot up in the polls because of a similar promise, but then the Progressive Conservatives went into an electoral nosedive and ended up with just 2 seats. She sealed her own fate when she said an election campaign was no time to discuss complicated issues.

Easter wondered at first whether it's realistic to run a positive campaign in the face of attacks from all sides: Justin Trudeau doesn't want to go for the person, he wants to stay above the fray. "It's fine for him, but I'm of the opinion that you have to meet fire with fire. I've faced these guys in the trenches many times and I know how they attack you personally." Easter worried about Trudeau's approach because "you can't remain nice guys when you're dealing with a bully," he says, referring to Harper and the Conservatives.

Inside the caucus, Justin Trudeau was seen as a confident and determined leader with a good grip on the party. He regularly attended Liberal activities, since he knew that winning elections required the party to be strong and on a secure financial and organizational footing.

People who didn't know him discovered he was an ambitious politician who spoke continually about election strategies leading up to the fall 2015 vote. "He never loses sight of this goal," a Liberal source noted.

Trudeau relied on an inner circle of advisers he had brought in from different camps. These strategists were obsessed with image, and did everything possible "to push him in the public eye, to make him a popular, likeable, electable, and desirable leader,"[8] says Patrick Gossage.

Big decisions were often taken jointly by the leader and Gerald Butts, a man known for evidence-based arguments. Gathered around the table was the same group of friends who had backed Trudeau during the Liberal leadership campaign. Dan Gagnier was happy to be back in the loop and helping out a politician from the younger generation: he had been chief of staff for former Quebec premier Jean Charest and also for former Ontario premier David Peterson in the eighties. He was known as a superb strategist and was said to be able to give his boss the facts while keeping his cool during a political storm. He would run the national campaign alongside Katie Telford. But Justin's brother Alexandre was no longer around.

Even though Sophie was not as visible, and didn't really care for politics, she wasn't left out. "Sophie and Justin work as a team," says one source. "He counts on her."

Paul Martin and above all Jean Chrétien (whom Justin Trudeau knew well) offered advice to the new Liberal leader. With his enormous respect for the winner of three consecutive majority governments, "Monsieur Chrétien" was one person that Justin never kept waiting on the line.

CHAPTER 8

THE TRUDEAU EFFECT

Justin Trudeau's popularity exploded in 2013: the Liberal Party of Canada jumped ten points in the polls, surging ahead of the Conservatives and the NDP.[1] Trudeau's appeal was particularly evident outside the House of Commons. He met with crowds and looked to make breakthroughs in regions hostile to the Liberals. He seemed to make a point of appealing to voters in western Canada, a region that had long been his father's nightmare.

The Conservatives seemed to have been thrown off their stride. Trudeau had star quality the Tories simply couldn't match. The aggressive tone of the Conservative attack ads seeking to demolish Trudeau made it seem he was the head of the Official Opposition, and not Thomas Mulcair, whom they preferred to ignore.

Veteran politicians also had the impression they were seeing a new force emerging on the political scene. Louis Plamondon of the Bloc Québécois, the longest-serving MP in the House of Commons, noticed Trudeau's magnetism starting in 2009. He says he was astonished to see the impact the son of the former prime minister had during an event organized by the Forum of Young Canadians in Ottawa. When the time came to take photographs, the meeting hall emptied out. "A spontaneous wave" of nearly a hundred students followed the star into an adjoining meeting room. MPs from the other parties were left completely alone.

"We remained behind with maybe ten students," says Plamondon, an MP for more than thirty years.[2] "That's when I realized he was a rock star. He had a charismatic bond with young people, whether male or female." According to Plamondon, this had nothing to do with Pierre Trudeau. Justin "was elegant, he was good looking," but also people were following him simply "because he existed.... I had never seen anything like this throughout my entire political career."

Even in Quebec, Justin Trudeau was winning a following. He was the young leader, the dynamic young father, and he played the role well. After his father's funeral, his relationship with Sophie Grégoire enhanced his visibility. "His entry into the Quebec star system coincides more or less with his entry into politics," says political scientist Thierry Giasson. Justin and Sophie are "a celebrity couple"; they bank on their more or less well-established celebrity by "promoting their private life." In fact, they have made the cover of several mass-circulation magazines, highlighting their children and their life together.

Clearly, part of the Quebec population would never vote for a Trudeau (or, for that matter, for any federalist). But, in general, Justin did not come to politics with the same baggage as his father. "He doesn't carry the baggage on the Constitution as his father did, nor does he want to," said pollster Jean-Marc Léger, who saw that Justin would have to find other ways to make his mark, because if he ever renewed a constitutional initiative, "it would swallow him up whole."

In Léger's view, Justin takes after his father in terms of performance and resolve — for example, when he secretly prepared himself for the boxing match that many people assumed he would lose. The boxing match went over well in Quebec, where people perceived Justin as "a hard worker." He is "an unusual sort of politician, an offbeat one, who gets ahead with a good bit of publicity. Pierre Elliott Trudeau was like that. It's the same for his son, who functions the same way his father did."

The pollster adds that many people in Quebec wanted to see the son succeed. They liked his progressive ideas, and they saw him as the embodiment of novelty and freshness — key advantages in an election campaign in Quebec. Trudeau didn't have Jack Layton's image. But the fact he was different from Stephen Harper helped him, just as Obama came across as totally unlike George W. Bush.

The MP for Papineau had a flair for capturing people's imagination, but he wasn't yet very well known in Quebec. He was hard to figure out, which gave him a certain aura of mystery, according to Léger, who saw that Trudeau stood a very good chance of making gains in the province. But he hadn't yet "defined a vision, the way his father had with the Just Society back in the sixties," so nothing could be taken for granted. In short, "the packaging was attractive, but people still hadn't seen the product."

In August 2013, four months after he became Liberal leader, Trudeau's popularity in the province had lifted his support to 41 percent, way ahead of second-place Thomas Mulcair with 27 percent.[3]

For many Quebeckers, Trudeau was someone with an open mind who "avoided taking things to extremes." He occupied the centre or centre-left of the political spectrum, which came as a refreshing change after the dreary law-and-order years of Stephen Harper.

Clearly, the federal Liberal leader liked bold ideas. At the end of July he made waves in Kelowna, British Columbia, by proposing to legalize marijuana. The Liberal Party had already adopted several resolutions to this effect, and Trudeau had come out in favour of decriminalizing possession of the drug, but this time he proposed regulating marijuana along the same lines as alcohol or cigarettes.

Trudeau said this was the best way to keep marijuana away from children. The war against drugs was counterproductive and was only making criminals richer. He said regulating the drug was a rational choice, whereas just a few months before he had warned about the harmful effects of marijuana on the brain, particularly among young people.[4]

Trudeau unleashed a firestorm in the media when he admitted to smoking pot a few times since becoming MP for Papineau. He added in an interview with the *Huffington Post* that Michel had been facing a marijuana possession charge at the time of his death. The Liberal leader suggested this experience had got him thinking it was time to decriminalize cannabis.

This admission was surprising since earlier on, as an ambitious MP, he had voted for toughening the penalty for marijuana possession. Now he told reporters, the day before national Liberal caucus meetings got underway in Georgetown, Prince Edward Island, "I don't think there's any risk in being open and transparent."[5]

The Tories saw this as a golden opportunity to launch into Justin Trudeau, but their attacks fell flat: the Liberal leader suffered no political damage from his remarks. On the contrary, he forced the Harper government to soften its position in a debate the Conservatives would never have dared launch themselves. On this issue, the two leaders were at opposite ends of the spectrum. In fact, there were important differences in tone and generational perspective between Harper and Trudeau, and nothing threw these differences into sharper focus than Harper's half-joking remark on the issue: "Do I seem like I smoke marijuana?" With his suit and tie and deadly serious expression, it was easy to believe the prime minister when he said his asthma had always prevented him from smoking anything at all.

The Conservative attack ads on cannabis had no impact. Professor Luc Dupont says Justin Trudeau's lapses were easily forgiven. "A double standard was at work because of Trudeau's youth. Just imagine if Mr. Harper had come out with the same statement a day later." The fact is, the Liberal leader was a star with a powerful public image and no real competitors.

During the first few months of 2013, the New Democratic Party was still under observation in Quebec, even though Thomas Mulcair had been elected party leader in March 2012. For more than six months after Jack Layton's death, the party was without a permanent leader, so it was the weaker "B team" that ran the party while the leading candidates slugged it out for the leadership.

Mulcair was no slouch when it came to standing up on issues, but according to an NDP strategist the party had a hard time attacking Trudeau without seeming brutal because the Liberal leader had almost a "romantic" and even "fairy-tale" image. The New Democratic leader was much more comfortable attacking Stephen Harper. According to political scientist Louis Massicotte, the two men were cast in the same mould: both were aggressive politicians speaking the same language. The NDP strategy consisted in repositioning the party as a credible alternative to the Tories by increasing its base — for example, by removing the word "socialism" from the preamble to the party constitution.

Trudeau didn't have to worry too much about the Bloc Québécois either, for it was just treading water. So his main opponent was the Conservative Party. And after seven years of Tory rule, the public was starting to get tired of the Harper government. There was a growing desire for a refocusing of public policies.

———

The Tories started struggling once the Senate expense scandal broke out. Four senators were being investigated: the Conservatives Patrick Brazeau, Pamela Wallin, and Mike Duffy, and the Liberal Mac Harb. The expenses file was a sensitive one and needed to be handled with finesse and rigour. But Justin Trudeau customarily reacted with haste.

In early June, the Liberal leader told Global TV he would absolutely welcome Mac Harb back in the caucus once the Liberal senator had reimbursed all inappropriate expenses. He saw a big difference between Harb's situation, which he considered "an honest mistake or a misunderstanding of the rules," and the expenses claimed by Senators Duffy, Wallin, and Brazeau.[6] But the message didn't go over well. Trudeau seemed far too eager to welcome Harb back into the fold, whereas the issue was a serious one: the misuse of public funds.

The leader's position came as an embarrassment to more experienced Liberal MPs. Trudeau had just invoked transparency in unveiling an action plan to get parliamentarians to post their expenses online. But now the Liberals seemed to be hammering Tory senators while continuing to make excuses for one of their own: a double standard seemed to be in play. The day after his interview with Global TV, Trudeau was conspicuously absent from the House and unable to answer questions from the media. Dominic LeBlanc came to his rescue, clarifying for the benefit of journalists that the leader's office would not draw any conclusions about Harb's fate until the investigations were completed. On returning to the House, Trudeau explained Harb would be welcomed back to the caucus if he was found innocent of the charges, but he would be kicked out if found guilty.

Officials close to Trudeau admitted he had "stumbled a bit" over this sensitive file, and that his words "had not been super-clear." Robert Asselin said the leader had in no way sought to defend Harb at all costs. Mac Harb resigned from the Senate in August 2013, reimbursing the $231,650 a Senate committee deemed him to have claimed improperly. In February 2014 the RCMP slapped him with criminal charges.[7]

This series of events demonstrated that the Liberal leader didn't yet have a seasoned politician's ability to navigate through interviews and press briefings. According to Asselin, Justin Trudeau had long been used to media pressure, but this pressure got much more intense once a person became a political leader and had to reply on the spot to events unfolding in real time.

Trudeau was still learning the ropes. True, his exposure to politics went back to his childhood, but his lack of experience was catching up with him.

"People have a false impression of him, as if he ought to know everything simply because he is the son of his father and he grew up in a political environment," says a colleague.[8] This colleague adds that Justin knew about political history, the impact of a political career on one's personal life, and big-picture politics, but he didn't understand day-to-day politics very well. He was neither a seasoned politician nor a long-time Liberal, and he lacked a good grasp of the inner workings of the party. To get this far, he obviously had some political abilities. But to what extent?

Time would tell.

———

Once the dust from the Harb affair began to settle, the Liberal leader started preparing his election platform in virtual secrecy. Marc Garneau explained that in the interest of rebuilding the party, "Mr. Trudeau and his team" would be banking on the leader's personal popularity with the electorate. The movers and shakers in the party decided the leader's time would better be used in "rebuilding the party and getting the message out" than in spending a lot of time in the House, where as leader of the third party he lacked visibility. So Justin Trudeau was now giving the party a human face. He was the best, if not the only, person promoting the Liberal brand.

Election rules prohibited companies and labour unions from making donations directly to political parties. Parties naturally turned instead to individuals.[9] Money talks during election campaigns, so there was an all-out effort to raise as much cash as possible. Under the guidance of Montreal billionaire Stephen Bronfman, the Liberal team made good use of online political marketing. Justin was marketed front and centre, as usual. Contests rolled along, offering a one-on-one meal with the Liberal leader or maybe a party T-shirt. The attitude was anything goes, as long as donations poured into the party's coffers.

Justin Trudeau's primary objective was creating a network that could support the party for years, as it had back in his father's time. He wanted to attract people from across the spectrum: disappointed Conservatives and New Democrats, progressives, and members of ethnic communities who had voted for the Tories in the 2011 election. He drew inspiration from Laurier's model of a Liberal coalition that brought many people together under one big tent.

According to Pablo Rodríguez, Trudeau targeted two segments of the population in particular: the elderly, who liked him for nostalgic reasons, and young people, who liked him because he was young. Besides which, there was no mystery about the fact that women found him appealing.

The party handed the young leader a schedule jam-packed with public appearances across Canada, but he was up to the challenge. Justin Trudeau was a health enthusiast who ate an optimal diet and never touched junk food. To keep trim, he regularly did yoga and boxing. According to Robert Asselin, Justin displayed far more energy on the hustings than Paul Martin and Michael Ignatieff, who had both found the life of a political leader physically very demanding. Asselin knew because he had worked for all three leaders. "Justin never gets tired, even when he is keeping up a frantic pace. He can head out west, come back east on a red-eye flight, then attend an event the next day with a beautiful smile."

Trudeau was sent out to meet riding associations, he did media tours, he took part in public forums, and he greeted crowds whenever he got the chance. He continued saying he wanted to hold a "conversation" with Canadians on the issues that concerned them the most ... which enabled him to avoid making any firm policy commitments.

But on August 21, 2013, his meeting with Quebec Premier Pauline Marois was anything but cordial. Apparently, she had not been available to meet him the previous April due to a scheduling conflict. The Parti Québécois gave him a frosty reception. The PQ minister Jean-François Lisée called him "a young prince coming down from Ottawa to meet people he considers to be his subjects." Lisée was particularly galled by the fact that Trudeau was leader of a small Opposition party but nevertheless apparently wanted to meet the leaders of Quebec's three main political parties at the same time, an arrangement Marois found unacceptable. This turned out not to be true and Lisée apologized. Trudeau had also irritated several people in April when he highlighted the anniversary of the *Canadian Charter of Rights and Freedoms* by saying Quebec had "chosen" not to sign on to the Constitution because Quebec had a sovereignist premier at the time — René Lévesque.[10]

Returning onto the Quebec political scene four months later, the "young prince" ripped into the projected Quebec Charter of Values proposed by Premier Pauline Marois, which had not yet been publicly unveiled but which Marois had described in broad brushstrokes. With this charter, Quebec would proclaim the religious neutrality of the state, and would prohibit government employees from wearing conspicuous religious symbols such as large crosses, hijabs, or kippahs.

The issue of the Quebec charter was a minefield for any federal politician hoping to make gains in Quebec without alienating the rest of Canada. But Trudeau wanted to be seen as a champion of the *Canadian Charter of Rights and Freedoms,* and he continued to present the Quebec Charter of Values as a threat to individual rights. This position catapulted him ahead of both Thomas Mulcair, who was courting the nationalist vote in Quebec, and Stephen Harper, who was keeping his distance.

During a press briefing, Trudeau said the Quebec charter stoked the fear of others. In his view, it tarnished the reputation of the Quebec government and conveyed a message of intolerance. "Prohibiting someone from wearing a hijab or a kippah is not compatible with Quebec and Canadian values," he said. He added Quebeckers were more tolerant than the project being floated by Marois, which would violate individual rights enshrined in the *Canadian Charter of Rights and Freedoms.*

"I know the people of Quebec are not afraid of others, they are proud and they are aware of the strength of their language and culture. [Marois] is somewhat mistaken: in wanting to be more defensive than necessary, she is underestimating us," he later told journalists.[11]

Trudeau added Quebeckers shouldn't have to choose between their job and their religion. He said the Quebec Charter of Values was divisive because it created two categories of citizens, those with religious beliefs and those without.

The debate on secularizing the state was tearing Quebeckers apart. Trudeau took the unusual step for a federal leader of writing a newspaper opinion piece about a provincial matter.

"There is no question that our government and our institutions must be neutral and secular," he wrote. "Church and state must be separate. But by what logic should we restrict the freedom of some Quebeckers to express their religious beliefs? Simply because they are not shared by the majority? [The Parti Québécois government] seeks to divide the people of Quebec over a problem that does not exist."[12]

Stephen Harper's Quebec lieutenant, Denis Lebel, was visibly uncomfortable with the situation and would have preferred to let the dust settle. He would only say the federal government would defend the rights of Quebeckers before the courts if the proposed charter put their fundamental rights at risk. He watered down his words a few days later, saying nothing in the charter upset him.[13] Once Thomas Mulcair read a draft of the Quebec charter, he said it was "intolerable" that a woman working in a daycare centre would lose her job because she wore a headscarf.

By taking this position, Justin Trudeau scored points in English Canada. But he sounded a little extreme when he compared opposition to the Quebec Charter of Values to the American civil rights movement in the sixties. Pauline Marois accused him of throwing fuel on the fire since Quebec was very respectful of minorities. He then explained there was no "direct link" between the draft charter and the segregation of black people in the United States, although the battles waged for openness, respect, and tolerance were similar.

Justin Trudeau's strength was also his weakness. He had catapulted ahead in opinion polls because of his personality, his refreshing manner of speaking, and his attractive appearance. But in 2013, the Liberal Party of Canada came down to just Trudeau himself. He had no team, no track record. Once the next election campaign got underway, he would have to be able to say he had a plan and a solid team, the recipe Jean Chrétien had used to such advantage in 1993.

The Liberal leader set out to recruit star candidates. According to a Liberal MP, speaking on condition of anonymity, Justin "is confident about his abilities, but he is always ready to surround himself with people smarter than himself."[14] The story goes that he told his MPs he ranked eight on a scale of ten, and "eights want to attract tens." "But I would say he's more like a seven and a half," the MP added somewhat maliciously.

On September 17, to everyone's complete surprise, the leader came up to the microphone in Ottawa to announce he had just recruited Chrystia Freeland, the former managing editor of the *Financial Times* of London, and also of Thomson Reuters in New York. She had just won the Liberal nomination in Bob Rae's old riding of Toronto Centre. Along with MP Scott Brison, she was tasked with developing the Liberal position on protecting the middle class in the lead-up to the 2015 election. Justin Trudeau had sought out and consulted Freeland over her recent book *Plutocrats: The Rise of the New Global Super Rich and the Fall of Everyone Else*, in which she tracked the decline of the middle class and the rising incomes of the wealthiest members of the business community. Trudeau found the book a useful reference.

The following day, Trudeau came out with a new coup: he appeared in the lobby of the House of Commons accompanied by retired Lieutenant-General Andrew Leslie, who had just joined the Liberal team. Leslie would join Marc Garneau in leading an advisory committee on international affairs whose conclusions on defence and foreign policy would help develop the Liberal Party's 2015 election platform.

The former commander of Canadian Forces in Afghanistan had served as chief of transformation for the armed forces, bringing out an ambitious 2011 plan to scale back regular and reserve forces and cut expenses at National Defence headquarters, but he fell out with the Harper government. He tested the waters with the Liberals because he was concerned about the fate of Canadian veterans and also about the "extreme" foreign policy positions of the Harper government. According to Leslie, Canada's international standing had taken a hit under Harper.

But the key thing that persuaded Leslie to go into federal politics was Justin Trudeau's stance on the Quebec Charter of Values promoted by the Marois government. Appalled by the way other national leaders remained silent on the issue, he was impressed by the Liberal leader's "reasoning" and "inclusive" vision of Canada. Leslie then held two months of discussions with the Liberal Party, after which he offered his support to the leader, saying he was ready to play whatever role the party found for him. Leslie came from a prominent Liberal family, and it was later learned he had been courted by other political parties, including the Conservatives, and he had shopped around for maximum advantage. He was obviously happy about his decision: "I'm not going to tell you who I'm comparing Justin to, but Justin is inclusive, not divisive. Justin likes people, he doesn't attack them. Justin listens, he doesn't order. He likes people and doesn't isolate himself from them."[15]

The new candidate, a self-styled "warrior," was about to find out just how tough politics can be. In early 2014, he was roundly criticized for having claimed more than $72,000 in moving expenses and real estate fees for moving from one Ottawa location to another Ottawa location.[16] "Some of our missions in Afghanistan, those are very interesting," he said by way of conclusion, "but Ottawa is dangerous!"

———

The fall of 2014 was a busy time for the Liberal leader, who used every opportunity to schedule more public appearances and make himself better known. In Washington, he stated his vision of the Keystone XL pipeline project, an issue that was making life difficult for Stephen Harper. The prime minister was ratcheting up the pressure to get the project approved, but the Obama government was holding out against it.

Justin Trudeau was in favour of Keystone XL, but he also wanted to show he was not as rigid as the prime minister. He told the Center for American Progress the project was not only good for Canada, it was good for the United States, because it would result in reduced American imports of oil from Venezuela. Alberta's oil was produced by a North American neighbour and was more secure, Trudeau said. When he was flatly contradicted by former U.S. vice-president Al Gore, who called the project ridiculous, Trudeau stuck to his guns. He wanted Albertans to know he was ready to defend their interests.

A few days later, the Liberal leader went to Calgary, Stephen Harper's backyard, just a day before the national Conservative convention got underway there. In Calgary, a city that hadn't elected a single Liberal

MP since 1968, he called on the citizens to keep an open mind about his party and about the responsible use of natural resources. On October 30, 2013, in an address before the Calgary Petroleum Club, he made a statement on the thorny issue of Keystone XL, giving the pipeline project his endorsement as long as it was environmentally safe. Trudeau wanted to appeal to "Red Tories" by positioning the Liberals as a business-friendly party, in contrast to the NDP, which opposed Keystone.

At the outset, Trudeau felt the need to explain he was not in Calgary to show he wasn't like his father, or to prove he had as much guts as his father. He was in Calgary, he said, because he wanted to deliver an important message. Canadians wanted a leader different from the one they currently had, someone who was a straight shooter, knew how to listen, and acted in their interests. Someone who would build rather than sow discord and "exploit divisions." The Liberal leader said this negativity was destructive, it led to "distrust and suspicion," it instilled fear, and it pitted Canadians against each another.

The Keystone XL project was in the national interest, Trudeau said, since it would create jobs, boost growth, and make the energy supply more flexible in North America. And one of the main responsibilities of the government of Canada was to find outlets for the country's natural resources, as long as it was done in an environmentally friendly way.

Trudeau was working on his game plan. He wanted to show he would need western Canada to build a truly national party. But in the shorter term he faced four by-elections. The Montreal riding of Bourassa had recently been vacated by Denis Coderre, who had been elected mayor of Montreal. Then there was Bob Rae's old riding of Toronto Centre. And then there were two other ridings, in Manitoba, where the Liberals were out of favour.

When the party's General Council convened in Drummondville, Quebec, in November 2013, Trudeau told the party faithful that Canadians were keeping an eye on the Liberals: to break through in Quebec they needed to earn the trust of Quebeckers. Emmanuel Dubourg, the provincial Liberal member for Viau riding, would be the federal Liberal candidate in Bourassa. His candidacy was already stirring controversy, however, since he had taken $100,000 in severance pay on leaving the Quebec National Assembly. This was all the more surprising since he was leaving his provincial riding in order to take a run at a federal riding.

Trudeau called on Liberal troops to remain visible and to go door to door. He said NDP leader Thomas Muclair would stop at nothing to win in Bourassa — but the Orange Wave of 2011 was a thing of the past. The Liberal leader predicted that without Jack Layton at the helm, support for the New Democratic Party would collapse. "They voted for Jack in 2011, but he's not the kind of leader they have now," he joked.

This speech was hardly electrifying, but it was well received at the General Council, where nobody could remember the last time federal Liberal supporters in Quebec had so much to be happy about. Two hundred and fifty people had been expected in Drummondville, but five hundred turned out. "It feels like 1993," said a jubilant Martin Cauchon, recalling the Liberal wave that had brought Jean Chrétien to power. Meanwhile, party organizers began to busy themselves with drawing up lists of potential candidates for the 2015 election.

The General Council provided a good setting to bring party supporters together, but no particularly important resolutions were passed. According to Pablo Rodríguez, Trudeau had ideas to propose, but first he wanted to sound out the party faithful in Drummondville as well as other key players, instead of making top-down policy decisions. The same exercise would be repeated at every meeting of the provincial wings of the federal Liberals in the lead-up to the national convention slated for February 2014. That's where the rank and file would vote on the resolutions that would make up the core of the party's election platform.

And people would simply have to wait for the national convention to hear about Justin Trudeau's vision for the economy. Meanwhile, the leader stumbled over another of his off-the-cuff remarks. In November 2013, he got into hot water by expressing his admiration for China during a Liberal Party fundraiser in Toronto. This was a "Ladies' Night" event, with tickets going for $250. The come-on was that women would "really" discover their future prime minister. The invitation with its Andy Warhol–style visuals called on participants to put questions to Trudeau — for example, about his strong points or his favourite heroes. So one participant asked him which country he admired the most besides Canada. The leader paused a second and then gave his answer: China.

"There is a level of admiration I actually have for China because their basic dictatorship is allowing them to actually turn their economy around on a dime and say we need to go green, we need to start, you know, investing in solar."

Foreseeing that his words could be misconstrued, he quickly added that what he admired most of all was the Canadian northern territories' consensual approach to government.

Was China such an exemplary country? The following day, reactions ranged from dismay to consternation. The Asian community of Toronto asked Trudeau to apologize for his insulting words. The Federation for a Democratic China said his use of the term "basic dictatorship" was foolish. He was not well informed, said a spokesman for the organization. Another person said he had fled China after being imprisoned and tortured there for having supported democracy. The Chinese dictatorship should be condemned, not admired, retorted Canadian activists originally from China, Korea, Taiwan, and Tibet, during a press conference. "Every one of us is the victim of the Chinese dictatorship," said Chinese democracy activist Sheng Xue.[17]

The remarks were brought to Thomas Mulcair's attention as he campaigned in Toronto Centre with the NDP candidate, Linda McQuaig. "I don't understand how someone can say that their favourite government was a dictatorship, frankly," Mulcair said. "I'm not a big fan of dictatorships," he added, taking another dig at Trudeau, "I rather prefer democracies." NDP supporters around Mulcair burst out laughing.

The Liberal leader went into damage-control mode, tweeting Canada was the best country in the world, but it faced powerful economic rivals that could quickly adjust to new challenges. It was ridiculous to imagine he would ever abandon rights and freedoms that were deeply rooted in Canada for another form of government. He sent his former rival Marc Garneau to the front lines, to explain that Trudeau was actually referring to the Chinese economic miracle. Garneau said any misguided comments by Trudeau would have no negative impact, since the leader had decided to be so accessible and open about the incident, adding that "people recognize his humility."

Nonetheless, the Ladies' Night event continued to irritate many people. Social media commentators blasted the tone of the invitations as "degrading" and "stupid." The event, Trudeau countered, had been organized as a bit of fun by female marketing executives who wanted to encourage women to go into politics. As for his remarks on China, he had only wanted to get a reaction out of people.

He clearly got a reaction out of Prime Minister Stephen Harper, who made good mileage out of the incident. "The next election isn't about electing the next winner of *Canadian Idol*," he said with a touch of irony, "it is about choosing someone who can boost economic growth."

MP Wayne Easter admitted the Ladies' Night fundraiser reinforced Justin Trudeau's image as "a lightweight." But the purpose of the evening — getting women interested in running for office — was a valid one, so the leader didn't owe excuses to anyone. Alexandra Mendès, outgoing president of the Liberal Party, also played down the incident.

"Everyone has tried sticking the 'ladies' boy' label on him," she said. "So why not take advantage of that for the benefit of the party?" After all, the event had brought in $250,000 to encourage women to run for the party.

The fact remains that the fundraiser was ill conceived. Whereas Trudeau had wanted to charm female voters, he ended up annoying many women. "Sure, it's good to keep a sense of humour, but it's also important to be cautious," said Eleni Bakopanos: Justin Trudeau was not just an MP, he hoped to become prime minister.

There would be no repeat of Ladies' Night any time soon.

———

A crucial date on the Liberal Party calendar was November 25, 2013, when four by-elections would be held.

On the morning of election day Trudeau walked the streets of Toronto Centre. Then he set off to spend the evening in the Montreal riding of Bourassa. His presence attracted attention in the two cities, where he was hounded by raucous New Democrat supporters.

The by-election results, which showed the Liberal Party was holding its own, came as no major surprise. The results confirmed the status quo in the House of Commons. The two ridings in Manitoba stayed Conservative, while the other two stayed Liberal, with Chrystia Freeland winning Bob Rae's old riding of Toronto Centre and Emmanuel Dubourg winning in Bourassa.

"People want a different kind of politics," a jubilant Freeland said in a hoarse voice, accompanied on the stage by her children. Later, in a press conference in her Toronto riding, she added that people wanted "a change in tone" in politics and "answers to the middle-class squeeze."

The Conservatives, who held on to the two Manitoba ridings in play, won easily in Provencher but just scraped through in their traditional stronghold of Brandon-Souris. The Tories had definitely lost support there because of the Senate expenses scandal, which allegedly involved a secret deal between Nigel Wright, Stephen Harper's former chief of staff, and Senator Mike Duffy, to repay the senator's disallowed housing expenses. The Liberal tally in Brandon-Souris shot up from 5.3 percent in the 2011 election to 42.7 percent in 2013, less than four hundred votes behind the Conservatives. Even though these Manitoba ridings had seemed promising for the New Democrats, voters there now preferred the Liberals to the NDP.

Justin Trudeau's advisers had even asked him not to campaign in Brandon-Souris, in case he was blamed for an eventual defeat. But Trudeau stuck to his guns, visiting the riding three times during the campaign. "I like winning," the politician told a Manitoba newspaper.

The by-election results came as a sharp disappointment for Thomas Mulcair. He had ferociously attacked his adversaries, and had practically waged the battle single-handed to shed light on the role the Prime Minister's Office had played in the Duffy and Wallin affairs. He visited Bourassa riding six times during the campaign, hoping to maintain the momentum Jack Layton had previously created in Quebec. But the NDP candidate there, Stéphane Moraille, a lawyer and singer in the band Bran Van 3000, went down to defeat.

Mulcair had also turned out repeatedly in Toronto in support of his star candidate Linda McQuaig, a former *Toronto Star* columnist, who had written a book on the decline of the middle class that bore comparison to Chrystia Freeland's book. McQuaig at least got a respectable result — 36 percent of the vote, compared to Freeland's 49 percent.

Justin Trudeau was in a fighting mood when he came to the stage in the riding of Bourassa, accompanied by his newly elected MP Emmanuel Dubourg. He conjured up the memory of the late NDP leader, adding the NDP is "no longer the hopeful, optimistic party of Jack Layton. It is the negative, divisive party of Thomas Mulcair."

He even borrowed a phrase Layton had addressed to Canadians from his deathbed: "The Liberal Party tonight … proved that *hope is stronger than fear.*" This absolutely enraged New Democrats, some of whom joined Thomas Mulcair is saying how disgusted they were by Trudeau's remarks, which spoke volumes about his character and lack of judgment.

Trudeau refused to back down, saying he been inspired by Jack Layton's positive approach to politics. Brad Lavigne, the NDP campaign director in 2011, wrote a withering opinion piece in the *Globe and Mail*, accusing Trudeau of co-opting "a great leader's words and [turning] them into meaningless jargon."[18]

The tone was being set for the fierce battle the Liberals and New Democrats would wage in the upcoming general election, slated for October 19, 2015.

The hotly contested by-elections of November 2013 showed Stephen Harper, Thomas Mulcair, and Justin Trudeau going all out to win. Each of the three men had a lot to lose: Harper wanted to keep his government in power; Mulcair wanted to look like the leader of a government-in-waiting; and Trudeau had yet to establish his credibility. The campaigns had been bitter. In the key Toronto Centre riding competition was particularly intense. The Liberals distributed pamphlets accusing Mulcair of being "too angry" and attacking "his radical plans for Toronto Centre." Evidently, in the heat of the moment, the Liberals were willing to toss aside "positive politics."

The take-home message for the Liberals: the by-election results confirmed the potential for increased support at the polls. Compared to their humiliating defeat in 2011, the by-elections of 2013 looked like a spectacular comeback. According to pollster Darrell Bricker at the Ipsos-Global opinion research firm, the Liberal leader had taken over a party in its death throes, but now, "on his own, he was bringing it back to life."

In 2013, Justin Trudeau carried his party on his shoulders. The Liberals played the only card they had left, a card they hadn't really been able to play since the time of Pierre Elliott Trudeau: personal charisma. The next general election slated for October 2015 was still two years off. Trudeau's organizers realized it would be hard to keep the momentum going.

Chapter 9

Another Side of Justin

Trudeau had shown he knew how to deal with setbacks. In 2014, behind the sunny image of the smiling and affable young man, people discovered he could also be intransigent and even merciless. That year, he made a surprising political decision on the Senate, he imposed the party line on abortion, and he suspended two MPs for sexual misconduct without giving them a hearing.

It is in facing obstacles that his competitive spirit comes out in the open. According to his adviser Robert Asselin, Justin Trudeau had faced hardships early on: his parents' divorce, his mother's mental illness, and his brother's accidental death. "He is very strong in the face of adversity, and I would even say he feeds on it."

Trudeau didn't feel intimidated by taking over a party in distress and having to square off against tough opponents, according to Asselin. On the contrary, these challenges motivated him. "He's a real Trudeau in that sense, a go-getter, a rebel."

This is how Trudeau acted when he realized he was having trouble with the issue of Senate reform: he made a brutal decision that came down like a ton of bricks. In one fell swoop he expelled the thirty-two Liberal senators from the Liberal caucus, three of whom had been named by his father, nineteen by Jean Chrétien, and ten by Paul Martin. The senators learned about his decision only half an hour before he announced it on

January 29, 2014, to a stunned group of journalists in the lobby of the House of Commons.

Trudeau admitted his move had provoked a harsh reaction, but he had taken the decision because the Senate was "broken" and needed to be fixed. By kicking out thirty-two senators he wanted to put an end to patronage and political favouritism in the Red Chamber, which had turned into a haven for friends of the party in power, whether Conservative or Liberal.[1] If the goal was to score points, he couldn't have chosen a better moment. As a matter of fact, Mike Duffy's ongoing legal saga had made it abundantly clear that Conservative senators, the Conservative Party, and the Prime Minister's Office all worked hand in hand.

From now onward, Justin Trudeau declared, Liberal senators would be accountable neither to the Liberal Party nor to himself as leader. They could act and speak freely on draft legislation, and come to their own decisions without being "subject to party discipline or to my own directives," he said in an interview.[2]

Trudeau said it was obvious that by imposing party discipline on the Senate, the Harper government had increased the power of the prime minister, who could at any time dictate exactly how senators would vote. This had the effect of transforming the Upper Chamber into a party organ.

"What we have seen in the Wright-Duffy case," Trudeau went on, "is a prime minister and his office intervening to an enormous extent in the operations of the Senate, to the point where the Senate has been turned into an extension of the Conservative parliamentary wing."

As a way of avoiding this situation in the future, he announced that Liberal senators would henceforth be excluded from the caucus, where issues, draft legislation, electoral strategies, and other initiatives were discussed. Moreover, senators would no longer be allowed to take part in fundraising activities on behalf of the Liberal Party of Canada, and the budget previously allocated to that task would simply be eliminated.

"The only members of the Liberal caucus will be MPs," Trudeau decided. "There will no longer be Liberal senators."

In a letter to Speaker of the Senate Noël Kinsella, Trudeau wrote categorically that the senators he had just booted out of the caucus would no longer be allowed to sit in the Upper Chamber as Liberals and would now be known as "independent senators."

Trudeau said the Senate needed to reconnect with its essential mission as an independent chamber of sober second thought on public policy for the benefit of Canadians, rather than for the benefit of a political party. If he formed the next government, he committed to reforming the way senators were appointed. The appointment process would have to be open, transparent, and non-partisan. An advisory committee would make recommendations to the prime minister on future appointments. Along the same lines, Trudeau called on Prime Minister Harper to free Conservative senators from the stranglehold of party discipline.

Trudeau had developed this commando operation in deepest secrecy. Not a single Liberal MP got wind of it in advance. "We knew nothing about it," said Marc Garneau, who was all for the decision. "We found out the morning of the announcement, which was important to ensure that things ran smoothly and also that there were no leaks."[3]

The announcement came as a devastating blow for Liberal senators. A good number of them got together, insisting they were still Liberals at heart, even though they were now independent. Henceforth they would sit as "the Senate Liberal caucus." Few senators criticized the decision publicly, but people wondered: was this the same Justin Trudeau who had boasted he could bring people together?

Liberals in the Senate had a hard time understanding what had motivated this unilateral decision. Some said it could have been the result of "a strategic panic attack inside Mr. Trudeau's office," since the auditor general was about to issue a report on senators' expenses. Others wanted to believe in the Liberal leader's good intentions, and spoke of a "noble ideal."

"I wasn't offended by the decision because it was in line with my own thinking," said Paul Massicotte, an Independent Liberal senator from Quebec.[4] But some of his colleagues in the Upper Chamber felt "insulted" and even abandoned. "I was kicked out," said another senator, who didn't appreciate the Liberal leader's diktat.

This stunning announcement got Justin Trudeau out of a bind. He had been having a hard time making a difference on the Senate expenses scandal, which was eroding the relevance of the institution. Thomas Mulcair was travelling across Canada, calling for the outright abolition of the Senate — a chamber some people derisively called "the Hall of Shame." Stephen Harper was promising to limit the terms of senators to nine years. Harper also defended the idea, which already had been put into effect in some provinces, of holding voluntary consultative senatorial elections. The winners of these elections would be eligible for an appointment to the Senate. The Harper government believed it could proceed with Senate reform without the consent of the provinces, and asked the Supreme Court of Canada for a reference on limited terms for senators and also on the eventual abolition of the Senate.[5]

Up until now, the Liberal leader didn't seem to have a definite position on the Senate, except to say he would establish a rigorous selection process, which sounded more or less like maintaining the status quo. But Trudeau didn't like to waffle: he wanted to take a strong position. He wanted to show it was possible to undertake significant reform of the Senate without opening up an endless round of constitutional negotiations, which he said Canadians had no stomach for. "They don't want constitutional negotiations till kingdom come, the way Mr. Mulcair is proposing," he said.

"The whole point of the Senate," Trudeau added, "is to counterbalance the extraordinary powers of the prime minister and his office, especially in the context of a majority government." He said it was the party structure in the Senate that was to blame for this state of affairs, so the structure needed to be addressed.

Trudeau's decision was a calculated risk, since he had never named senators and the opportunity would arise only if he became prime minister — which couldn't happen until a year later at the earliest, and might never happen. He didn't owe senators anything, but he was cutting off faithful organizers, experienced people with great connections who knew the Liberal Party like the back of their hand. Among these senators were Serge Joyal, a constitutional expert who supported the leader's reform agenda for the Senate; retired General Roméo Dallaire; and David Smith, an election organizer with fifty years of behind-the-scenes experience with the Liberal Party of Canada. Moreover, Quebec senators had played a key role in fundraising and organization in a province where Liberal MPs were few and far between.

The way Justin Trudeau wrenched the Senate away from the party caucus showed his willpower and creativity, and was generally well received by the public as a result. But a former executive of the party said the handling of the split left a lot to be desired: it showed "disrespect" toward senators who were part of the Liberal family. According to Sheila Gervais, former national director of the Liberal Party of Canada, these senators had helped keep the Liberals from losing momentum between 1984 and 1993, when the party was the Official Opposition in the House.

Trudeau acknowledged he had lost friends in the Senate and good organizers "who won't be active anymore…. But we're getting in so many more that it's not something I think about too much," he told the *Toronto Star*. He said this was the price to pay to show how determined he was to repair the Senate.[6]

He admitted he had hesitated because he knew experienced Liberal senators were bound to be upset. The move had to be "clean, strong and simple," the leader said. "What got me over the hump was thinking about five years from now, 10 years from now, [when we have] a functioning, non-partisan Senate that actually does a great job of evaluating proposed legislation solely on its merits, not on the political angles of polls or election results or seats that can be won." He said this was his motivation, rather than any apprehension about the soon-to-be-released report from the auditor general.

Many experts responded well to the move. According to constitutional expert Benoit Pelletier at the University of Ottawa, Trudeau's coup "sent the right signal…. The party line has no place in the Senate because the Senate is supposed to be independent of the House of Commons." Moreover, the Senate has no power to block money bills. In Pelletier's view, the Upper Chamber should operate a little like a judge who weighs arguments presented in his court, instead of blindly approving the demands of the parties involved.

Actually, prime ministers had always used the Senate as a partisan chamber to reward their friends and election organizers. Stephen Harper, for example, had named several defeated Conservative candidates to the Senate. The selection process was the prime minister's direct prerogative, so patronage appointments had been a long-standing tradition.

Liberals had also taken advantage of patronage appointments. One has only to think of the way Pierre Trudeau appointed many prominent Liberals to the Senate and to the top positions in Crown corporations just before retiring from politics. These appointments were confirmed by his successor John Turner before the general election was called in 1984.

Brian Mulroney scored a knockout blow against John Turner during the televised election debates that year, ridiculing the way he had endorsed the patronage appointments.[7]

With his Senate bombshell, Justin Trudeau had made a bold move, which was all to his advantage, at least in the short term, and which set him apart from the New Democrats and the Conservatives. He presented himself as the candidate promoting openness and transparency, and succeeded in repositioning himself on the Senate file a year and a half before the election slated for late 2015, while distancing himself from a discredited institution.

His advisers had told him the general public was uneasy about the Senate, and it was time for action. The Liberal leader would later say this had been a carefully considered decision, taken after consultations with constitutional experts and a rigorous examination of proposals for Senate reform submitted by several Liberal senators. According to Senator Paul Massicotte, Trudeau had been influenced to a degree by Massicotte's own suggestion that senators, as unelected officials, should remove themselves from strategy meetings held with MPs, which have as their sole objective winning the next election. Massicotte said by attending such meetings, his peers in the Upper Chamber were "brainwashed" to promote the interests of the party, even if the practice ran against the interests of the general public.

Still, when all was said and done, no one knew whether Justin Trudeau's bold move could be sustained in the longer term, since future Liberal leaders would be under no obligation to follow his lead on the Senate.

———

New leadership meant new rules. Trudeau insisted that all MPs had to earn the privilege of running under the Liberal banner, even in ridings they had represented for the longest time. Too bad for candidates who were seeking re-election for the second or third time — now they too would have to line up and win the riding nomination like novices. Liberal Party of Canada rules dictated that the person selling the most membership cards in a given riding would officially be recognized as that riding's Liberal candidate.

The principle of an open nomination process was consistent with the image of openness and transparency Trudeau sought to uphold. But it was a double-edged sword. Jean Chrétien and other Liberal leaders before him had always maintained some flexibility in appointing candidates as they saw fit. The leader had to build a team, and it was his prerogative to place star candidates in key ridings.

Many insiders felt Trudeau had moved too hastily on the Senate. In the event he won the upcoming general election, he would need to put together a solid Cabinet that included people from a wide variety of backgrounds: academics, experts, business leaders. But experienced professionals at the top of their game might not want to give up job security for the kind of limbo awaiting them if they didn't win the party nomination. According to a master election campaign organizer, "a party needs to be able to nominate candidates right off the bat ... without leaving anything to chance."

Increasing support for the party was leading to renewed enthusiasm. Some ridings in Quebec, Ontario, and elsewhere had five and six candidates seeking the Liberal nomination. Naturally, this led to tensions.

There was an outburst of discontent in February 2014 shortly before the biennial Liberal convention held in Montreal. Christine Innes was hoping to run as a Liberal in a by-election in Trinity-Spadina against Olivia Chow, the incumbent New Democrat there and Jack Layton's widow. But the party blocked her candidacy because of allegations her husband Tonny Ianno, a former Liberal MP, had bullied young volunteers.

Innes, however, believed she was actually being punished for not committing to run in the new riding of Spadina-Fort York in 2015, which would leave Chrystia Freeland free to run in the riding she wanted for herself, University-Rosedale.[8]

There were many twists to this story. The party stood by its allegations, Christine Innes vigorously denied them, and the conflict ended up before the courts. Innes sued Justin Trudeau for defamation. In the end, the party prevented her from running as a Liberal in 2015. According to one Liberal insider, this kind of bullying was simply not tolerated, because Liberal infighting not only harmed party fortunes at the polls, it also damaged the very "soul" of the party.

A second lawsuit was filed by former Liberal leadership candidate David Bertschi, who was disqualified from running in the

Ottawa-Orléans riding. Things got so heated at the nomination meeting that a fist fight broke out between the different camps.[9] Retired Lieutenant-General Andrew Leslie was parachuted in as a star candidate in the bilingual riding. Afterward, Leslie assured people that he had enough delegates to win the nomination handily even if his rival had been allowed to run, but he didn't sound particularly convincing. Actually, Trudeau had sent a very strong message favouring Leslie's candidacy by introducing him on the stage during the biennial convention in Montreal.

There were also complaints the party had manipulated the rules to get Trudeau's childhood friend Marc Miller nominated in a Montreal riding, although the party denied this.

Dan Gagnier, one of Trudeau's advisers, maintains the leader never waived his right to express "his preference" for a given candidate. If this was really the case, then the party hadn't explained things very well.

Some people said openly that Trudeau had made a mistake in not explicitly saying he would retain the power to nominate competent candidates. But Montreal Senator Paul Massicotte didn't agree: "I see this as being normal, as being smart. I know some advisers told him not to [promise an open nomination process], but this is democracy … let the people decide."

Trudeau seemed rather naive, however, to promise an open nomination process, because it gave the impression that anyone could run under the Liberal banner — which in turn created expectations. According to Peter Donolo, Jean Chrétien's former strategist, it would have been "more transparent to say: 'These five seats are important for these reasons, and I want to put these candidates in.' I think that's more transparent, it's more honest."

———

Justin Trudeau came down just as harshly on his MPs where abortion rights were concerned. He had no intention of backing down on any issue involving the *Canadian Charter of Rights and Freedoms,* and he meant to show his resolve in this case.

In the name of the absolute right to an abortion, he decreed in May 2014 that any person seeking to run for the Liberal Party in the upcoming election would have to commit to voting pro-choice, whatever the candidate's religious beliefs. He made an exception, though, for pro-life MPs in his caucus already sitting in Parliament, who would benefit from a kind of amnesty.

The Liberal Party was pro-choice and would remain pro-choice, he stated clearly. This position seemed to come out of the blue when he announced it all of a sudden during a press briefing on Parliament Hill. MPs and party faithful alike were stunned. The Trudeau team claimed this was not only Justin Trudeau's personal position, it had also been adopted by the Liberal Party ages ago. According to Dan Gagnier, Trudeau had "simply decided to be clear on the issue, even if his position came with risks."

Trudeau saw the whole issue in the light of the *Canadian Charter of Rights and Freedoms,* and he wouldn't take no for an answer. True, he didn't want to be perceived merely as his father's son, but anything involving the Charter, according to a well-informed Liberal, "is written in his DNA."

Liberal parliamentarians had always been free to vote according to their conscience on matters like abortion, but this would no longer be the case. People uncomfortable with the idea of being overtly pro-choice had to toe the line after a talk with the Liberal leader and the application of some "vigorous means of persuasion." Some MPs saw Trudeau's tough attitude as a sign of leadership, whereas others saw it as "the attitude of a dictator," as one anonymous Liberal source put it.

Wasn't the Liberal Party of Canada the big red tent of Sir Wilfrid Laurier, where everyone was free to express his or her views?

———

These incidents put a dent in the leader's image, but he made a reasonably good showing in the by-elections held on June 30, 2014.[10] Remarkably, in one of the contests Liberal Adam Vaughan beat New Democrat Olivia Chow in Trinity-Spadina with 53.7 percent of the vote. The NDP fared poorly, dropping to 34.1 percent.

That victory and the other Liberal win that day were promising, but the coming year would nevertheless be a difficult one for Trudeau. The Liberals were squeezed in between the Conservatives on the right and the NDP on the left. The New Democrats had ignored Trudeau for a whole year, but now they ramped up their attacks on him. Although Thomas

Mulcair had been performing well in the House of Commons, he had fallen to third place in voting intentions. He had led the attack on Stephen Harper in the Wright-Duffy affair, but it hadn't yet helped him much, although the wind would soon start to blow in his favour.

Trudeau was often criticized for his lack of policy positions, so he now clearly laid out his political priorities: promoting investment in infrastructure and education, and committing to roll back the Harper decision to raise the retirement age (and eligibility for old-age pensions) from sixty-seven to sixty-five.

Then problems broke out in the Liberal caucus. In November 2014, two Liberal MPs (Massimo Pacetti from the Montreal riding of Saint-Léonard-Saint-Michel, and Scott Andrews from Avalon riding in Newfoundland) were suspended after allegations of sexual misconduct were made against them by two female New Democrat MPs. The women were never publicly identified. The file reached Justin Trudeau's desk and he acted swiftly. He would later say he had no regrets: there was zero tolerance for bullying and sexual harassment in the Liberal caucus.

Some Liberals felt Trudeau had acted too quickly in this affair: he had not even called on the two MPs (who vigorously denied the allegations) to give their side of the story. Nonetheless, after an independent study reported on their behaviour, the leader kicked them out of the party.

It seemed out of character for Trudeau to be this decisive, but he was learning to consolidate his leadership. He had to show he knew how to manage his caucus and his party. In order to enhance his chances of winning the upcoming election, he reserved the right to make structural changes, to choose the best candidates, and to kick the wrong people out of the party.[11] Otherwise, he knew he could end up on the Opposition benches for a long time. According to historian Michael Behiels, Trudeau resembled Wilfrid Laurier in this respect: "Publicly, he was the charmer but behind the scenes, he was tough."[12]

According to Trudeau adviser Dan Gagnier, nobody should be surprised by the ruthless streak in his character: many people see him as inexperienced, but the truth is just the opposite. "He is a young man who has been forged by significant life experiences. This is what makes him so much more determined, more courageous, and much tougher than a lot of people think."

Former Prime Minister Brian Mulroney holds the same view. He knew Justin well as a long-standing friend of his son Ben. "Critics say that Trudeau doesn't have a program," Mulroney said, but "his program is that he's not Stephen Harper."

It was no fluke that Trudeau had led in opinion polls fourteen months in a row, Mulroney added. Anyone underestimating him would do so at his or her own peril. Canadians wanted change, and Trudeau represented this change. "He's a young man, attractive, elected two or three times to the House, attractive wife, beautiful kids — this is a potent package."

The Conservatives' other mistake, according to Mulroney, was in not devoting enough attention to Thomas Mulcair, "the best Opposition leader since John Diefenbaker. I have known them all, met them all. The idea that this is going to be a two-party tap dance is wrong," he said.

Mulroney said the Conservatives should do their homework, because the attack ads they used against previous Liberal leaders were no longer working. He said Trudeau was a "different kettle of fish" compared to Stéphane Dion and Michael Ignatieff. In fact, Justin Trudeau was a completely new phenomenon.

But Justin Trudeau's honeymoon with public opinion would not last forever.

CHAPTER 10

THE ALLURE OF THE BLANK SLATE

Justin Trudeau came across as the embodiment of change. With his good looks, optimistic tone, dynamism, and passion he seemed quite the reverse of Stephen Harper, who appeared wooden, serious, and controlling almost to the point of being inhuman.

Canadians recalled the frosty image of the Conservative prime minister giving his son a handshake as the youngster headed off to school. The party's best attempts to dress up "Sweater Stephen" in colourful pullovers made no difference. Meanwhile, NDP leader Thomas Mulcair always seemed ferociously angry — even his friends conceded the point. He was respected in Quebec, but he lacked Jack Layton's endearing emotional side.

People who had met Justin Trudeau in person often noted his welcoming presence and his good listening skills. "It isn't a put-on," says a Quebec political observer. Justin was like the boy next door. "You want to go over and talk to him."

People were always gathering around him at the Patro Le Prevost community centre in his riding, asking him questions, says communications director Laurence Cardinal. "He engages them, he bursts out laughing if they are too direct. People talk to him about his father, at least the older ones among them."

Trudeau had the advantage of a terrific memory. According to a colleague who knows him well, Justin was the young MP who remembered his scripted lines "word for word — even five or six years later." He was also the guest who had no trouble remembering people's names, whereas his father sometimes forgot the names of his own ministers. Wayne Easter noticed this quality a few years ago in Prince Edward Island. Easter had invited Trudeau to have coffee with fifty guests or so. He presented Trudeau to every one of them. At the end of the meeting, Trudeau spoke to them all in groups of two and three people. Easter says he called them all by their first names. "And when he talked to them, they had his total focus of attention for that forty-five seconds or one minute. He's not looking over his shoulder to see who else is coming by, he's not thinking; you have his undivided attention, and that is a skill that very, very few people have, and it's ingrained in him," recalls the MP.

Trudeau set off what pollsters call "an explosion of feelings," much as Jack Layton used to. Voters went wild about Jack, but he had to gain their affection by fighting three election campaigns and launching an all-out charm offensive. Trudeau's appeal was practically spontaneous in many parts of Canada … but in Quebec the so-called Trudeau effect took longer to settle in and was somewhat unpredictable.

According to pollster Jean-Marc Léger, celebrity was the "key factor" in Justin Trudeau's spectacular rise: people wouldn't be talking about him if his name wasn't Trudeau. His instant breakthrough to prominence "may be due to the fact he has been a star ever since childhood," says political scientist Thierry Giasson. This was more widely acknowledged in English Canada, where his childhood had garnered more media attention than in Quebec.

The difficulties Justin Trudeau experienced in full public view made Canadians feel connected to him personally. That feeling was essentially an illusion, because people didn't know him any better than they knew other "stars." The public probably had an even better grasp of Stephen Harper's personality. But Trudeau's obvious charisma, combined with his fame, worked well for him.

You can't buy charisma. It is a very precious and rare force, according to Virginia Postrel, the American author of *The Power of Glamour*, who says charisma is "a kind of personal magnetism that inspires loyalty."[1] After the Liberal leadership race and the public's reaction to Trudeau's rock star appeal, both the NDP and the Conservatives were concerned about what federal Cabinet minister Tony Clement called "the Hollywoodization of politics" in Canada. It's very hard in the political arena to take on a celebrity, because glamour and charisma are intangible benefits.

Do celebrities make better politicians? Not necessarily, according to Newfoundland political scientist Alex Marland, who has studied the phenomenon. George W. Bush and Arnold Schwarzenegger weren't more effective once elected to office, but they had a "competitive advantage" to reach the top. "It's easier to become the leader of the party," says Marland, "and it's easier potentially to become head of government, but whether that helps you once you're in government, I'm not sure." Celebrities are a few steps ahead of other politicians. Whatever they do, they are important players on the political scene. One has only to think of the Bush and Kennedy families in the United States and, in a more local sense, the Mannings in Alberta, the Bennetts in British Columbia, the three Johnsons in Quebec, Paul Martin Sr. and Jr., and the Ghiz family in Prince Edward Island. But even though such celebrities have advantages from the get-go, there is no guarantee of their reaching the finish line.

John English devotes several pages of his biography of Pierre Elliott Trudeau to celebrity. This is an important factor in Justin's popularity, and it was also an important factor in his father's. "Pierre was a celebrity who dated celebrities" and seemed to love that universe, he says.

Politics in 2014 didn't work the way it did in the sixties, but Justin showed that he has flair, just like his father. According to English, "it was so shocking in the 60s [for someone like Pierre Trudeau] to drive a Mercedes when you're supposed to drive a Chev.… Justin is the same way, he's unpredictable, very athletic … young and hip. It perfectly describes his father." The rise of Justin Trudeau was due to what English calls "a huge charisma deficit in politics" in Canada. Trudeau filled this gap.

As a matter of fact, Canadian history has seen a steady procession of boring prime ministers. In itself, this is not a bad thing. Pollster Nik Nanos says Stephen Harper was boring but reassuring. There have only been a handful of charismatic leaders on the federal scene: John A. Macdonald, Wilfrid Laurier, John Diefenbaker in his own odd way. Then it was fast forward to Pierre Elliott Trudeau. After him, Brian Mulroney was extremely popular at the beginning of his first term, and had an undeniable presence.

In today's era of showbiz politics, though, many politicians are — or try to be — celebrities. Justin Trudeau seemed well suited to this new political universe. He liked to be seen, he liked people, he felt comfortable in the limelight. But Alex Marland says an important distinction should be drawn. Pierre Elliott Trudeau became "a real celebrity because he had earned it through his talents, and his intellectual ability and his engagement." His son Justin was a born communicator, and he certainly had charisma, but he still had to earn his celebrity status "not because of his last name" but through his own talents.

Justin Trudeau was already showing he could take on, and overcome, tough challenges, but Canadians still didn't have much of an idea about the man or his ability to govern. There were signs here and there, but he still had to demonstrate that he had what it took to lead the country.

———

In many ways, during his first years of national prominence, Justin Trudeau remained a blank slate. People read into his personality whatever they wanted to. He had never made great speeches or left a body of substantial writings, so it was hard to get an idea of what he was really about. For almost two years, until the early spring of 2015, he had played up his image without revealing what he stood for politically. For some Canadians — though not for everyone — this was enough to project their hopes and desires onto him.

In the celebrity era, observes Robert Asselin, Trudeau's appearance could also be a distraction, to an extent, drawing attention to the packaging, not the content:

> I once said that to a journalist, and I kind of regretted it afterwards. In English, I said, "Justin is like a girl, a beautiful girl you meet for the first time. You find her so beautiful that all you can think is, 'My God, is she *ever* gorgeous!' Which means you are less inclined to listen to what she has to say, and so forth." I sometimes have the same impression with Justin — he has good looks, he is charming, and has an engaging smile, and people don't get past that.

Some in the media nicknamed him "Pierre light," as if to say he was an intellectual lightweight compared to his father. Ever since he was a teenager, people had been telling Justin he was his father's son but he lacked his father's depth. He always took the remarks in stride.

"In any case," Justin Trudeau confided to *La Presse*, "before entering politics, wherever I turned up, expectations were either huge or they were very low. Over time I developed defences. My whole life, people have been watching me, so I had to shield myself, otherwise life would have been unbearable. Sometimes it's frustrating because as soon as I say the wrong thing, everybody attacks me. At the same time, I know who I am, and who I am has nothing to do with the perception other people have of me."[2]

Justin Trudeau wrote *Common Ground* to share his wealth of experiences with readers, making it easier for them to relate to him. He described growing up as a child, living through his parents' divorce, working as a schoolteacher — all of which equipped him to "stand up for people who maybe need a little more help than I was lucky enough to not need."[3] He also talked about his years at Brébeuf, the deaths of his father and his brother, but he had little to say about his major policy positions.

But while Justin Trudeau claimed to be open and accessible, it still wasn't that easy to know the man. Members of the Liberal caucus said he wasn't the kind of person you wanted to have a beer with. He had that old "Trudeau reserve." He didn't reveal his true self. One Liberal source says, "In all our meetings, I never had fifteen minutes of personal time with him."

His adviser Robert Asselin admits he initially hesitated to join Justin Trudeau's team.

> The first thing I realized was that I really didn't know Justin. People have all kinds of preconceptions before meeting someone. He is extremely intelligent, but when he's compared to Pierre Trudeau — well, clearly his father set a demanding standard.... In terms of intelligence he is constantly underestimated because his good looks give people the impression he has no ideas of his own.

Justin lacked his father's cold and even brutal intelligence, but according to Asselin, Justin "has at the same time a very rational and systematic way of thinking things through. When he studies his files, he always asks questions, he is intellectually well ordered. You can tell he has had a very (classic) liberal education."

But Justin's clear-thinking side didn't always come to the fore. The Liberal leader made ill-conceived statements, he went back on things he said, he contradicted himself, and he offered excuses. "For sure, there's an impulsive side to him," a colleague recalls. "But it's never a put-on just for show."

Trudeau sometimes came across as his own worst enemy. He didn't like being scripted, and he tended to think aloud, without filtering what he was saying or considering the consequences. This was because he wanted to get things moving. He was in a hurry. "In his mind he sometimes jumps a few steps ahead," chuckles a close confidant. "He says 'OK, let's do it!' That's what happened with the decision about the Liberal senators."

Donald Savoie, a world-renowned expert on public administration, noticed when sharing a meal with Pierre Trudeau and his two eldest sons that young Justin was "alert, full of opinions and charisma, and never hesitating to express his views," whereas his brother Sacha didn't open up so easily. "There was nothing scripted about him, he had opinions on everything and it was easy to know where he stood, very easy. I had only to mention a subject, and he fired off his views."

Savoie, a professor at the Université de Moncton, says the MP for Papineau was more tightly scripted on becoming party leader, "but I don't believe it's possible to keep that kind of personality under control, I don't believe Justin Trudeau can be scripted 100 percent." Left to his own devices, the Liberal leader's tendency was always to hold nothing back. An example of this, according to Savoie, was Trudeau's statement that he was glad the Senate favours Quebec at Alberta's expense.[4]

Liberal organizer Reine Hébert noticed Trudeau's independent streak the minute he entered politics. "You can try telling Justin, 'Say this, say that....' He will often look at you and answer, 'That's *not* what I'm going to say.' I often tell people he's a big boy, he's going to decide what to say."

Still, his repeated gaffes when talking about Ukraine, China, or bilingualism gave the impression the Liberal leader didn't know his files or had a hard time articulating his ideas.[5]

His advisers wanted to correct this impression. According to Dan Gagnier, "no matter what people say, he's really very smart. He's educated, he's a young man who was not only raised in a political family but who has had his knocks in life, all of which has strengthened his character."

Paul Martin recalled how impressed he was by Justin Trudeau's independent spirit and self-confidence: "One of the reasons I understand him so well is that when I decided to run for office I also wanted to choose my riding myself. It's really important for an MP to have this independence, to be able to express his own ideas, and Justin's been doing this from the start."

If Trudeau won the upcoming election, Martin predicted, he would be more "pragmatic" and flexible on big international files than Stephen Harper had been, notably on China and also the African continent, where several Canadian embassies were shut down by Harper.

The former prime minister conceded the Trudeau name definitely opened doors for Justin, just as he himself had benefited from being the son of Paul Martin Sr., the former secretary of state for external affairs. But he maintained Justin Trudeau had developed his own unique approach to politics. As Liberal leader, Justin was quick on the uptake: he was sure of himself, he knew what he knew, but he never hesitated to admit he "needed to study a particular issue more in depth. There was no arrogance in his attitude." Martin added: "It's not a question of not knowing his files: he knows them in great detail. I have had discussions with him about the economy, Aboriginal people, Africa, subjects I have taken up with some of the brightest people in the world. And I can tell you Justin wouldn't have any trouble mastering these subjects. It's very important as a leader to understand when the situation changes. I found him very good at that."

But, as the new Liberal leader, Trudeau didn't instill confidence in everyone. "Is he marketable? Yes," said Donald Savoie. "But the second thing worth asking is, does he have the substance needed to govern effectively? We don't have the answer to that question yet. He has never been a minister, he has never been a school principal.... Actually we don't know how capable he is as a manager, a leader."

Faced with doubts like these, Justin Trudeau's supporters immediately countered that people had also wondered whether Stephen Harper, the guy from out west, had what it took to govern effectively. But Harper had a few qualities Trudeau lacked.

According to Donald Savoie, "You could say Stephen Harper was not defined by his charisma, but it's clear he brought something solid [to his leadership]. It gave him a slight advantage. People told themselves Harper 'wouldn't make any gaffes.' He's like an accountant, and nobody can say Justin Trudeau gives the impression of being an accountant!"

On the other hand, according to Laurence Cardinal at the Patro Le Prevost community centre, Trudeau gave the impression he was not at all a pre-programmed politician with a ready-made answer to every question, a person "who pressed the play button.... If he loses that spontaneity, he will become like all other politicians."

Justin Trudeau had always said he made errors, but he preferred to show himself as he really is — the real Justin. "I think voters are looking for real people, not spun, sound-bited and massively controlled politicians."[6]

Chapter 11

THE NETWORKED CANDIDATE

As has often been said, Justin Trudeau was ever-present on social media networks. A true child of his generation, he couldn't do without Facebook, YouTube, Twitter, or Instagram. In fact, his friend Thomas Panos called the Web "a natural extension of his personality."

He came onto the public stage at a time when social media was completely transforming the political landscape, bringing the people closer to the political class. Politicians could now use social media to address the public directly, posting messages, videos, and photos online without passing through the filter of the traditional media. According to Marc Lalonde, politicians are no longer "at the mercy of journalists" providing their own interpretations.

Pierre Elliott Trudeau had been perfectly suited to television, the medium of choice in the second half of the twentieth century. But nowadays, any party that wants to increase its standing in the polls has to invest in social media. Political parties often preach to the converted, but once the messages are out, party faithful can relay them and set the Twittersphere abuzz.

At the same time, by posting online people could be exposed to instant criticism and even insults. But when a social media presence is well managed, it creates public curiosity about a candidate and generates media buzz. For example, Justin Trudeau made the "damaging admission" that he doesn't drink coffee in the same interview in which he spoke about having smoked cannabis as an MP. The comment about coffee drew a storm of teasing, distracting some people from the potentially damaging cannabis story. Trudeau ended up tweeting as a joke that he may have made "a mistake in wanting to be open and transparent" — about the coffee part of his interview. The joke quickly went viral.

Even so, skill at managing social media does not necessarily result in greater success at the ballot box unless it is backed up with other political tools. Pollster Darrell Bricker notes only 1 percent of Canadians tweet.

Liberal strategists understood clearly that nothing was going to replace handshakes, smiles, and casual chatting with the voters. But they saw that a leader needs to be present both on social media and in person, and experts were predicting that social media would be used more than ever in the election that was slated for October 2015. In honing the Liberal strategy, therefore, Gerald Butts and Katie Telford tapped the Obama team for advice.

According to Robert Asselin, the American experience didn't automatically apply to Canada, because the scale of mass communication can't be compared and the two political systems are so different. The United States has a population of 320 million — almost ten times the Canadian population. But there were a few lessons to learn from Barack Obama's large-scale charm offensives on Facebook and YouTube: "The rationale is fabulous: once you get someone, you don't let them go," says Asselin.

In fact, once a person's name was entered into the Liberal Party of Canada's database, that person became a "target" — whether or not he or she had actually made a decision whom to vote for. Everyone signing up on www.justin.ca was bombarded with emails and directed to a link where Justin gave a "two-minute talk" calling on them to make a contribution, take part in an activity, or sign up as a volunteer. "And five minutes later, the money is already in party coffers. People have given their card number, and it's over," sums up Asselin.

The Liberals were pinning a lot of hope on the next generation — voters thirty-five and under who no longer watch TV or read newspapers but are constantly on social media. The Trudeau team believed their leader was way out in front of other parties in this respect, and had not yet reached his full potential. According to Asselin, the Liberal leader was going to attract a lot of people "simply because he's Justin" — even when they weren't particularly attracted to the Liberal Party — a little like Jack Layton, who made a breakthrough in Quebec although the NDP didn't have much of a base there. "When Justin speaks, I don't think he seems like an old-style politician," says Asselin. "He often wears jeans and sometimes lets his shirt hang out a bit. Like people say, he's really *cool.*"

Each politician has a particular style, and social media is not suited to everybody. Using social media to advantage depends on look, image, and choice of words. The image ends up personifying the brand. Michael Ignatieff and Stéphane Dion, two intellectuals, couldn't have the same impact online as Justin Trudeau, according to image expert Luc Dupont.

When Dion, a former environment minister, tried playing the spontaneity card, "he came across as an intellectual hard at work. He didn't name his dog Rover or Lassie. He named his dog Kyoto," says Dupont. Trudeau, on the other hand, seemed to have found the winning formula. "Highly choreographed and polished" images show him on stage the evening he won the Liberal leadership race, proudly holding his wriggling son, accompanied by his wife Sophie and their daughter. The images show something so natural, so spontaneous, "they seem to be anything *but* politics," according to Dupont.

Trudeau was perfectly aware of the fact. He told his fans he couldn't imagine "wearing a mask" in his public communications. When he tweeted, he opened up as if he were talking to a friend. He had neither Prime Minister Stephen Harper's reserve nor the formality that suited Thomas Mulcair as leader of the Official Opposition. As head of the third party in the House, Trudeau had more room for manoeuvre … and therefore, he could afford to take more chances.

Justin Trudeau had grown up with technology. As an MP he had always posted regular updates on his Facebook page. His Twitter account went back to 2008, and he tweeted all the time. This platform was second nature to him. He still tweeted several times a day, although once he became party leader he got help from his staff.

According to Luc Dupont, less than 10 percent of Canadians get around to reviewing a party's election platform on its official website, which explains how social media casts such a wide net. "Politics is increasingly making the shift toward show business." The average voter "knows more about stars than about election campaigns," which interest fewer and fewer voters, he says. "In this context it's important to keep people talking, sharing, to play on hype, as if the voter were no longer able to see the difference between politics and entertainment, between a reality TV show and information."

Trudeau was adept at personalizing the content he posted on Facebook or Twitter, finding words and symbols that resonated. He posted a lovely photo of his family in a red canoe, by way of announcing that Sophie was expecting their third baby. "Thrilled to let you know we're going to need another seat in our canoe: Sophie is pregnant!" Trudeau tweeted, with the hashtag #threeisthenewtwo. Then when their third child was born, Trudeau posted a photo showing the infant's hand gripping Dad's finger. The baby's name — first spelled "Hadrian," then corrected in a subsequent tweet to "Hadrien" — led to an outpouring of responses. The fact that many of these responses were negative reminds us that social media never stops being a two-edged sword.

It was also on Twitter that Justin Trudeau responded when Thomas Mulcair attacked the Liberals and Conservatives at an NDP caucus retreat for what he called their long legacy of corruption. A reporter asked Mulcair why he had chosen not to mention Trudeau by name, although he mentioned Prime Minister Stephen Harper several times. "If and when he does do something," the NDP leader said, "we'll of course talk about that."

"See, he doesn't actually think I'm Lord Voldemort," Justin Trudeau tweeted once Mulcair finally mentioned him by name: "@thomasmulcair just said '@justintrudeau'- twice."[1]

Most Canadians still don't follow political parties on social media, but online posts and tweets are an effective way to take down barriers and humanize men and women in politics. Also, they are a far cheaper way to mobilize people than running an advertising campaign!

According to Robert Asselin, the MP for Papineau was not averse to engaging people in conversation, showing at the same time he was not a rigid politician. "When Justin writes on social media, 'I just dropped Xavier off at school, I am proud of my big boy,' people relate to that, because he is living something everyone experiences." In Asselin's view, even without being an open book, Trudeau was "letting people understand who he was." Stephen Harper "wouldn't be as demonized if he opened up a bit," he added.

Once Trudeau became Liberal leader, the NDP and Conservatives scrambled to catch up on social media. On July 15, 2013, Stephen Harper made the unprecedented step of announcing the composition of his new Cabinet on Twitter. A few months later, the NDP tweeted a "virtual Question Period" after the Conservatives prorogued Parliament until mid-October. Since Parliament wasn't sitting, the NDP leader put his questions to the prime minister online, asking what he knew about the Wright-Duffy affair. The questions remained unanswered.

Image is everything on social media. In this respect, Trudeau was making gains, "but on matters of substance, things were not so clear," said Donald Savoie. It was hard to articulate a position in a tweet of 140 characters or less, and Twitter subscribers often had very set views.

"Nowadays, in politics, you form an opinion, you make a decision based on a clip that lasts fifteen or twenty seconds. This is not the era of Pearson, Diefenbaker, or even Pierre Trudeau, when people had to be much more balanced," Savoie added. "Now, on Facebook, Twitter, things go so fast that people reach an instant opinion, but that opinion is more fluid than it would have been thirty years ago."

According to pollster Jean-Marc Léger, the impact of social media during political campaigns is relative. Social media doesn't create a movement, it amplifies a movement that has already begun. But ignoring social media means ignoring a potential outlet and potential supporters.

Justin Trudeau talked about anything and everything on social media. When he posted a photo of a screwdriver and asked his Twitter fans whether they thought it was rewarding to install a new tri-light switch, some people saw him as an anti-politician interacting with ordinary people — whereas others concluded he didn't have the right stuff to be prime minister.

One thing was clear. With some 832,000 Twitter followers, Justin Trudeau gave people reasons for clicking. "Do you want to become prime minister? Just screw up your courage and do it!" came one tweet in response to the funny photo, while another wondered: "Trudeau, handsome, intelligent and a jack-of-all-trades? Not just ready to govern, but to electrify the House?"

Justin wasn't afraid of cameras or crowds, and everything was choreographed to show him at his best: his father's buckskin jacket in *Maclean's*, the pictures in *Chatelaine* taken at his place in Ottawa,[2] where the "crazy family" was photographed fully dressed in the swimming pool.

Justin was a master showman, much like Sophie, a former fashion model and TV host. He was constantly being put on display in contests organized by the party. He willingly offered himself as a gift to be won, like a trophy.

As chief Liberal fundraiser Stephen Bronfman put it in 2013, "Justin Trudeau is very saleable. He has a good name and people want to discover who he is." In fact, the Liberal machine spared no effort to showcase him. His charm and social grace served his political goals. When he introduced the winner of the "Win a Date with Justin" contest, Dorothy Corbeil, a retired nurse from Golden Lake, Ontario, he made a point of saying she represented the Canadian middle class he was determined to help out. And Corbeil, a long-standing Liberal supporter, posted a message of her own, which in turn reinforced Justin Trudeau's brand.

"Justin was all I'd hoped he would be — authentic, kind, personable, and funny. He said we could ask him anything, and we all relaxed and did," Corbeil wrote in an email posted on the Liberal Party website in December 2013. "Justin is humble" and he has "good energy." Over supper, Corbeil explained what a hardship it was for small and medium-sized businesses to have to charge GST on income over $30,000, a threshold that inhibited them from growing, given all the time-consuming paperwork required for filing. The threshold actually hadn't been changed since the original GST was introduced in 1991.

"Justin wasn't aware of that fact and took it to heart," the happy winner wrote. "The food was delicious and the service excellent. I was treated like a queen."

On the same Web page, Justin called on his supporters to check out the video of his meal with Dorothy and to make a $3 donation and join the drive to raise $1 million for change in just twelve days. The following day, the Liberals offered to give away "twelve limited-edition Justin Trudeau scarves as part of the Win Dinner with Justin contest."

Contests like this became the daily fare of the Liberals with Justin Trudeau as leader. Almost every time, the gift to be won was Justin himself. True, the format of the contests could be risky, as the November 2013 Ladies' Night had shown. But the results couldn't be argued with. On December 15, 2013, the Liberal Party of Canada proudly announced that 12,707 people had donated a total of $1,003,462 to party coffers in just twelve days.

This winning recipe was used on other occasions. There was a contest calling on participants to sign a petition against the Northern Gateway crude oil pipeline that would drive through the Great Bear Rainforest, which extends from Vancouver to the Alaska Panhandle. Another contest gave people donating $3 to the Liberal Party the chance to win breakfast with Justin Trudeau and also attend a speech Hillary Clinton was about to give in Ottawa. And then there was the contest to develop the best T-shirt slogan.

But let's not forget the official Liberal Party store, offering toques, scarves, coffee mugs, Liberal barbecue aprons, zip-up hoodies in bright Liberal red, and, of course, white baby onesies with convenient snaps at the crotch for quick diaper changes with the message MADE BY LIBERALS in big red letters.

Image was everything in Liberal strategy, to put it mildly. Party strategists remembered the classic photograph showing Robert Stanfield fumbling a football. It became a defining image during the 1974 election campaign, helping Pierre Elliott Trudeau secure a majority government. And they recalled how photographs taken in 1997 of Gilles Duceppe wearing a hairnet while touring a cheese factory had subjected him to intense ridicule. So the Justin Trudeau team was not taking any unnecessary risks: they micro-managed his image.

Professor Alex Marland says this new style of fundraising campaign marked a watershed in Canada. Rarely had a Canadian politician ever been "commodified" to this extent. Marland wondered if the selling of Trudeau-as-a-product might herald the onset of American-style election campaigning.[3]

The Trudeau team was both tech-savvy and keen on political marketing. The model to follow was clearly the Obama formula, which had tapped into social media to generate interest in his candidacy. Luc Dupont points out that there were also other points of comparison between the Trudeau and Obama campaigns: the emphasis on the family, with "emotion" and "hope" as leading lines of communication. And there's no denying the similarity of "Dinner with Justin" and "Dinner with Barack." The party's marketing strategy targeted particular groups of voters the Liberals wanted to switch on to politics, notably young people.

Justin Trudeau banked on his image a lot — too much, according to some people — but this strategy was definitely paying off. According to Senator Paul Massicotte, "We work with the cards in our hand. After all, Justin has great presence, he has style."

CHAPTER 12

THE PLAN FOR THE MIDDLE CLASS

Justin Trudeau and Gerald Butts liked nothing better than pulling off a major coup. By early 2015, in the lead-up to the fall election, they no doubt felt the Liberals had to shock and awe the electorate if they were going to leap from third place — behind the Conservatives and New Democrats — into first.

After waiting around a few months, the Trudeau team finally put their cards on the table. Two years after winning the Liberal leadership, Justin Trudeau unveiled the cornerstone of the party platform. On May 4, 2015, in a Gatineau restaurant, surrounded by families, he announced his plan to help the middle class make ends meet.

"It was about time," wrote the daily newspaper *Le Droit*.

Holding a microphone, Trudeau moved between the tables, stopping here and there and taking the time to explain in broad brush-strokes "Justin Trudeau's Plan for Fairness for the Middle Class," as it was officially called.

"We have a plan for fairness. A Liberal government will give a tax cut to the middle class and provide middle-class families with more money to raise their kids," he said during the campaign-style event.

The leader made two promises: first, to lower taxes for middle-class families and overhaul benefits for families; and second, to increase taxes for the wealthy by creating a new tax bracket ranging from 29 percent to 33 percent for individuals earning more than $200,000 per year. In 2013, this category made up 1.3 percent of individuals reporting income.[1] According to the plan, this measure would bring in $3 billion, which would then offset the cost of lowering the tax rate for the middle class from 22 percent to 20.5 percent for individuals declaring income between $44,701 and $89,401.

The Liberals estimated that a typical family with two children and an annual income of $90,000 would receive a monthly non-taxable cheque for $490. According to their calculations, the same family would receive $275 after tax under the Harper government's plan. Another example: a single-parent family with a child under six years of age and annual income of $30,000 would receive non-taxable support of $533 per month, compared to $440 under the Conservatives' plan.

The new Canada Child Benefit would replace two Harper government initiatives, the Canada Child Tax Benefit for low-income families and the Universal Child Care Benefit. The basic amount of the Liberals' proposed benefit would be $6,400 per year per child under six years of age and $5,400 for children between the ages of six and seventeen. The measure would be progressive, so parents whose combined income reached $200,000 would receive no benefit.

The driving idea behind this plan was to distribute wealth more fairly, by taxing well-to-do Canadians at a higher rate in order to give the middle class more breathing room. La Presse couldn't help comparing Justin Trudeau to Robin Hood.

To fund his plan, Trudeau proposed cancelling three Conservative measures: first, abolishing income-splitting (freeing up $2 billion); second, cancelling the Tory decision to raise the Tax-Free Savings Account limit from $5,000 to $10,000 (which, according to several credible studies, profited only a small group of workers); and third, abolishing the Harper government's child tax benefits. (Cancelling these last two measures would free up an additional $18 billion.) A Liberal government would also cut back on government advertising campaigns. Overall, this would still leave a shortfall of $2 billion, however. The Liberal Party indicated that a full explanation of the plan would come later, during the election campaign.

The Conservatives cringed at the Liberal plan, nicknaming it the "Trudeau Tax." Conservative minister Pierre Poilievre said the plan would hurt people with low incomes, since two-thirds of people making their maximum Tax-Free Savings Account contribution earned less than $60,000 a year. The NDP meanwhile pointed out that two-thirds of Canadians earned less than $44,000 per year.

Some experts held the Trudeau plan could have adverse effects. With a new tax bracket at 33 percent, individuals earning $200,000 and over in New Brunswick would see their total tax rate (counting both federal and provincial taxes) jump to 58.75 percent, while in Quebec the rate would jump to 53 percent. The concern was that such a high tax rate could push the wealthy to flee to countries with lower tax rates, or resort to tax evasion, or both.

For the time being, however, the Liberals were breathing easier. Trudeau could now itemize his plan for the middle class in detail, instead of speaking in platitudes. When the Conservatives accused the Liberals of opposing tax cuts, the Liberals had a counter-argument handy: thanks to the Trudeau plan, families earning less than $150,000 would have more money in their pockets at the end of the year than they would under the Conservatives.

Trudeau was now in attack mode, and he revealed once again his tactical flair. The boxer hadn't tried to outflank the Conservatives with a Green Plan or something of the sort: instead, he had moved directly onto their home turf — taxation. He had waited for the Harper government to present its budget in April 2015, and then had turned the tables on the Conservatives, who just a few months earlier had promised enhanced — but taxable — benefits to families.[2]

The Liberals had given themselves an extra advantage. They were proposing measures to win the support of the middle class — benefits that were easier to understand, more visible … and also non-taxable. But whether the Liberal measures were really all they claimed to be, or whether they were affordable, would only become clear if and when they were adopted. So for the time being, the Liberals were busy selling a product, persuading voters they would be better off under a Trudeau government than they would be if the Harper government was re-elected.

Thomas Mulcair was from a family of ten children and liked to say that Justin Trudeau was not from the middle class and therefore lacked credibility. The NDP had taken up the issue and presented its own proposals to lighten the tax burden of the middle class: a $15 federal minimum wage, a tax cut to small businesses, and a national $15-a-day daycare plan. The New Democrats believed they were better suited to talk about the middle class — a message that was, after all, more consistent with their party's values.

Actually, defending the middle class was not a typical election issue for the Liberals. Over the past few election campaigns the party had focused on health, employment, and Canadian unity. According to Gordon Ashworth, one of Trudeau's campaign organizers in Ontario, defending the middle class might not seem all that exciting at first glance, but it had wide appeal.

"You need a theme, and most people think they're middle class," he explained. "So you try to find something that encompasses everybody. Everybody can see into it what they want to see."

According to pollsters, the middle class represented a "huge block of voters." Many people felt they belonged to the middle class, whether they earned $40,000 per year or $100,000.

Several studies had shown that the Canadian middle class was doing quite well. But no matter what the statistics indicated, the Liberals said Canadians were anxious about their economic prospects and their ability to pay for the children's education or plan for their own secure retirement.

Focusing on the middle class was also a way for the Liberals to present an economic plan without directly attacking the Conservatives on the economy, where they were perceived to be the strongest. Typically, the majority of voters considered the Tories the most credible party when it came to taxation and trimming the fat from public expenditures. On the other hand, according to pollster Nik Nanos, public perception of the Liberals was strong when they talked about economic prosperity and growth. This helps explain why the Liberals took up the message on inclusive prosperity they heard from Larry Summers, former chief economist at the World Bank and former director of the National Economic Council under the Obama administration. He had been invited to attend the Liberal Party convention in Montreal.

The Liberals were also betting many voters wanted to return to values of generosity, sharing, and fairness after many years of hard-nosed Conservative government. It remained to be seen whether progressives would find Justin Trudeau persuasive. At the Montreal party convention he had suggested the party would take better care of people. But he had also insisted that any state intervention into the economy had to be targeted and subjected to budgetary discipline and measures focusing on growth. He rejected out of hand the idea of using tax increases to fund vast social programs, because that would only increase the financial burden on the middle class.

The Trudeau plan was a clever move, but it was also risky. Clever because Trudeau was moving onto the home turf of the Conservatives, which meant he was less vulnerable to their attacks on taxation issues; risky because by moving closer to the Conservatives (as he had already done on the military mission in Iraq and the anti-terrorist Bill C-51) he was opening up more room for the NDP to make its mark and rally the left-wing vote.

Two years into Justin Trudeau's leadership the Liberals found they had dropped in the polls, so they now changed tack, committing to unveil the main points of their election platform. Starting in spring 2015, they ramped up the number of their announcements: an environmental plan, their vision of Canada-U.S. relations, democratic reforms, and specific measures to improve the electoral system. When Trudeau found it necessary to unveil a new campaign slogan for the party — "Real Change" — it was an indication the party was losing ground.

In the lead-up to the election, the political context remained as uncertain as ever. Thomas Mulcair seemed an increasingly credible contender to be the next prime minister of Canada. But Gilles Duceppe was back on the federal scene as leader of the Bloc Québécois, threatening to erode NDP support in Quebec. And with fears of a recession in the air, there was no guarantee Stephen Harper could persuade voters he was the best person to manage the economy.

Nothing could be taken for granted.

CHAPTER 13

TRUDEAU 2015?

The bar was set high for Justin Trudeau. He had attracted several thousand new members to the Liberal Party and he was increasingly filling up party coffers.[1] Now, in the lead-up to the fall 2015 election, the Liberals had to organize and plan their campaign activities in no less than 338 ridings from sea to sea to sea. For two years now Trudeau had been busy revamping the party — but he had started from a low baseline. In the aftermath of the 2011 election disaster, according to Pablo Rodríguez, "very few ridings had any organization on the ground, with a critical base of volunteers. Let's be honest about it: we took a real beating."

Justin Trudeau had cut himself off institutionally from his senators, some of whom were superb organizers. Instead, as full-scale campaigning was about to begin, he was left with thirty-six[2] Liberal MPs as well as an army of thirty thousand[3] volunteers to coordinate campaign events and turn out the vote. Trudeau had attracted good candidates across the country, but most of the three hundred fresh recruits running under the Liberal banner had never before taken part in a federal election campaign. The Liberal leader was under no illusions: he himself had predicted at the Montreal convention that the 2015 election campaign would be the fiercest one in Canadian history.

Meanwhile, the Conservatives were revving up their Big Blue Machine. Their machine was well funded and it was simply everywhere.

The Conservatives were ready to seize the opportunity any time Trudeau showed the slightest weakness. Nothing horrified them more than the idea that Trudeau could actually win the coming election and undo everything they had put in place over the past nine years.

Stephen Harper sized things up cleverly. He wasn't trying to win a popularity contest. The Conservative leader didn't hesitate to introduce measures that were widely frowned on, as long as he knew they would produce results in the ballot box. He systematically targeted voters and ridings by announcing measures that would appeal to specific groups. His strategy lay in showing he was the most experienced candidate, the one best able to take on the crises of the day and with whom Canadians ran the least risk. He continually reminded voters that under his government the economy had been running smoothly, he had welcomed world leaders to Ottawa, and he had won the debate on the war against terror after the October 22, 2014, shootings in Ottawa.

Harper's advisers thought that by the time the campaign got underway, the Big Blue Machine would have had the time it needed to develop a package of devastating messages that would stick to Trudeau. Republican Party–style attack ads hadn't yet worked against the Liberal leader, though. Perhaps that was because they had taken things to ridiculous extremes. Even the hardest of hard-core Conservatives had to admit the ad campaign claiming Justin Trudeau was "in over his head" and not ready to run the country had missed the mark. One Tory supporter, radio host Charles Adler, tweeted that anyone who believed this was the way to run a campaign needed "to have their heads examined."[4] Adler also ridiculed the wacky Conservative claims that Trudeau had become "an instrument of Al Qaeda" by visiting a mosque in his riding in 2011. American sources later revealed Al Sunnah Al Nabawiah mosque was believed by the U.S. military to be one of seven places of worship in the world where well-known extremists had been recruited, a claim denied by the Muslim Council of Montreal.[5]

Justin Trudeau had never before run an election campaign where his every word was analyzed, dissected, and scrutinized. His team knew that his opponents could use his habit of making off-the-cuff remarks against him in televised debates. A single unguarded comment — like the one about "China's basic dictatorship" — could prove fatal in a brief election campaign where candidates never had time to explain what they really meant. This time, however, Harper had changed the rules of the game. On August 2, 2015, he launched a seventy-eight-day campaign leading up to the general election on October 19, 2015. It was the longest campaign anyone could remember. On average, federal election campaigns last forty-nine days; in recent years, thirty-seven-day campaigns have become the norm.

Trudeau promised to be more disciplined and to stop putting his foot in his mouth. As he admitted in *Common Ground*, people who are too clever or too funny can get themselves into trouble. He said he needed to find the right balance between being himself and getting the right message across.[6]

His advisers were ready for anything, but they also knew Trudeau was a less easy target than his predecessors had been. "There's no denying Mr. Dion and Mr. Ignatieff had their strong points, it's just that Justin is a very different man," Dan Gagnier said. "Remember the two sports he practises: boxing and yoga. That gives you an idea of his personality. He's someone who's able to keep his balance, and continue growing, on a personal level and as a politician." Justin had been making progress ever since he took over the Liberal leadership, Gagnier added, and was now growing as a politician at an accelerated pace.

An official working for the commissioner of official languages had a similar story to tell. In 2013, when Stéphane Dion and Justin Trudeau came for a meeting with the commissioner, the official recalled it was Dion who led discussions on behalf of the Liberal Party. But a year later, Trudeau had "assumed leadership: it was obviously *his* meeting."[7]

The Liberal leader still had the ability to surprise people. "I know what I'm capable of and I get busy doing it," Trudeau told journalist Althia Raj, adding he wasn't concerned about being underestimated because it meant he could play on the surprise factor.

In fact, one of Trudeau's most distinctive characteristics was that he kept his cards close to his chest. For example, everybody assumed he was going to wipe out in the boxing match with Patrick Brazeau, a man reputed for his toughness. According to Nik Nanos, Justin didn't "succumb to his ego": he even let out rumours he was going to get beaten, while secretly training for the fight. "He managed expectations," and when the time came, it was easy for him to "step over those expectations." Kicking the senators out of the Liberal caucus also surprised many people.

"Those are very simple signals that people can understand," said Nanos, "as opposed to policy issues, which are more complex." They showed "his level of resolve," he said, and gave an idea of the man's character.

———

But the fact remained that Justin Trudeau had had his ups and downs since taking on his party's leadership. There was still no way of knowing whether he would succeed.

In 2013, he had rock star appeal at the polls — and it lasted for fourteen consecutive months. But by mid-2014, the Liberal leader was having a harder time staying in the public eye, because the issues of the day had now shifted to the world stage: terrorism and the fight against the Islamic State, and other tough issues. The Liberals were the third party in the House of Commons and not the Official Opposition, and therefore they didn't have much impact on those issues. Trudeau also made a few injudicious off-the-cuff remarks, and additionally he had to face internal Liberal problems: the Senate, conflicts about open nominations of candidates to run in the next election, the expulsion of two MPs. On the other hand, he showed himself to be a leader capable of being decisive and acting quickly. It remained to be seen how much some of these decisions were going to cost him politically in the longer term.

For instance, there was no guarantee the senators expelled from caucus would want to help the Liberals under a future Trudeau government. After all, the dividing line drawn between the caucus and the thirty-two senators was not just a cosmetic change. On the contrary, it was a drastic cut, according to several former Liberal senators who had learned to accommodate themselves to the new dynamics. "I couldn't tell you what's happening inside the Liberal caucus," said one of the expelled senators, adding proudly that Liberal senators had had to "reinvent" themselves overnight.

Among the former Liberal senators, the independent-minded ones enjoyed their new freedom to study draft legislation without having to haggle behind the scenes with strategists in Trudeau's office. According to

Paul Massicotte, the expelled senators quickly got together and drafted their own written guidelines, stating they would never be bound to vote as a block on legislation proposed by the Liberal Party. They still met to share information and discuss issues. "But when we leave the meeting room, we vote the way we want, and often we vote against the majority," said Massicotte. In fact, he added, the former Liberal senators took a position different than that of the Liberal Party between 15 and 20 percent of the time.

That could spell trouble for any future Liberal government, because it meant these senators couldn't be counted on to pass legislation introduced by the Liberal Party. Also, some senators still felt resentful about being sidelined. When one was asked whether he would be ready to co-operate with the Liberals if Pierre Elliott Trudeau's son formed the next government, he answered with a caustic "Just watch me."

Although some were predicting that this stark dividing line between the Liberal caucus and the Senate would come back to haunt Trudeau, the leader believed "passionately" in his decision, in the words of one of his close colleagues, and was therefore willing to take the risk. For the time being, according to Senator Massicotte, the new arrangement was working well for the expelled senators, who were subject to no interference from the Liberal Party. "We receive no directives from Mr. Trudeau's office. We would be insulted if that were the case."

———

Meanwhile, as the election was approaching, discontent was beginning to simmer among the party faithful for yet another reason: Trudeau's close-knit coterie of advisers were sometimes taking decisions without any real concern for the consequences on the ground.

This problem came into the open when Conservative defector Eve Adams, MP for Mississauga-Brampton South, a Greater Toronto Area riding, was welcomed into Liberal ranks with little or no consultation with party members on February 9, 2015. It wasn't clear why the inner circle had taken the decision. The lack of clarity raised questions about how truly committed the leader was to transparency. Hadn't Trudeau vowed to do politics differently, not to get involved in old quarrels, and not to impose his choice of candidates?

The Eve Adams saga began after the Conservative MP had learned that the boundaries of her riding, Mississauga-Brampton South, were due to be redrawn in time for the October 2015 election. She was notified by the Tories in 2014 that she wouldn't be allowed to run in the new riding of Oakville-North Burlington after allegations of meddling in the nomination contest. Her fiancé, Dimitri Soudas, lost his job as executive director of the Conservative Party as a consequence. With no riding in sight, Adams switched parties and announced she wanted to run in the downtown Toronto riding of Eglinton-Lawrence.

This did not go over well with the Liberal rank and file. As one seasoned political observer put it, the move left the impression that the Liberals were steering solid candidates away from running in Eglinton-Lawrence in order to offer the Liberal nomination to a Tory defector. Party veterans criticized Justin Trudeau's inner circle for not having consulted with the provincial Liberal MLA in the area, Mike Colle, before opening the door to Adams. Colle grumbled that he would do nothing to help parachute Eve Adams into Eglinton-Lawrence because she had no real connection with the riding. "Over my dead body," he wrote on his Facebook page. Besides, the riding was currently held by Conservative Minister of Finance Joe Oliver, and gave every indication it would be an electoral quagmire.

And there was still a lot of bad blood over Justin Trudeau's decision to block Liberal Christine Innes from running in Toronto's Trinity-Spadina over allegations of intimidation and bullying by her husband, Tony Ianno, the former MP. According to one seasoned Liberal organizer, no better candidate than Innes could possibly be found: you can't "meet a more decent person than her. Sure, Tony Ianno had a couple of problems, but so has Eve Adams's partner. Christine Innis, she ran a couple of times, worked her guts off, she can't run but this princess [Eve Adams] can? In terms of Toronto Liberals who have spoken to me about it, I haven't heard anyone say this is great." (At the time, it appeared that running in Eglinton-Lawrence may also have been a consideration for Innes, but in fact it later became known that she had been blocked from running in any riding.[8]) The Liberal organizer added that the leader's decision concerning Eve Adams could only reinforce the perception he wasn't ready to govern: "If some people still had doubts, this latest series of events hasn't helped."

If bringing Adams into the Liberal fold was a supposed to be a coup, then somehow the message wasn't getting across. Recruiting her looked like a low blow aimed at taunting the Conservatives, the kind of provocation all too often seen in politics. What is more, the move went ahead with indecent haste: just one week after approaching Trudeau about switching parties she was already attending Liberal caucus meetings. The gambit gave some party faithful the impression the leader's inner circle was reacting to opinion polls instead of staking out positions of principle.

As things turned out, the whole political operation fell flat. On July 26, 2015, former Conservative MP Eve Adams got 792 votes for the Liberal nomination in Eglinton-Lawrence, losing easily to Toronto lawyer Marco Mendicino, who pulled in 1,127 votes.

The Eve Adams episode created tensions in Liberal ranks and it was all very public. Some people felt tactics like this could push the Trudeau campaign off the rails even before it got underway.

For a lot of Liberals, this had been a total waste of time.

———

Many Liberals still worried that Trudeau's obvious charm, glamour, and empathy might not be enough to persuade skittish voters. The young leader made mistakes, and his message sometimes lacked consistency.

Some people felt, after Justin took over as Liberal Party leader, that the Trudeau camp continued to push his image to the exclusion of nearly everything else. One of the rivals Justin had defeated at the leadership convention in 2013 recalled the final evening when votes were tabulated at the convention. "There was that little photo with all his kids around.... Clearly, everything had been preplanned. The question now is: Will he be able to bring the party back, or will image win out over substance? The big problem he has in terms of image is that people don't find him reassuring. People say, 'He's young.' But he isn't young. He lacks maturity."

Justin Trudeau was being sold as an unbelievably charismatic star, not as a politician. But according to Professor Louis Massicotte, thinking of the challenges the candidate would face in the 2015 election, glamour eventually wears thin. "If charisma is going to have any staying power in politics, it has to support something. People were willing to let themselves be charmed by Pierre Trudeau, because behind the pirouettes they knew the prime minister had something impressive to offer."

"The man had a solid education," Massicotte added. "He knew what he wanted, he gave the impression of being a man of substance, he was also persistent, he had a strong character. Does his son have those qualities? I am not so sure. If all [Justin] has to offer is star quality, then he is not destined for a brilliant future. Because people eventually get used to things like that. We saw that with his father: at a certain point, people didn't talk about his charisma any longer."

According to an experienced politician who preferred to remain anonymous, celebrity naturally enables a candidate to establish his or her profile more quickly and to make a breakthrough in politics more easily than a candidate who has had to work hard to become known. But celebrity in itself isn't enough. "You have to convince people that are attracted to your name and celebrity status that you are authentic and that you have substance."

According to the same politician, Trudeau is great at interacting with people, he learns quickly, he has good general knowledge and good political instincts. But he had never yet shown that he possesses "a firm command of policy." Justin Trudeau had gone through all kinds of experiences in his life, but not necessarily the ones needed to manage a competitive and dynamic economy. "Which wasn't that different from the case of Stephen Harper, who became prime minister without ever having managed anything in his life."

Another possibility was that the Liberal leader's age — he would be just forty-three on election day in October 2015 — might also work against him. Voters certainly found Justin Trudeau intriguing, but he still had years ahead of him, and people might end up saying, "Let him acquire more experience, his time will come later."

Still, this experienced politician also noted that many voters expect the person aspiring to become prime minister to have "good Canadian values."

"Take Mr. Chrétien, for example. I think people underestimated him at first. He's a very intelligent and clever person, but that wasn't the reputation he had when he ran for office. People made fun of the way he expressed himself." But Jean Chrétien had good instincts and lots of experience, and the public realized "he had good judgment."

The danger for Justin Trudeau was that he could be labelled in an enduring way as someone without original ideas and as someone who had a hard time expressing himself. People had said that about Ronald Reagan too, according to pollster Jean-Marc Léger. But Reagan was a major political player. He was masterful at delivering the message. "This is the task awaiting Justin Trudeau. We don't know what his ideas really are. He has to show he is able to define a message and to get it across if he's elected. His main problem is his lack of credibility."

The Trudeau team insisted Justin Trudeau's strong point was that he represented hope for the future and he was ready to bring change.

"Does he have the same experience as Harper or Mulcair? I would say he doesn't, but then he doesn't have the same baggage as they do either," said Dan Gagnier. "He hasn't spent the last twenty years in politics. He represents the young generation."

The question everyone was asking was whether Justin Trudeau would be given enough time to show he was a serious candidate before election day came. It could turn out that his "conversation" with Canadians had simply lasted too long and he had delayed more than he should have in unveiling the key part of his election platform — his plan for the middle class. It is hard for a party to lay out its proposals clearly during a campaign, when things can so easily go off the rails.

In the final sprint leading up to the October 2015 election, Justin Trudeau left people with two different and somewhat contradictory images: one image was of the charming, energetic, sensitive young man radiant with charisma; the other image was of an impulsive, erratic man, making ill-considered remarks off the cuff, who lacked substance. An ambitious man, but not a reassuring one.

Justin Trudeau knew how to charm people. But would he be able to persuade them?

CHAPTER 14

THE VICTORY

Once the election campaign got underway on August 2, 2015, Justin Trudeau started from a pretty low base. The Liberals were trailing the Conservatives and New Democrats in the polls, and Trudeau's opponents felt they could afford to ignore him. True, he had spiked in popularity on clinching the Liberal leadership. But since then neither Stephen Harper nor Thomas Mulcair had considered him a serious rival — even though experience showed Trudeau was at his best when other people underestimated him.

Prime Minister Harper arrived at Rideau Hall that August morning to ask the governor general to dissolve Parliament. He thought he had left nothing to chance, and the Tories were assured of another victory. But as things turned out, Harper was about to face a volatile, moody electorate, a tough economic environment, and a challenger with star quality — Justin Trudeau — who was anything but down and out.

Speaking outside the governor general's residence, Harper highlighted his experience managing the economy and described himself as the right man to protect Canadians from the international jihadi movement. Any change of course would be a setback for Canada, he added with a solemn air.

"A national election is not a popularity contest," Harper said. "It's a genuine choice between practical, serious, real-world experience and a dangerous approach that has failed before."

He launched into his main opponents, Thomas Mulcair and Justin Trudeau, claiming they were risky choices at a time of global economic instability. Voting for other parties would "lead to higher taxes, reckless spending and permanent deficits," said the outgoing prime minister.[1]

The Conservatives were ready to do battle, but 2015 had been an exhausting year marked by the scandals surrounding Senator Mike Duffy, the image of Dean Del Mastro led away in handcuffs,[2] virulent debates in the House of Commons, internal dissension, and the departure of several ministers.

Harper's inner circle calculated the party was likely to win a second majority government as long as the Tories continued flogging their economic record and stuck to the fundamental message that it was all about the economy.

They projected the NDP's support would eventually falter. Besides, the seventy-eight-day campaign was long for a reason: voters were bound to forget about the Wright-Duffy affair, and the storm of negative attack ads generated by major labour unions would peter out.[3]

At the beginning of 2015, the NDP was hammered by acrimonious attacks about the party's satellite offices in Quebec,[4] yet Thomas Mulcair was leading in the polls. He continued to make gains as leader of the Official Opposition in the Commons, particularly because of his masterful handing of the Wright-Duffy affair.

Mulcair was a fiery presence in the House of Commons, asking pointed questions that destabilized the Conservatives. He distinguished himself by his strong opposition to the Conservative anti-terrorism bill and by attacking the government's omnibus bills and the *Fair Elections Act*. Moreover, in May, Alberta NDP leader Rachel Notley became premier in that province, breaking the decades-long Conservative stranglehold and giving Mulcair a boost nationally.

Mulcair's strategy was to avoid upsetting voters, to seem prime ministerial, and especially, to give critics no reason to continue portraying him as a man quick to anger. For Thomas Mulcair, the man to beat was Stephen Harper. He never missed an opportunity to say so. Nothing was decided yet, but victory for the NDP nationally seemed within reach.

He launched his campaign in Gatineau, gleefully attacking Harper for holding "the worst economic growth record of any prime minister since

1960. He's had eight deficits in a row and added $150 billion in debt....
Clearly, Mr. Harper, your plan isn't working."

Mulcair focused his entire speech on Stephen Harper. The NDP leader's attitude toward Justin Trudeau was completely different. Showing his disdain for the Liberal leader, Mulcair avoided mentioning Trudeau's name a single time. He nonetheless derided Trudeau indirectly by saying Canadians needed an experienced first minister.

For the first day of the campaign, Thomas Mulcair had painstakingly rehearsed his lines to make the best possible impression. But he ended up reading his speech, and then left the podium without answering questions from journalists — a fact that was widely noted by the media. This reminded people of Harper's authoritarian habit of cutting off reporters' questions. It was the first sign that Mulcair's campaign was too tightly controlled and lacked spontaneity.

As for Justin Trudeau, he was nowhere to be seen the day the election was called in Ottawa. He was on a plane to Vancouver, from where he belatedly launched his campaign after fulfilling a promise to take part in Vancouver's Gay Pride parade. This unusual choice drew some criticism, but Trudeau repeated that Stephen Harper was not about to make him break his promise. According to tradition, every self-respecting party leader makes a speech in the federal capital shortly after the election call. But Trudeau preferred sticking to his game plan so he could avoid doing anything that looked rushed or improvised.

In Trudeau's opening speech of the election campaign, he attacked Stephen Harper's economic program as a failure and Thomas Mulcair's program as a "mirage." He accused Stephen Harper of needlessly stretching the election campaign to eleven weeks, passing the $125 million bill on to taxpayers.

Trudeau's campaign started off without much fanfare. He wouldn't get his campaign jet before September 7, and the Liberals would have to use their advertising dollars sparingly.

But Justin Trudeau would have seventy-eight days to demonstrate he was ready to take the reins of power. He was consistently positive during the campaign, seeking to adopt Sir Wilfrid Laurier's vision of dialogue and compromise. He continued portraying himself as the father of young children. He was definitely charismatic, yet voters still had their doubts....

Trudeau's inner circle considered the Liberal leader had growth potential and would make gains among a cohort of first-time voters — especially among the young people targeted during the 2013 Liberal leadership race. But for Justin Trudeau, there would be no room for error.

——

The next few weeks would be gruelling for all parties, and there would be many hurdles to overcome. The seventy-eight-day campaign was the longest since 1872. The sheer length of the campaign turned party leaders into hardened marathon runners. Campaigning required stamina, the ability to adjust to quick-moving situations, strong nerves, and good political instincts.

The image and tone of the party leaders would make the difference. Voters would have a choice between a serious, hard-working but cold prime minister who liked crushing his opponents; a self-confident leader of the Official Opposition who didn't project much warmth; and Trudeau, the star who posed for selfies with voters and seemed friendly and accessible.

The Conservatives were swimming in cash. Thanks to the new election funding rules they had set in place, they were able to pour yet more funds into their war chest while financially exhausting their opponents, who had far less financial resources.[5] Harper naturally denied that the rules deliberately sought to hamstring the other parties.

Despite this advantage, the outgoing prime minister didn't have much breathing room. He had lost several key ministers, including James Moore, John Baird, and Christian Paradis. Then he had to deal with an increasingly bleak economic environment. The drop in oil prices had put several oil sands projects on hold, sowing widespread concern, particularly in Alberta where droves of workers were being laid off.

This was not good news for the Conservatives: for two years they had been stagnating in the polls at between 28 percent and 32 percent.[6] In contrast, in 2011 they had formed a majority government with 39.6% of the popular vote. The Tories now hoped to get the Liberals and New Democrats to split the vote in a majority of ridings, so they could "run up the middle" between the other two parties.

Harper firmly believed the campaign would focus on the record of the Conservative government and public finances. He had no intention of deviating from that message or compromising his convictions. And if voters rejected the Conservative mantra, so be it. "He was at peace with himself," says John Reynolds, a former Conservative MP in the northern Vancouver area. "He knew he did a good job."

The Conservatives were monitoring Mulcair closely, but they continued attacking Justin Trudeau, whom they presented as a leader without any stature who was simply not up to the task.

An ad regularly broadcast on television before the election call and subsequently repeated during the campaign shows a hiring committee reviewing Justin Trudeau's CV and photo. Sitting in a boardroom, committee members say Justin isn't ready to assume the mantle of prime minister because he has never balanced a budget or had to pay employees. "Nice hair, though," the committee scoffs, striking his name from the list of leaders vying for the job. "I'm not saying no forever," adds one committee member, "but not now."

According to Liberal pollster David Herle, the ad mocking Trudeau's CV had a real impact. It conveyed a powerful image and led to a drop in the polls for the Liberals. It accentuated the negative impression left by Trudeau's handling of the Eve Adams episode, his disappointing position on the anti-terrorism bill, and the slowness of his team to produce concrete policy statements.

Herle adds that the Conservatives stubbornly continued cranking out the ad even when Mulcair was the one leading in the polls. "They wanted to keep us down."

On August 1 the Liberals responded with an ad of their own to demonstrate they were ready to do everything possible to bring prosperity to the middle class.

Many Liberals believed it was a pipe dream to imagine their party could win a majority and form a government, but the game was far from over. Party strategists decided to capitalize on the desire for change, which they identified early on as a leading issue in the campaign. Moreover, party polling indicated voters were willing to take a second look at Pierre Trudeau's son.

"People did not view Justin Trudeau as a finished product but as a work in progress," Herle adds, which meant there could be movement. But Trudeau still had to prove himself.

The first test of the campaign came on August 6 in Toronto during the first televised leaders' debate. When Stephen Harper's participation was still up in the air, Thomas Mulcair hesitated to confirm he would take part, saying he was focused on beating Harper and would not participate in any debate unless Harper was also present.

As expected, the Conservatives didn't do Justin Trudeau any favours.

Two days before the first debate organized by *Maclean's*, Harper's spokesman Kory Teneycke made a remark that actually began to turn the tide against the Conservative Party, according to John Reynolds. Teneycke commented during a press briefing that Trudeau had likely spent hours memorizing "a lot of attacks" and rehearsing "pithy responses," adding, "but there's a big difference between that and understanding how to manage an economy. There's only one candidate on the stage with a proven track record with respect to managing our economy, and that's Stephen Harper."

But before he said that, Teneycke had come out with the line that expectations for Trudeau have "probably never been lower for a leader going to a debate.... I think that if he comes on stage with his pants on, he will probably exceed expectations."[7]

Teneycke's contemptuous remark summed up all the disdain Harper's team felt for this inexperienced politician. According to Reynolds, the remark proved to be a mistake that would haunt the Conservatives because Canadian voters generally show respect for people aspiring to high political office.

However, as a politician and a boxer, Trudeau knew the element of surprise could make a difference. On the morning of August 6, as if to show he was primed for the debate, he donned boxing gloves and worked out in the ring at Paul Brown's Boxing Gym on Yonge Street in Toronto. The scene reminded people of his fight against Patrick Brazeau. This was no ordinary campaign appearance. Trudeau was never shy in front of the camera. His media performance demonstrated he was looking forward to the first debate, which would give voters a chance to compare the leaders' style and approach. After sparring in the ring, he refused to answer questions from journalists. But he had met his objective: the photo of the boxer in the ring made the rounds of several newspapers. And the message was clear: he was ready for the fight.

There would be five televised debates in all. The first debate was in English, and it offered voters a new image of Trudeau. Many people expected him to wipe out, but instead he conducted himself well without exactly putting on a dazzling show. The Liberal leader had been preparing for months now.

This was the first time Thomas Mulcair was taking part in a nationally televised debate during an election campaign. He was nervous, although he came across as a robust debater. But the evening got off to a bad start for Stephen Harper when he dropped a glass that smashed on the floor before the broadcast. The other leaders focused their attacks on Harper. He managed not to stumble, but he made some astonishingly candid remarks he otherwise wouldn't have made in a more controlled setting. For example, he admitted Canada was on the brink of a recession, something his government and his finance minister, Joe Oliver, had always refused to do. "I'm not denying that," he conceded during heated exchanges with Mulcair. He immediately added that most sectors of the economy were doing well except the energy sector, because of the fall in oil prices.

Harper also defended his position on the Canadian mission against the Islamic State of Iraq and Syria (ISIS). On this subject, Trudeau hesitated. He seemed vulnerable because he had already indicated he would withdraw Canadian fighter jets from the mission against ISIS. But he made up for that momentary hesitation by accusing Thomas Mulcair of hypocrisy on the Energy East pipeline project — saying one thing in Quebec where there was widespread opposition to the project, and saying the opposite in the rest of Canada where attitudes to the project were mixed.

Justin Trudeau attacked the NDP leader in his comments following the debate for promising to repeal the *Clarity Act* if he ever took power. Along the same lines, during the debate he accused Mulcair of wooing the separatist vote on Saint-Jean-Baptiste Day. "This is not worthy of a prime minister. No prime minister should make it easier for Quebec to separate from Canada." This attack put Mulcair on the defensive. He made a federalist profession of faith, which had little appeal for his nationalist base in Quebec. "I've fought for Canada my whole life," the fiery Mulcair counterattacked.[8]

The first debate had no clear winner. Trudeau projected dynamism and self-confidence, but that wasn't enough to guarantee success. "Will this performance in the televised debate enable Trudeau to gain new ground?" the Quebec newsmagazine *L'actualité* asked. "It's going to be an uphill battle."[9]

Even so, in the view of pollster Jean-Marc Léger, the debate would prove to be "a turning point" in the election campaign. From that point onward, people began to see Trudeau in a different way. But they also began to have a different take on Thomas Mulcair. Both leaders would be scrutinized by progressive voters who wanted to elect a new government to lead the country. Which of the two leaders was best placed to make that happen? Justin Trudeau had his work cut out for him.

The day after the debate, Mulcair congratulated himself for getting Stephen Harper to admit the country was on the verge of a recession, an admission Conservative strategists found deeply unsettling. Harper dodged questions from journalists about it, preferring to tell them "80% of the Canadian economy is healthy and growing." Trudeau meanwhile repeated the Liberal pledge to balance the budget, without setting a deadline.[10]

Trudeau's inner circle believed he should capitalize on his performance during the first debate. Four days later, on the Quebec-based French-language network TVA, Trudeau said he was ready both for the long campaign and for discussing a wide range of issues. He promoted his own policy of tax cuts for the middle class while asking wealthy Canadians to do more. "We are the only ones doing this," he said, adding that people wanted a prime minister who knows how to listen and who "connects with people."[11] This statement didn't have much impact.

For the time being, media attention was focused on the Wright-Duffy affair, which had been eating away at the Conservative Party since 2013. Whatever the Conservatives claimed, Senator Mike Duffy's trial would cast a negative light on Harper's inner circle as well as on Harper himself, who was often left alone to field journalists' questions on the topic day after day.

———

Once Mike Duffy's trial got underway again on August 12, the Conservatives were convinced they would get through it unscathed. But the highly publicized trial gave ammunition to their political opponents. And there was no shortage of opportunities. Full of fire and indignation, Thomas Mulcair acted as if he was back in his comfort zone in the House of Commons. Except that during an election campaign, he should have been focusing more closely on his own party program, which he seemed reluctant to reveal to voters. Trudeau was less obsessed with the Duffy trial, but he made statements at critical junctures in the proceedings. The Liberal leader preferred sticking to retail campaigning, meeting thousands of Canadians and making sure he was as visible as possible.

For Harper, the Duffy trial would prove a distraction he really didn't need.

The trial showed how the Harper machine had tried to stifle the scandal of Senator Duffy's unreasonable expenses, reinforcing its image as a controlling government, desperate to stay in power. For almost a whole month Harper was at pains to explain how he didn't know about a $90,000 cheque from his former chief of staff, Nigel Wright, to Duffy to cover the senator's disallowed expenses. Harper's predicament worsened after Benjamin Perrin, legal counsel for the Prime Minister's Office, contradicted Wright, saying it was clear the prime minister had "directly approved" the idea of reimbursing Duffy's unauthorized expenses. In his testimony he stated that Ray Novak, a close colleague of Harper for fourteen years and one of his campaign directors, knew about the $90,000 transaction.

On August 28 the Conservative leader heaved a sigh of relief when the trial adjourned until November. The fact remained, though, that this case monopolized the attention of the Conservatives, overshadowing the news of the day and spreading havoc throughout the team. Whatever the eventual outcome (Duffy was acquitted of all charges after the election), the damage had already been done. During the trial, Canadians had seen the Harper method of total control in action.

In his withering attacks on Harper, Mulcair had shown how ferocious he could be.

On the sidelines, Trudeau, meanwhile, lacked visibility. He would soon change that.

On August 27, at a construction site in Oakville, just west of Toronto, Trudeau appeared smiling at the controls of a red crane, surrounded by construction workers in red helmets. This was the beginning of a major Liberal offensive to win the hearts of voters. Trudeau had made many announcements and promises since the beginning of the campaign, but the Liberals had not edged past 30 percent in the polls. Mulcair was still out in front. The Liberal campaign was lagging and lacked focus, and needed a real shove to get things moving.

For the Oakville event, everything had been meticulously prepared: the image, the logistics, the message. Trudeau stepped up to the microphone and announced a Liberal government would invest heavily in infrastructure projects such as bridges, roads, and green projects, creating "thousands of jobs." The price tag would rise from $65 billion to $125 billion over the coming decade. Earlier in the campaign Trudeau had stated he would balance the budget, but he now conceded there would be modest annual deficits of $10 billion over the next three years.

"Our economy needs investment in order to create growth," he told the beaming construction workers in Oakville. "Our plan features three years of historic investment in the Canadian economy. That growth will eliminate the Harper deficit and we will balance the budget in 2019–2020."[12]

According to Trudeau, with Canada experiencing low interest rates and a favourable debt-to-GDP ratio, the time was right to make public investments to stimulate Canada's sluggish economic growth. He said he was the only leader telling Canadians the truth. He was betting Mulcair wouldn't be able to fulfill his promises without plunging the country into a budget deficit. Inevitably, Mulcair would have to cut programs, Trudeau added. As for Harper, he was projecting a budget surplus of $1.4 billion, but the country's economic situation was bleak. Harper would have to revise his optimistic projection downward.

Trudeau's about-face on deficits was bold, and it surprised many observers. It reminded people of Jean Chrétien's strategy back in the 1993 election campaign. Chrétien had promised a similar program of public investment, repeating the mantra of "jobs, jobs, jobs!" tirelessly during the campaign that year. The strategy proved effective and contributed to Chrétien's resounding victory.

The advantage of Trudeau's plan was that it was in such complete contrast to the Conservatives' zero-deficit obsession. And just two days earlier Mulcair had announced he intended to eliminate the deficit by 2016.

It was too late for Mulcair to turn back — the NDP was trapped. The party found itself in a very difficult position, admits an informed source, because "people are always afraid of the NDP's economic reputation, particularly in Ontario, because of Bob Rae. So the NDP would never have been able to promise deficit spending during the [2015] campaign and still hope to win."

The public investment strategy was a real coup for Trudeau. By making a decisive turn toward the left, Trudeau could now say he was more progressive than the NDP!

Mulcair was caught off guard. He defended his program, saying he was offering a more balanced approach. He admitted in the same breath he might be forced to make cuts in government spending, providing a few examples, such as eliminating the Conservative measure to offer income splitting for families.

Harper quickly joked that Trudeau's deficit would be so tiny, "you can hardly see it."[13]

In a more serious vein, Harper added: "Friends, we've gone through this before. Look at the mess in Ontario with a modest deficit from a Liberal government." This was a clear allusion to Kathleen Wynne's government. Taking evident pride in his own economic record, the Conservative leader concluded Trudeau simply didn't know what he was talking about.

But Trudeau's promise of public investment positioned him as the candidate of change at a time when over two-thirds of voters wanted a new prime minister leading the government of Canada.[14]

———

Throughout the month of August, Mulcair maintained his lead in the polls. But this statistical lead concealed real problems behind the scenes. The early onset of the campaign had caught the New Democrats off guard. They had two campaign buses as of August 6, but the campaign aircraft would only become available on the Labour Day weekend in early September.

Operationally and logistically, "some problems were visible," says an NDP source, but they were never addressed "because things were going well."[15] In Quebec, at least one pro-sovereignty candidate resigned. Other candidates were dropped by the party.[16] On August 20 it was reported that four ridings in Manitoba and two in New Brunswick had still not managed to find candidates. Recruiting candidates was also proving difficult in Ontario after the collapse of the provincial New Democrats during the 2014 provincial election.

Despite these bumps in the road, Mulcair seemed unbeatable. Quebec opinion polls showed he enjoyed the support of about 47 percent of Quebec voters.[17] Trudeau's inner circle figured the only way to stop Mulcair from cruising to victory was to take a bold gamble.

"The calculation was that we could not go another month. We had to get people thinking that we could win," says Liberal pollster David Herle.

The Liberals decided to go on the offensive by responding directly to Conservative ads and attacking the NDP. Mulcair had not released any ads in August, so the Liberals judged the timing was right to launch their own publicity campaign — they now saw the advantage of positioning themselves on television, even though some thought it was a waste of time to broadcast campaign ads during the summer with so many people still on vacation.

Some members of Trudeau's inner circle suggested their leader develop a very negative message reviling Harper, "but Trudeau had been clear he would not accept that," says David Herle.

Ultimately, the Liberals went for a very evocative message highlighting the theme of the impoverishment of the middle class. The ad was broadcast starting on September 1.

In the ad, Trudeau appears on camera in a white shirt and red tie, trying to climb up the down escalator. Then he stops and catches his breath, and when the escalator changes direction, he gets to the top. Trudeau says:

> This is what is happening to millions of Canada in ten
> years under Stephen Harper. His idea to give benefits to

the wealthy but make cuts to everything else is making it harder for most people to get ahead. And Mulcair promises more cuts. Now is not the time for cuts.

In my plan, we'll kick-start the economy by investing in jobs and growth and lowering taxes for the middle class. That's real change.

The ad had two underlying messages: Trudeau is pulled back yet he continues advancing one step at a time, while the middle class is working harder and harder, but is losing ground....

According to David Herle, the ad got a mixed reception, but it accomplished something important: it enabled the Liberals to score points and take their place in the race — a race that was about to take a whole new direction.

———

By early September, election day on October 19 seemed far away. According to a Liberal organizer, the party took things one day at a time. There was no panic. Trudeau was reassuringly calm. He was good at keeping his cool under pressure. Everywhere he went crowds were receptive and social media was on fire. There was some movement in the polls. The Liberals were slowly making progress. Trudeau was a skillful politician. He would soon get the chance to demonstrate he had real political acumen and was in tune with public opinion.

When the Syrian refugee crisis worsened in September, Harper justified his government's slow response on the grounds that thorough security checks needed to be undertaken on all refugee applicants. The message did not go over well.

Then a horrifying image of the drowned body of Alan Kurdi on a Turkish beach flashed around the world. The little boy had been fleeing the conflict in Syria with his family. His mother and brother had also died, leaving his father as the only survivor. The father's sister lived in British Columbia and had been trying to bring the family to Canada. The image put a human face on a major humanitarian crisis, and put the Conservatives in a difficult position.

Harper said he found the images of little Alan devastating. He announced that Canada would receive more refugees but would also address the root cause of the crisis — the Islamic State. Harper reiterated the soundness of receiving a limited number of refugees while bombing the Islamic State from the air.

The reaction of the prime minister highlighted his cold personality and the Conservatives' overly bureaucratic approach. Under questioning on September 2, Immigration Minister Chris Alexander finally admitted that barely 2,500 Syrian refugees had reached Canada in addition to 20,000 more from Iraq. That didn't amount to much. In January 2015 Canada had pledged to receive 10,000 refugees from Syria over a period of three years, while giving priority to people from persecuted religious or ethnic minorities.[18]

Trudeau struck a chord when he said Canada should receive 25,000 Syrian refugees. On September 3, on a campaign stop in the Montreal suburb of Brossard, he said this was the kind of generosity that reflected Canadian values. He was scathing in his criticism of the Conservatives, who had suddenly "developed compassion" for refugees during the election campaign. In Toronto Mulcair was moved to tears both as father and grandfather, and said Canada should immediately open its doors to 10,000 refugees from Syria. But Trudeau was the one making the headlines. He could not have chosen a more appropriate theme than directly linking generosity toward refugees to reviving the values many Canadian identify with.

Faced with popular discontent, Harper revised his position. On September 8 the Conservative leader promised to improve the refugee-selection process while stressing the need for security checks to ensure "real refugees" got in. But ultimately, as Mulcair put it, the refugee situation demonstrated that Harper was the leader of a "heartless" government.

———

On September 10, halfway through the campaign, there was still no clear front-runner in the polls. Harper thought he could gain some ground by boasting about an unexpected budget surplus of $1.9 billion, but the Conservatives dropped to third place in voting intentions with 28 percent.

Moreover, campaign manager Jenni Byrne was suddenly taken off the campaign and sent back to the Conservative bunker in Ottawa — a clear sign of conflict growing among party strategists. Trudeau was now at 31.5 percent in voting intentions, just one-tenth of a percentage point behind Mulcair. There was no groundswell of support for Trudeau, but perceptions of the Liberal leader were changing.

This was clear on September 17 in Calgary, when the leaders got together for the second televised debate, on the economy. The election was still a three-way race, but Trudeau faced aggressive attacks from his opponents, which indicated he had improved his standing. That very morning New Democrats and Conservatives attacked his "disastrous" approach on deficits and major public investment. Despite the $1.9 billion surplus, Trudeau said he would maintain his position on the need for deficits to stimulate sluggish growth. The budget would be balanced by 2019.

On arriving in Calgary, Trudeau radiated confidence. He began his day at dawn, paddling a canoe on Calgary's Bow River — a moment photographers and journalists were invited to cover. A Nanos poll in the *Globe and Mail* that morning revealed that his commitment to deficit spending in order to finance large infrastructure projects appealed to many Canadians. Some 49 percent of Canadians were in favour, while 42 percent supported eliminating deficits.[19] Canadians still had doubts about Trudeau's economic management skills, the poll indicated, but he had made progress on this score since July.

Trudeau's performance in the second debate confirmed that his strong showing in the first debate had not been a fluke. Harper cast himself as the champion of the economy and he knew his files well, but he acknowledged that job creation was not going as well as it should. On the issue of Syrian refugees, Harper drew a lot of fire from his opponents when he accused them of wanting to open the door to hundreds of thousands of undocumented people who had never been subject to security clearance. He criticized Trudeau's deficit-spending plan, claiming it would result in unjustified expenses.

Mulcair appeared tense, as if afraid of making mistakes. He had just unveiled the NDP economic program, which would increase business taxes, reduce subsidies to oil companies, and eliminate tax breaks on stock options, leading to four years of budget surpluses.

In terms of image, however, several media commentators agreed that Trudeau represented change. It wasn't hard to understand why: he was young and dynamic, and his campaign bubbled with enthusiasm. And crowds awaited him at every turn.

———

Mulcair relied on NDP support in Quebec to create a contagion effect in other provinces. However, Gilles Duceppe, leader of the Bloc Québécois, was close on his heels. It would be hard for Mulcair to counterattack. After all, the Bloc and the NDP had the same nationalist clientele in Quebec, which created many headaches for the NDP leader.

Gilles Duceppe was going for broke. He was running in his old Montreal riding of Laurier-Sainte-Marie, even though he knew he would lose there. At least, he believed, he was furthering the cause of Quebec independence.[20] With the Bloc now down to two MPs, two less than in the 2011 election, he had nothing to lose.

On September 18 Duceppe unveiled a vitriolic attack ad, slamming the NDP for its position on the niqab during the swearing-in of new citizens as well as for its position on the proposed Energy East pipeline. The televised ad showed oil flowing like lava, which then turned into a niqab.

"The NDP agrees to a pipeline that will cross our waterways without offering us any benefits. And the NDP finds it normal that a woman should wear the niqab while voting and being sworn in," the ad ran.

The Bloc's ad had a devastating impact on the NDP. But the hemorrhage of votes had only just begun.

Harper too wanted to claw back the nationalist vote. His aim was to break up Mulcair's electoral base in Quebec, which included Coalition Avenir Québec supporters, the Bloc Québécois, various nationalists and even "soft" sovereignty supporters, and provincial Liberals. If he could decrease support for the NDP in Quebec by grabbing the nationalist vote, he calculated, then the Conservatives could race up the middle between the NDP and Trudeau's Liberals.

He declared he would appeal the Federal Court of Appeal ruling that women have the right to wear the niqab during citizenship oath ceremonies. Harper even said he would prohibit federal employees from wearing the niqab. His government had already challenged the Federal Court's decision.

Harper played the situation for what it was worth. Coincidence or not, on September 24 the Privy Council — the Cabinet secretariat that advises the prime minister — published the results of an opinion survey conducted between March 12 and 25. The survey indicated significant support for making women remove the niqab when taking the citizenship oath: fully 93 percent of Quebeckers were in favour, and 82 percent in the rest of Canada.

Faced with this challenge, Mulcair was caught between a rock and a hard place. He offered legal arguments to justify the wearing of the niqab. But he was on the defensive, and he seemed hesitant, which was anything but reassuring. He came across more as a lawyer than as a nuanced political leader.

Trudeau took essentially the same position as Mulcair on the niqab, but he handled himself better. He repeated formulas that were easy to understand, simply saying it was a matter of fundamental rights and freedoms. No one was shocked to hear him say he wasn't about to tell a woman how to dress. Moreover, his electoral base in Quebec included anglophones and allophones who were not overly bothered by the issue, although his position did upset some of his candidates there. At this point in the campaign Trudeau lost the support of some francophone voters, but the Liberals weren't about to experience anything like the NDP, who stood at 50 percent in voting intentions among francophone voters and were now facing the prospect of a rout.

"For [the Liberals], this meant a drop of 3 to 4 percentage points, but for us it meant 20 points," says an NDP adviser.

For Mulcair, taking this position would have disastrous if not suicidal consequences. The NDP rank and file in Quebec were full of anger and dismay. Many openly challenged his leadership.

The controversy over the niqab haunted Mulcair during the final debate on October 2 in Montreal, organized by TVA Nouvelles. This debate would be crucial, since it would give the leaders significant visibility before election day on October 19. Mulcair had now slipped to third place and was losing support in the polls. Harper was recovering lost ground; Trudeau was now the front-runner.[21] The niqab gave rise to heated exchanges during the debate. Harper denied acting out of political opportunism, declaring that the citizenship oath must be done with the face uncovered. "This reflects our values," he said. Although Mulcair's position on the niqab had undermined his campaign during the last few weeks, he maintained it staunchly: "This is a subject that makes many people uncomfortable and understandably so," said Mulcair. "It makes me uncomfortable too, but the reality is that the courts have ruled." Doubtless, Mulcair was making a courageous statement of principle, but according to several observers voters were unwilling to forgive him and were now turning to Trudeau.

Mulcair couldn't turn the situation around. On October 14, when he announced the cost of his proposed national child-care program, voters were no longer listening. The creation of the first 370,000 new spaces would be spread over four years at a cost of $1.9 billion per year. After eight years, investments in child care would reach more than $5 billion annually. The NDP leader noted these costs would be borne 60 percent by the federal government and 40 percent by the provinces. The promise of a balanced budget seemed to have fallen by the wayside. But this ambitious national child-care program wasn't the lifesaver the NDP was looking for.

Trudeau meanwhile had the wind in his sails. In Brampton, Ontario, some 5,000 people crowded into an arena to attend a Liberal rally. Television coverage captured the image of the flashy and dynamic Liberal campaign. The rally had been organized on short notice, thanks to social media where news of Liberal events spread like wildfire. Trudeau radiated confidence. He claimed before an audience brimming with enthusiasm that Harper was no longer putting any energy into the campaign. Harper's government "is like a bad movie franchise: by the time you get to the third or fourth sequel, most of the stars are gone, and the plot is getting pretty thin. This government is out of touch and out of ideas. And if we stay focused and work hard, in two short weeks they'll be out of time."[22]

Even so, the Liberals were blindsided by a controversy they could have avoided. Five days before the election, the co-chair of the national campaign, Dan Gagnier, had to resign to avoid becoming "a distraction" in the Liberal campaign. In an email he had sent to five executives of TransCanada, the promoter of the Energy East pipeline project, he had advised them to be proactive and to quickly address the next government, whether Liberal or NDP, to avoid any delay in getting the project underway. TransCanada admitted to *Maclean's* that Gagnier had signed a contract the previous spring to provide communications advice to the company.

Trudeau initially defended Gagnier but then distanced himself, calling Gagnier's actions "inappropriate" since they didn't meet the ethical standards to which Canadians are entitled. He said Gagnier would be kicked out of the Liberal Party "long-term." Mulcair slammed this breach of ethics, but it was too late to make a difference.

When Stephen Harper ended his campaign in Toronto alongside Doug and his brother Rob Ford, the cocaine-snorting former Toronto mayor, it seemed like a last-minute act of desperation.

———

Conservative strategists had believed the eleven-week electoral marathon would benefit their party above all. Some people had even called the sheer length of the campaign a stroke of genius. But things had not turned out as planned. True, the campaign had messed up the NDP game plan, but it had also given Justin Trudeau the opportunity to build up visibility for the Liberal brand. He was also able to get a key message across to voters — that the Conservatives had had their day.

The Conservatives had certainly made mistakes. By the end of the campaign, the prime minister had become a liability for his party. By being sent to the front to respond to all the current issues of the day, Harper ended up personifying everything people disliked about the Conservatives. It got to the point where the Conservatives launched an ad on October 13 during a Blue Jays game, telling voters this election was not about Harper … which is actually a strong indication the election had turned into a referendum on Harper.

The Conservatives never showed any real desire to reach out beyond their traditional base except in Quebec, where they made a determined effort to seduce the electorate. Jason Kenney admits the Tories hadn't anticipated the impact of a whole new cohort of voters arriving. Many of these voters were casting a ballot for the first time. According to analyst Éric Grenier, they voted massively for the Liberals.

Kenney, who says the Conservative Party is the only party with no youth wing, thinks that for a long time now it has not done enough to attract young voters. "I think probably the single biggest demographic challenge we had was amongst first-time younger voters." People aged thirty and younger tend to be on the left of the political spectrum, and the Conservatives could have taken positions capable of inspiring young people, such as equality between generations. "But we have not communicated these messages," adds Kenney.

After nearly ten years in power, it was time for Stephen Harper to move on. Accompanied by his wife Laureen, he left the stage in his riding of Calgary on election night without mentioning his future. He later announced his resignation in a press release as if drawing a veil over his term in office. "That's the way he is," says Reynolds. "He keeps to himself."

"I had the incredible honour to serve as your prime minister," Harper told the supportive crowd. "While tonight's result is certainly not the one we had hoped for, the people are never wrong.... Canada is stronger than ever.... The budget is balanced and federal taxes are at their lowest in 50 years."[23]

With 99 seats out of 338 in the Commons and gains in Quebec, he consoled himself with the thought that the Conservative Party of Canada would form the Official Opposition in the Commons, sending the NDP to the back benches. Harper would keep his seat in Calgary Heritage, the successor to his old riding of Calgary Southwest, but the Conservatives would hold a leadership race to find a successor.

Overall, the Conservatives had made the wrong calculation. Several elements had escaped them, and there had been internal divisions on how best to conduct the campaign. Moreover, they hadn't understood they were waging a war on two fronts. When the campaign kicked off in August, many people thought Thomas Mulcair was poised to win the election. Others, such as Jenni Byrne, continued worrying about the Trudeau effect. But try as he might to tell people that Trudeau "wasn't stupid," John Reynolds faced a wall of incomprehension. Jason Kenney never understood the Trudeau phenomenon:

> To be honest, my view was that the Liberal Party's brand in this country is tremendously resilient, but I thought those voters looking for change would be looking for safe

or prudent change — and, to be honest with you, I thought that Thomas Mulcair, with his government experience, his maturity, his depth, trying to steer the NDP in a more moderate direction, would appear to be a much safer kind of change than the untested, sometimes juvenile Justin Trudeau. And so I actually thought that there was a good chance that the NDP would for the first time be a national alternative. I was obviously wrong. So, unlike Miss Byrne, I was one of those who thought, for a long time, the NDP would be our primary challenge. So I don't think there's one single view in the Conservative Party on that.[24]

This Conservative perspective is a little difficult to understand, according to political scientist Louis Massicotte, because the Trudeau effect had been "overwhelming" if not "stratospheric" for nearly a year and a half before the election. From the end of September, Trudeau quietly gained one percentage point per week, "and this trend never really stopped," says the analyst Éric Grenier. The Conservatives didn't believe there was any need to adjust their electoral strategy.

After a while, the Tory ad claiming Trudeau was just not ready to govern rang false. True, the ad had lowered expectations for the Liberal leader, says Grenier, but at the same time it "signalled to many voters that the real opponent was the Liberals."

The Conservatives decided to stick with the ad making fun of Justin's CV because it appealed to their most loyal core of supporters. Kenney doesn't think those ads turned voters against the Tories. "I think we were saying what we believed to be demonstrably true about Justin Trudeau, and that message resonated with the public for a long while."

Blinded by their contempt for everything associated with the Trudeau name, the Harper team wasn't able to see that the Liberal leader had potential of his own. They simply couldn't understand how "some kid could beat Stephen Harper," says Nanos. But Trudeau is a retail politician who likes to shake hands and meet people. The Trudeau brand has a real power of attraction.

Harper was completely out of touch with Canadians and didn't position himself well during the campaign. He offered continuity when the public wanted real change. But in addition to that, as Kenney explains, "there was just a feeling that we had been picking on enemies unnecessarily, alienating people unnecessarily. And some of that was true, and I think that was where we gave people the opening" to vote against the Conservatives.

Voters remembered how aggressive and ruthless the Harper government had been: acrimonious debates, the lack of transparency, the muzzling of scientists and people who didn't think the same way as the government did, virulent attacks on the Supreme Court of Canada, and more.

Many Canadians were afraid of losing the Canada they knew. They punished the Conservatives at the ballot box.

———

The NDP came close to a historic victory, but then saw its support melt away in Quebec. It would never recover.

In Quebec the NDP went from 59 seats in the 2011 elections to just 16 in 2015. In Ontario, it lost 14 seats. The NDP ended up with just 8 seats in the province, none of them in Toronto. In 2011 the NDP had won 103 seats out of a total of 330. But four years later it got just 44 seats out of a total of 338.

Defeat came as a crushing blow to the NDP, which had seen itself as the party of change poised at the gates of power. But it's possible the party itself wasn't ready to assume that role. The party had never tasted power at the federal level, and this was Mulcair's first national campaign. On election night he was pleased to see Canadians bring an end to the long reign of Stephen Harper. "They have rejected the politics of fear and division," he said, repeating words he had often heard the Liberal leader say.

The party had certainly never counted on such a long and gruelling campaign. Mulcair himself had expected the election call to come a month and a half later, on September 13. According to an NDP strategist:

> The party was not ready for a campaign launched in early August. There was a lot of catching up to do, there was a lot of improvisation early on in the campaign, and the problems that developed after that were somewhat

neglected because of the NDP's popularity in polls at that time.... When you're ahead in the polls, you are more reluctant to make the changes that are needed.

Given these conditions, the pace of the NDP campaign suffered. It was hard to unveil a new campaign theme every week for eleven weeks when campaigns normally lasted only five weeks. An informed source in the party says that the New Democrats had done a good job preparing a pre-election tour in July, but the intensity of an election campaign was something else again. "You have to fill all those days [with fresh announcements], because you're fighting for every column inch of space in the newspapers and every second in TV newscasts. So you have to literally fill the days, and we had some filling to do."

According to an NDP adviser, the niqab had a more destructive impact on the NDP campaign than any other issue. The emergence of the niqab as an issue completely changed the dynamics of the campaign by turning it into a three-way race and allowing the Liberals to break away from the pack. "When you look at the polls, everything taken together, the NDP was the front-runner or very nearly the front-runner from July through to September. In mid-September came the ruling on the niqab, and within two weeks the NDP lost twenty points in Quebec."

The Quebec press accused Mulcair of fence-sitting on the issue, whereas Trudeau got away with mere scratches.

Thomas Muclair didn't succeed in getting his message across, but he treated defending the niqab as a matter of conviction and he stuck to his guns. He took "a firm stand based on principles and he wouldn't budge from that position."

For the NDP, this was the beginning of the end.

In effect, the sudden decline in NDP fortunes in Quebec signalled that Mulcair was hardly likely to make gains in Ontario and win the election. And so began the exodus ... to the Liberals. Whereas Jack Layton had been able to win the Liberal vote in Quebec in 2011, the tables were now turned and the Liberals won that support back again.

———

The Bloc Québécois definitely capitalized on the niqab controversy. The Bloc appealed strongly to nationalist NDP supporters who realized "they didn't back Tom Mulcair's stance on the issue. So they quietly went back to the Bloc."[25]

The Conservatives and even Trudeau's Liberals picked up some of the nationalist vote in the province. According to the Bloc MP Louis Plamondon, some Bloc supporters and other Quebec nationalists decided to vote strategically, because it was vital "to get rid of Harper, and this hurt the Bloc."

Duceppe's return to the helm at the Bloc stabilized things. Ultimately, the Bloc ended up with 10 seats — more than the 2 it had won in 2011 but with less of the popular vote. This meant the Bloc didn't have enough standing in the Commons for official party status, and would only be allowed to pose a few questions each week during Question Period.[26] For the second time in a row, Duceppe lost his former Montreal riding of Laurier-Sainte-Marie to Hélène Laverdière of the NDP. He resigned as Bloc leader. "People thought we almost disappeared but we are more present than we were before. We came a long way," Duceppe said to cheering supporters on election night.[27]

He even had a few kind words for Justin Trudeau: "I think he worked hard. This was quite the uphill battle for him," he added, congratulating Trudeau on his victory.

———

Nobody had seen Trudeau's victory coming. Nobody had expected a Liberal majority government. Thanks to the long campaign, Justin Trudeau got his basic training, he established his credibility, he charmed voters, and he introduced a detailed election platform.

On the ground, Liberal candidates had more time to explain their party's platform, the centrepiece of which was the plan for the middle class. "We had seventy-eight days to talk about our plan," says Navdeep Bains. "People were interested in our plan. In my riding, a family of four with two children earning an income of about $90,000 would receive $2,500 tax-free. This had a resonance. I was able to repeat this message door-to-door every day of the campaign."

Navdeep Bains and his team like to say they knocked on 150,000 doors in the Ontario riding of Mississauga-Malton.[28] They didn't face a lot of resistance from Conservatives who were struggling to attack the Trudeau plan for the middle class. When the Conservatives are asked why they weren't bitter about this, the answer is simple: "Our core supporters don't like taxes," says Jacques Gourde.

The Liberals were given free rein to defend the plan, but according to experts the plan for the middle class had the most impact on a symbolic level. Since the plan was to provide tax cuts to 99 percent of all taxpayers and tax the 1 percent of Canadians who are wealthy, Trudeau could sell it as "the plan for the 99 percent."

"The plan for the middle class was important because it conveyed the message that he wanted to be prime minister for everyone," says pollster Nik Nanos. "That's why we saw him during the campaign, telling the New Democrats and Conservatives, you are not our enemies. Symbolically, it was very important."

It must be said that the Liberals had been preparing the ground since 2014. Several times a month the Liberal Party announced its candidates, many of whom were prominent people. Mulcair had few star candidates, and the same old names were mentioned as Conservative candidates.

Trudeau played his cards well. He didn't deviate from his game plan, he captured the mood of the electorate, and he positioned himself as the candidate of change. This included his proposal to kick-start the economy with infrastructure spending, whereas his two main opponents were busy preaching the virtues of balanced budgets. This was a bold move for Trudeau to make, but Luc Dupont says there was something reassuring about it: Trudeau's message was "perhaps we have done enough belt-tightening."

It is hard not to see a parallel between Trudeau's boxing victory over Brazeau and the 2015 campaign where he started out in third place. In both cases he had been underestimated, and in both cases he exceeded expectations. Even Brazeau indicated on his Twitter feed that he was going to vote for Trudeau.

———

Pierre Trudeau's son won 184 seats across the country, including 80 in Ontario. He even made gains in Alberta, where he gained 4 seats. The Liberals won Jack Layton's old seat in Toronto-Danforth and also his widow Olivia Chow's seat in Spadina-Fort York. In British Columbia, the Liberals picked up 17 seats.

The stars aligned for Justin Trudeau in the last few weeks of the campaign. "Ultimately, voters opted for a change of government. If the Liberals hadn't done all their work, the NDP would have won the election. Anyway, the strongest desire felt by voters was to get rid of the Conservatives," says pollster Jean-Marc Léger.

In Quebec, Trudeau exceeded all expectations by winning 40 of the province's 78 seats. Vote-splitting by the NDP and the Bloc handed victory to the Liberals in several Quebec ridings. The last time the Liberals had made that many gains was in 1980 when Pierre Elliott Trudeau won 74 of the province's 75 seats.

The Liberals swept the four Atlantic provinces, a historical first. The party won all 32 seats there, in strongholds where the Conservatives were well established.

The Liberal game plan — whatever its shortcomings — had what it took to get the Liberal Party of Canada from third place to victory in a single election. This was another historical first.

"To turn a situation like around the way Trudeau did is exceptional," says Jean-Marc Léger. "There was a desire for him to succeed, and he did succeed."

For Justin Trudeau, the Trudeau name had long been both an asset and a liability. The son had inherited his father's old party but now he had rebuilt it in his own image. He had run his campaign his way. This was his victory, and his alone.

NOTES

CHAPTER 1: 24 SUSSEX DRIVE

1. According to John English, in *Just Watch Me: The Life of Pierre Elliott Trudeau, 1968–2000* (Toronto: Knopf, 2009), 3.
2. Margaret Trudeau, *Beyond Reason* (New York: Paddington Press, 1979), 129.
3. Canadian Press, "Justin's Happy Too: Mrs. Trudeau, 2nd Christmas Son, in 'Top Form,'" *Globe and Mail*, December 27, 1973.
4. Nancy Southam, ed., *Pierre: Colleagues and Friends Talk about the Trudeau They Knew* (Toronto: McClelland & Stewart, 2006), 248.
5. Associated Press, article appearing in *Free Lance-Star* (Fredericksburg, VA), March 8, 1976, 9.
6. In her memoirs, Margaret recounts asking Pierre for a sewing machine as a wedding present. She even set up a sewing room on the third floor of the prime minister's official residence.
7. Margaret Trudeau, *Beyond Reason*, 64.
8. Margaret Trudeau, *Consequences* (Toronto: Seal Books, 1982), 23.
9. Keith Richards, *Life* (New York: Little Brown, 2010), 393.
10. Margaret Trudeau, *Consequences*, 248–49.
11. Margaret Trudeau, *Consequences*, 24.
12. Margaret Trudeau, *Consequences*, 61.
13. She reveals her disorder in her autobiography *Changing My Mind* (Toronto: HarperCollins, 2010).

CHAPTER 2: THE FORMATIVE YEARS

1. Michel Vastel, *The Outsider: The Life of Pierre Elliott Trudeau*, trans. Hubert Bauch (Toronto: Macmillan, 1990), 18.

2. Althia Raj, *Contender: The Justin Trudeau Story*, e-book distributed by *Huffington Post Canada*, March 2013, 17.

3. In *Contender*, Althia Raj says Trudeau got input for the eulogy from Butts, Montreal radio host Terry DiMonte, and a few friends, but he had already been thinking about what he would say for some time (24). In his own book, *Common Ground* (Toronto: HarperCollins, 2014), Trudeau explains he holed himself up at DiMonte's place to write the eulogy and got help from a few close friends to find the right anecdotes (144).

4. Raymond Giroux, "Le mythe du Canada bilingue créé par Pierre Elliott Trudeau reconfirmé, Justin plus fort que tout," *Le Soleil*, October 7, 2000, A17.

5. *Pierre Elliott Trudeau: Portrait intime* (documentary transcript), (Montreal: Télé-Métropole/Les Éditions Alain Stanké, 1977), 31.

6. Interview with Brébeuf teacher Gilles Levert.

7. Justin Trudeau, *Common Ground*, 79, 81.

8. Raj, *Contender*, 8–9.

9. Justin Trudeau, *Common Ground*, 108ff.

10. Pierre Elliott Trudeau had been a professor of law at the Université de Montréal; Justin's maternal grandfather James Sinclair had been a Rhodes Scholar at Oxford University; and his own father, also named James Sinclair, had been a teacher in Scotland.

11. Nathalie Petrowski, "Justin Trudeau: franchir une étape à la fois," *La Presse*, November 15, 2008.

12. Ken MacQueen, "Justin Trudeau's B.C. Playground," *Maclean's*, October 11, 2012.

13. Margaret says Canadians contributed $1.5 million toward building the cabin. "Every bit of lumber, every window and door, every nail had to be helicoptered up to the building site." Margaret Trudeau, *Changing My Mind*, 253.

CHAPTER 3: RUNNING IN PAPINEAU

1. Jonathon Gatehouse, "Justin's Time," *Maclean's*, December 23, 2002.

2. Michael Valpy, "Dalai Lama Wows Them in Toronto," *Globe and Mail*, April 26, 2004.

3. Stéphanie Bérubé, "Justin Trudeau, animateur à CKAC," *La Presse*, February 27, 2004.

4. In this report, Trudeau concluded that the most pressing challenge facing the Liberal Party "wasn't persuading young people to vote Liberal; it was getting them to vote at all." *Common Ground*, 161–62.

5. "La Chambre reconnaît la nation québécoise," Radio-Canada (website), November 28, 2006.

6. According to Bloc leader Gilles Duceppe, the Conservative motion signalled "real progress for Quebec" since it meant Canada had become "the first country whose democratic institutions officially recognized Quebec as a nation." (The Bloc had previously tabled a motion in the House of Commons on November 21, recognizing *les Québécois* as a nation, without adding the Conservative wording "within a united Canada.") The Bloc's motion was defeated by 233 votes to 48 on November 27. Source: interview with the Journals Branch, House of Commons.

7. Justin Trudeau, *Common Ground*, 6.

8. Hélène Buzzetti, "Discours controversé sur le bilinguisme. Justin Trudeau se fait rappeler à l'ordre," *Le Devoir*, May 8, 2007.

9. Ibid.

10. Ibid.

11. Hugo de Grandpré, "Justin Trudeau est de nouveau dans l'embarras à cause de propos controversés sur le bilinguisme au Canada," *La Presse*, February 12, 2008.

12. Kathleen Lévesque, "Les Jeunes patriotes chahutent Justin Trudeau," *Le Devoir*, September 25, 2008.

13. Bloc Québécois, "Pour le respect de la langue et de la nation québécoise, il faut battre Justin Trudeau," press release of October 10, 2008.

14. *House of Commons Debates*, 1st session, 40th legislature, no. 002, November 19, 2008, 24.

CHAPTER 4: THE FIGHT

1. Thomas Walkom, "Justin Trudeau Reawakens Liberal Leadership Rumblings," *Toronto Star*, April 3, 2012.

2. Margaret Wente, "Justin Trudeau for Leader! Okay, Maybe Not," *Globe and Mail*, April 5, 2012.

CHAPTER 5: THE PARTY'S GREAT NEW HOPE

1. James Bradshaw, "Michael Ignatieff Gets Full-Time Harvard Job," *Globe and Mail*, June 24, 2014.
2. Katherine Dow, "Trudeau Not Prodded into Race," *Winnipeg Free Press*, June 11, 2012.
3. Justin Trudeau, *Common Ground*, 262.
4. Author's interview with John English.
5. Ignatieff insisted on being named deputy leader after the party faithful voted against him at the 2006 leadership convention. Dion gave in because he really had no choice, claims Ignatieff in his book: the "compromise candidate" lacked crucial support.
6. Dion's role had been to develop a hard-line strategy, dubbed Plan B, to deal with any future separatist threat by clarifying the rules of secession. (Plan A was to respond to Quebec's long-standing traditional demands.) Basing his position on the Supreme Court of Canada's reference on Quebec secession, he argued forcefully that Ottawa would not feel compelled to negotiate with Quebec following a yes vote on secession without a clear referendum question and majority. These terms were never defined, but Dion argued it would take more than a simple majority vote to break up the country. He spearheaded the adoption of the *Clarity Act*, which spells out the conditions of secession, earning him criticism from nationalists in Quebec who have consistently argued that the province could secede unilaterally.
7. House of Commons, *Debates*, 1st Session, 40th Parliament, December 2, 2008, 553.
8. Michael's great-grandfather Count Nikolay Pavlovich Ignatyev had served under Tsar Alexander II of Russia, and had been minister of the interior under Tsar Alexander III, who succeeded to the throne in 1881. His son Paul Ignatieff — Michael's grandfather — had been the last minister of education of Imperial Russia under Nicholas II. In the aftermath of the October Revolution, he took his family into exile in England and then in Canada. His son George — Michael's father — reached Canada at the age of sixteen. A Rhodes Scholar at Oxford University, he worked at Canada House, the Canadian High Commission in London. He later served as Canada's representative at NATO and as ambassador to the United Nations.

9. Michael Ignatieff, *Fire and Ashes: Success and Failure in Politics* (Toronto: Random House Canada, 2013), 109.

10. Tamsin McMahon, "Ignatieff Steps Down as Liberal Leader," *National Post*, May 3, 2011.

11. The National Energy Program (NEP) was adopted in October 1980 after OPEC jacked up the price of oil. The NEP aimed to make Canada self-sufficient in petroleum resources, to restrict foreign ownership of the Canadian petroleum industry, and to share petroleum revenues more equitably between Alberta, the federal government (whose share increased from 10 percent to 25 percent), and the petroleum industry. Moreover, given that the energy costs of eastern Canadians had soared, Ottawa moved to force the sale of Albertan oil below the market price. Alberta responded by slowing the development of two projects in the Alberta tar sands and by reducing its production of crude. A new agreement was reached, but Albertans would long remain resentful. Brian Mulroney repealed the NEP.

12. Rick Bell, "Justin Trudeau Bashes National Energy Program in Calgary," *Toronto Sun*, October 4, 2012.

13. Daniel Leblanc, "Inside Justin Trudeau's War Room," *Globe and Mail*, March 1, 2013.

CHAPTER 6: A LEADER IN WAITING

1. Agence QMI, "Trudeau comme chef placerait les libéraux en tête," December 8, 2012.

2. Justin Trudeau, *Common Ground*, 284.

3. *La Presse canadienne*, "Justin Trudeau a déjà amassé 600 000 $," January 7, 2013.

4. Leslie MacKinnon, "Justin Trudeau a Household Name but Still an Enigma," *CBC News* website, April 3, 2013.

5. Moya Dillon, "Trudeau Touts Middle Class During Pickering Campaign Stop," *Durhamregion.com*, October 11, 2012.

6. Joan Bryden, "Mr. Nice Guy Garneau Has No Intention of Finishing Last," *Canadian Press*, in *Macleans.ca*, December 21, 2012.

7. "Liberal Leadership Candidate Joyce Murray: 'Our Numbers Are Higher Than Anyone Else's,'" *Toronto Star*, March 26, 2013.

8. André Pratte, "Le CV de M. Trudeau," *La Presse*, February 19, 2013.

9. Joan Bryden, "Justin Trudeau Light on Policy, but Offers Key Glimpses of Next Liberal Platform," Canadian Press, in *Huffington Post*, April 14, 2013.
10. Justin Trudeau, *Common Ground*, 262–63.
11. Françoise Le Guen, "'On a le droit de mériter mieux — Justin Trudeau,'" *Journal Le Nord* (Saint-Jérôme), December 12, 2012, 7.
12. Justin Trudeau, "Texte du candidat à la direction du PLC," *LaPresse. ca*, October 31, 2012.
13. The party had chosen a voting system giving 100 points to each of the country's 308 ridings. This meant the winner would need to get 50 percent of a total of 30,800 points.

CHAPTER 7: ENTERING THE FRAY

1. James Sinclair was MP for Vancouver North from 1940 to 1949, and then, once the electoral map was redrawn, for Coast-Capilano, which covered the northern part of the greater Vancouver area. He sat as an MP in Ottawa for a total of eighteen years.
2. Justin Trudeau, *Common Ground*, 30.
3. *Les Francs-Tireurs*, Télé-Québec, November 24, 2010.
4. Vastel, *The Outsider*, 39.
5. At the time, Prime Minister Harper had justified not observing the anniversary by saying, "The Charter remains inextricably linked to the patriation of the Constitution, and the divisions around that matter are still very real in some parts of the country."
6. Joan Bryden, "Justin Trudeau Recalls Father's Glory Days at First Caucus Meeting," Canadian Press, April 17, 2013.
7. Justin Trudeau only became a member of the Liberal Party of Canada in 2006.
8. Author's interview with Patrick Gossage.

CHAPTER 8: THE TRUDEAU EFFECT

1. In June 2013, the Liberals under Trudeau had 37 percent of voter intentions (almost twice the support the Liberals actually got in the 2011 election), compared to 29 percent for the Conservatives and 21 percent for the NDP. In Quebec, Trudeau pulled in 46 percent of voter intentions, while in Ontario the Conservatives (37 percent) and

Liberals (36 percent) were more evenly matched (Léger Marketing). The polling website ThreeHundredEight.com calculated the average of polls conducted in 2013 and estimated that by 2013, overall support for the Liberals had increased by 10 percent over 2011–12.

2. Plamondon was an MP under the Progressive Conservative banner before moving over to the Bloc in 1990.

3. The Bloc Québécois had 17 percent of voter intentions, while support for Stephen Harper moved up from 8 percent to 14 percent, mainly in the Quebec City region. Source: CROP poll, *LaPresse.ca*, August 27, 2013.

4. "Justin Trudeau Wants to Legalize Marijuana in Order to 'Keep It Out of the Hands of Kids,'" *Postmedia News* website, July 24, 2013; Mitch MacDonald, "Trudeau Supports Decriminalization of Marijuana," *Guardian* (Charlottetown), November 13, 2012.

5. "Tories Failing P.E.I.: Trudeau," *Journal Pioneer* (Summerside), August 28, 2013.

6. Mike Duffy received a cheque for $90,000 directly from Stephen Harper's then chief of staff Nigel Wright in order to refund the senator's disallowed housing expenses. Duffy pleaded not guilty to thirty-one counts of fraud, breach of trust, and corruption. On April 21, 2016, he was acquitted of all charges. An audit of Wallin's expenses showed she had claimed $532,508 in travel expenses between January 2009 and September 2012, only $390,182 of which could be justified. Although she denied doing anything wrong, she reimbursed $152,908 (source: the Senate Communications Directorate). On May 19, 2016, the RCMP announced they would not lay criminal charges against her. Patrick Brazeau was alleged to have made false declarations about his place of residence and to have claimed a housing allowance to which he was not entitled; he pleaded not guilty to charges of fraud and breach of trust. His trial was originally scheduled for March 2016 and later postponed. He was also charged with assault and sexual assault in February 2013 in a case of domestic violence, for which he denied any responsibility. Finally, in April 2014 he pleaded not guilty to charges of assault and possession of cocaine in an unrelated case. On October 28, 2015, Brazeau was granted an unconditional discharge on assault and drug charges. The charge of sexual assault was dropped due to lack of evidence. After two years without pay, Brazeau, Wallin, and

Duffy were back on the Senate payroll once the election call in August 2015 annulled the suspension orders against them.

7. On May 20, 2016, following the Duffy acquittal, the Crown dropped the charges against Harb, saying there was no longer a reasonable prospect of conviction.

8. Interview with an insider who did not want to be identified.

9. Donations were capped at $1,500 per person per political party.

10. La Presse canadienne, "Justin Trudeau souligne l'anniversaire de la Charte dans la controverse," *L'Express*, April 18, 2013.

11. Jessica Nadeau, "Trudeau attaque Marois sur la Charte des valeurs québécoises," *Le Devoir*, August 22, 2013.

12. Justin Trudeau, "I Have Faith in Quebec. So Should You," *Globe and Mail*, September 12, 2013.

13. Canadian Press, "Values Charter Doesn't Upset Harper's Quebec Lieutenant," *CBC.ca*, September 25, 2013.

14. Interview with an anonymous source.

15. Author's interview with Andrew Leslie.

16. "Retired General Claimed $72K in Expenses for Move Within Ottawa," *CTVNews.ca*, February 15, 2014.

17. "Justin Trudeau's 'Foolish' China Remark Sparks Anger," *CBC.ca*, November 9, 2013; Matthew Little, "Trudeau, China and Political Warfare," *Epoch Times*, November 14, 2013.

18. Brad Lavigne, "Justin Trudeau: You, Sir, Are No Jack Layton," *Globe and Mail*, November 27, 2013.

CHAPTER 9: ANOTHER SIDE OF JUSTIN

1. The NDP had never formed a government and had therefore never been in a position to name senators.

2. Interview with Justin Trudeau, *Le Téléjournal*, Radio-Canada, January 29, 2014.

3. Author's interview with Marc Garneau.

4. Officially, the senators expelled from the Liberal Party caucus are known as "Senate Liberals." They sit as a separate caucus.

5. In a ruling handed down on April 25, 2014, the Supreme Court of Canada ruled that abolition of the Senate required the unanimous consent of the provinces. This ruling was a defeat for the Harper government,

which had believed it could act unilaterally. As for the idea of limiting the terms of senators (who currently faced mandatory retirement at age seventy-five), the Court noted that it would require the agreement of seven provinces representing 50 percent of the population of Canada.

6. Susan Delacourt, "Trudeau Dismisses Worries He's Lost Party Organizers with Release of Senators from Liberal Caucus," *Toronto Star*, February 2, 2014.

7. Pierre Elliott Trudeau set off an avalanche of patronage appointments shortly before retiring from the federal scene. Just before the writ was dropped in 1984, his successor John Turner endorsed all the appointments.

8. Leslie MacKinnon, "Christine Innes Liberal Candidacy Rebuffed over Deal, Letter Says," *CBC.ca*, March 14, 2014.

9. Mark Kennedy, "Police Intervene After Fight Breaks Out at Meeting to Nominate Andrew Leslie as Liberal MP Candidate," Postmedia News, December 7, 2014.

10. On June 30, 2014, the Liberals came in second behind the Conservatives in two Alberta ridings, obtaining 35.3 percent of the vote in Fort McMurray-Athabasca and 16.9 percent in Macleod. The Liberals won the Toronto riding of Scarborough-Agincourt with nearly 60 percent of the vote.

11. These incidents did not greatly hurt Liberal fortunes in the by-election of November 17, 2014. The Liberals were hard on the heels of the Conservatives in the Ontario riding of Whitby-Oshawa, Jim Flaherty's former riding, with 40.7 percent of the vote compared to the Tories at 49.3 percent. In the Alberta riding of Yellowhead, the Liberals came in second, with 20 percent, well behind the Conservatives at 62.6 percent of the vote.

12. Author's interview with Michael Behiels.

CHAPTER 10: THE ALLURE OF THE BLANK SLATE

1. Virginia Postrel, *The Power of Glamour* (New York: Simon & Schuster, 2013), 116. Postrel (117) draws a distinction between charisma and glamour: "Charisma draws the audience to share the charismatic figure's own commitments, seeking that person's affection or approval.... Glamour requires mystery, allowing the

audience to fill in the details with their own desires…. Charisma enhances leadership; glamour enhances sales."

2. Nathalie Petrowski, "Justin Trudeau: franchir une étape à la fois," *La Presse*, November 15, 2008.
3. Mark Kennedy, "Q and A: Justin Trudeau in His Own Words," *Ottawa Citizen* (website), October 18, 2014.
4. In May 2013, Trudeau said in an interview with *La Presse* that he didn't support abolishing the Senate because it gives an advantage to Quebec over provinces like Alberta and British Columbia, with twenty-four Quebec senators and only eight senators for each of these two provinces.
5. In February 2014, Justin Trudeau cracked a joke on the Radio-Canada TV show *Tout le monde en parle*, saying Russia might intervene in Ukraine because it was in a bad mood after failing to make it to the medal round in Olympic hockey at Sochi. The attempted joke went over very badly.
6. Greg Weston, "Justin Trudeau, Long Shot with a Short Résumé," *CBC.ca*, December 7, 2012.

CHAPTER 11: THE NETWORKED CANDIDATE

1. In J.K. Rowling's books, Harry Potter's mortal enemy Voldemort is such an evil wizard that nobody dares to pronounce his name.
2. To be closer to his family, Trudeau sold his Montreal house in late summer 2013 and rented a six-bedroom house in the elegant Ottawa district of Rockcliffe Park, not far from the prime minister's residence on Sussex Drive where he had grown up (Campbell Clark, "Justin Trudeau Moves Family to Ottawa," *Globe and Mail*, August 9, 2013).
3. As quoted in Anne Kingston, "Win a Date with Justin," *Maclean's*, November 6, 2014.

CHAPTER 12: THE PLAN FOR THE MIDDLE CLASS

1. Statistics Canada, Income Statistics Division, "Annual Income Estimates for Census Families and Individuals," June 26, 2015.
2. Under the enhanced Universal Child Care Benefit, the Conservatives offered a boost of up to $60 a month per child between the ages of six and seventeen as of January 1, 2015. For children under six years old, the increase was up to $160 a month per child. These benefits were taxable.

CHAPTER 13: TRUDEAU 2015?

1. According to Elections Canada statistics, the Liberals raised $15,063,142 from 77,064 contributors in 2014, compared to the Conservatives' $20,113,303 from 91,736 contributors and the New Democrats' $9,527,136 from 46,355 contributors.

2. At dissolution, the Conservatives held 159 seats (from 166 elected in 2011); the NDP, 95 (from 103); the Liberals, 36 (an increase from 34); the Bloc Québécois, 2 (from 4); and the Green Party, 2 (an increase from 1).

3. By the end of the campaign, according to Trudeau, the Liberals had 80,000 volunteers.

4. Charles Adler is a radio host at CJOB in Winnipeg. Formerly a controversial host on the Sun News TV network, he had 23,000 subscribers on his Twitter feed. These tweets are from September 1 and August 7, 2014.

5. Minister of Public Safety Steven Blaney said on August 6, 2014: "It is completely unacceptable that Liberal Leader Justin Trudeau would associate with a group that allegedly radicalizes Canadians to join al-Qaeda and engage in acts of unspeakable violent extremism." According to Pentagon documents released by WikiLeaks, Mohamedou Ould Salahi, a Mauritanian detained in Guantánamo, had been an imam in a Montreal mosque for one month. The Americans suspected him of being the mastermind of a Montreal Al Qaeda cell that had perpetrated terrorist attacks on American soil (Susana Mas, "Justin Trudeau's 2011 Mosque Visit Draws Fire from Steven Blaney," *CBC.ca*, August 6, 2014; Sidhartha Banerjee and Jonathan Montpetit, "Mosquées pro-terroristes: les musulmans montréalais s'indignent," *La Presse canadienne*, in *La Presse*, April 26, 2011).

6. Mark Kennedy, "Foot in Mouth? Trudeau Vows More Discipline Over Off-the-Cuff Remarks," *Ottawa Citizen*, October 17, 2014.

7. Author's interview with anonymous source.

8. Leslie MacKinnon. "Liberal Organizers Rejected Innes Because She Wouldn't Agree to Later 'Riding Assignment,'" *CBC.ca*, March 14, 2014.

CHAPTER 14: THE VICTORY

1. *National Post*, August 2, 2015.
2. Dean Del Mastro, the former Conservative MP for Peterborough and Stephen Harper's former parliamentary secretary, was sentenced on June 25, 2015, to one month in prison and four months house arrest. On October 31, 2014, he had been found guilty on three counts of violating the *Canada Elections Act* during the 2008 election: exceeding the election spending limit, forgetting to declare a personal gift of $21,000 to his campaign, and falsifying a document. He had been sitting as an independent MP since September 2013, but resigned as an MP in November 2014. He tried to appeal his conviction on June 3, 2015, but the appeal was rejected and the sentence upheld.
3. Unifor, a coalition of private-sector unions, promised to do everything it could to defeat the Harper government because of what it considered Conservative anti-labour measures. The Public Service Alliance of Canada launched a $2.7 million ad campaign to denounce Conservative budget cutbacks that threatened essential services. In June, the political action committee Engage Canada came out with a similar position, denouncing health-funding cuts. Some right-wing groups such as Working Canadians slammed Trudeau for understanding nothing about the middle class. These ads were launched before the election call.
4. The Board of Internal Economy, Parliament's governing body, ordered sixty-eight current and former MPs to reimburse $2.75 million of parliamentary funds they had used for straight partisan purposes, by financing satellite offices in Montreal, Ottawa, and Toronto. The NDP challenged this decision before the Federal Court of Canada.
5. During a typical thirty-seven-day campaign, each party has the right to spend a maximum of $25 million. But the Conservatives adopted new election-funding rules in 2014: when an election campaign went beyond thirty-seven days, each party could spend an additional one-thirty-seventh of that sum (roughly $675,000) per day. In short, the three main parties could now spend up to $54,936,320 each, whereas the Bloc Québécois was fielding candidates only in Quebec and could therefore spend up to $13.7 million. About half this sum would be reimbursed by Elections Canada. Candidates

would also be allowed to spend more during the campaign (source: Elections Canada).

6. Interview with Éric Grenier, opinion poll analyst and author of the site *308.com*.

7. "Trudeau Will Win Debate Points 'If He Comes on Stage with His Pants On': Tory Spokesman," *CBC.ca*, August 5, 2015.

8. Martin Patriquin, "Thomas Mulcair's Clarity Problem," *Maclean's*, August 7, 2015.

9. Alec Castonguay, "Débat: Mulcair solide, Harper sur la défensive, Trudeau dynamique," *L'actualité* (website), August 6, 2015.

10. Canadian Press, "Stephen Harper Forced to Defend Economic Record as His Rivals Pile On," *Toronto Star*, August 6, 2015.

11. "Justin Trudeau se dit à l'écoute et authentique," *TVANouvelles.ca*, August 10, 2105.

12. "Justin Trudeau Says Liberals Plan 3 Years of Deficits to Push Infrastructure," *CBC.ca*, August 27, 2015.

13. Ibid.

14. According to a Léger Marketing poll conducted on August 15, 2015, 61 percent of Canadians wanted a change of government in Ottawa. The strongest desire for a change of government was in Quebec (75 percent), followed by the Atlantic provinces (74 percent), and Ontario (56 percent). Only 23 percent of Canadians preferred the status quo, with this segment rising to 37 percent in Alberta. When asked which party best represented change, 33 percent of those polled said it was the NDP, 19 percent the Liberals, 7 percent the Conservatives, and 2 percent the Bloc Québécois.

15. Interview with an anonymous NDP source.

16. Three days after the election call, the outgoing MP for the Montreal suburban riding of Vimy, José Núñez-Melo, denounced the NDP uncompromisingly for kicking him out of the nomination race in the riding.

17. Joël-Denis Bellavance, "Sondage CROP/La Presse: le NPD domine sans partage," *LaPresse.ca*, August 20, 2015.

18. Canadian Press, "Mulcair, Trudeau, Take Aim at Tories as Tens of Thousands Struggle to Find Refuge in Europe," *CBC.ca*, September 2, 2015.

19. Campbell Clark, "Voters in Favour of Liberals' Economic Plan, but Unsure on Trudeau: Poll," *TheGlobeandMail.com*, September 17, 2015.

20. Interview with a Bloc Québécois strategist.

21. Marco Fortier, "Le NPD perd encore des plumes," *Le Devoir*, October 2, 2015.

22. "For the Record: Justin Trudeau's Rally Speech in Brampton," transcript, *Macleans.ca*, October 4, 2015.

23. "Stephen Harper's Concession Speech," transcript, *Toronto Star*, October 20, 2015.

24. Interview with Jason Kenney.

25. Interview with Louis Massicotte.

26. A political party needs 12 seats to gain official party status in the House of Commons.

27. "Gilles Duceppe, for the Record: 'Le Québec que j'aime, c'est vous,'" *Macleans.ca*, October 20, 2015.

28. Bains, named by Trudeau as minister of innovation, science and economic development, had earlier represented the riding of Mississauga-Brampton South from 2004 to 2011.

INDEX

Katimavik, 33, 77, 113
Kemper, Alicia, 18
Kemper, Fried, 18
Kemper, Kyle, 18
Kennedy, Gerard, 36, 37, 75
Kenney, Jason, 198–99
Kent, Peter, 53
Keystone XL pipeline, 91, 132–33
Kidder, Margot, 7
Kinsella, Noël, 140
Kurdi, Alan, 192

L'actualité, 187
La Presse, 98, 100, 154, 167
"Ladies' Night" fundraiser, 134–36, 164
Lalonde, Marc, 113–16, 158
Landry, Louise, 44
Lanthier, Louis-Alexandre, 42, 45–47, 64, 75, 102
Laporte, Pierre, 15
Laverdière, Hélène, 203
Lavigne, Brad, 138
Layton, Jack, 50, 66, 125
Le Devoir, 47, 58
leadership, debate on, 92
leadership races, 68, 77, 82
Lebel, Denis, 130
LeBlanc, Dominic, 64, 72, 77, 81, 126
Lefebvre, Jim, 20, 22, 29
Legendre, David, 20
Léger, Jean-Marc, 123–24, 151, 162, 179, 187, 205
Leslie, Andrew, 131–32, 146
Levant, Ezra, 59

Levert, Gilles, 24
Liberal Party of Canada
2009 interim leadership, 71–72
2011 interim leadership, 61–63
2015 leadership convention, 102–04
caucus announcement, 125
decline, 67, 105
discontent among, 175–77
Justin on, 79
leadership races, 61, 62, 64, 66, 78–80
rebuilding, 85–86, 105–06, 118–19
rules, 144–45
seat numbers, 60, 69, 204–05
support for, 36, 124, 137, 147, 174, 196, 205–06, 212–13n1, 215n10–11
under Pierre Trudeau, 60
Liberal Party Renewal Commission, 36
Lisée, Jean-François, 128–29
long-gun registry, 92, 99

Maclean's, 33, 62, 117, 163, 198
Maksymetz, Richard, 64
Marchand, Jean, 113
marijuana legalization, 91, 101, 124
Marland, Alex, 113, 152–53, 164
Marois, Pauline, 128–29
Martin, Paul, 35, 38, 67, 120, 156
Massicotte, Louis, 70, 125, 177–78, 200
Massicotte, Paul, 141, 144, 146, 165, 175

Wallin, Pamela, 126, 212–13*n*6. *See also* Senate expense scandal
western Canada, Justin's appeal to, 122
Whistler-Blackcomb, instructor at, 30–32
"Win a Date with Justin" contest, 163

"Win Dinner with Justin" contest, 163–64
Wright, Nigel, 137, 188
Wright-Duffy case. *See* Senate expense scandal
www.justin.ca, 83

Young, Bruce, 77

VISIT US AT

Dundurn.com
@dundurnpress
Facebook.com/dundurnpress
Pinterest.com/dundurnpress